The Design Student's Journey

Being a professional designer is one of the most intellectually rewarding careers. Learning to become a designer can be tremendous fun but it can also be frustrating and at times painful. What you have to do to become a designer is not often clearly laid out and can seem mysterious. Over the past 50 years or so we have discovered a great deal about how designers think. This book relies upon that knowledge but presents it in a way specifically intended to help the student and perhaps the teacher. Bryan Lawson's classic book *How Designers Think* has been in print since 1980 and has gone through four editions to keep it up to date. This book can be seen as a companion volume for the design student.

Bryan Lawson studied at the Oxford School of Architecture followed by a Master's and Doctorate in psychology. He has studied the relationship between people, place, and wellbeing. He has also extensively studied the nature of the creative design process. His book *How Designers Think* was published in 1980 and is still in print, reaching its fourth edition.

Bryan was Head of School and Dean of the Faculty of Architectural Studies at the University of Sheffield in the UK. He is now Professor Emeritus and has held professorial posts at universities in Singapore, Australia, Malaysia, and Hong Kong.

T0394003

"The understanding of how designers think and work has grown substantially in recent years. Based on this knowledge, and addressed to students, this book is very welcome. Structured around the process of learning to design, it provides clarity on developing the cognitive and practical skills of designing. It is an approach that should be more evident in all design schools."

Professor Nigel Cross, The Open University, author of *Design Thinking: Understanding How Designers Think and Work*

The Design Student's Journey

understanding How Designers Think

Bryan Lawson

Routledge
Taylor & Francis Group

LONDON AND NEW YORK

First published 2019
by Routledge
2 Park Square, Milton Park, Abingdon, Oxon OX14 4RN

and by Routledge
52 Vanderbilt Avenue, New York, NY 10017

Routledge is an imprint of the Taylor & Francis Group, an informa business

British Library Cataloguing-in-Publication Data
A catalogue record for this book is available from the British Library

Library of Congress Cataloging-in-Publication Data
Names: Lawson, Bryan, author.
Title: The design student's journey : understanding how designers think / Bryan Lawson.
Description: New York : Routledge, 2019. | Includes bibliographical references and index.
Identifiers: LCCN 2018032886| ISBN 9781138328556 (hb : alk. paper) | ISBN 9781138328570 (pb : alk. paper) | ISBN 9780429448577 (ebook)
Subjects: LCSH: Design—Study and teaching (Higher) | College environment.
Classification: LCC NK1170 .L39 2018 | DDC 745.4071/1—dc23
LC record available at https://lccn.loc.gov/2018032886

ISBN: 978-1-138-32855-6 (hbk)
ISBN: 978-1-138-32857-0 (pbk)
ISBN: 978-0-429-44857-7 (ebk)

Typeset in Charter and FS Albert
by Swales & Willis Ltd, Exeter, Devon, UK

To Rosie

. . . and for all the years between.

Contents

Acknowledgements

I am greatly indebted to all the wonderful designers who have spent time helping me to understand how they design and for use of images of their work. In particular they include:

Kit Allsopp of Kit Allsopp Architects, London

Professor Peter Blundell Jones, University of Sheffield

Richard Burton of Ahrends, Koralek and Burton, London

Santiago Calatrava of Santiago Calatrava Architects and Engineers, Zurich

James Mary O'Connor of Moore, Ruble and Yudell, Santa Monica, USA

Theo Groothuizen of Groothuizen Beheer BV, Netherlands

Frans de la Haye of De La Haye Design, Netherlands

Louis Hellman, Architectural Cartoonist

Herman Hertzberger of Herman Hertzberger Architects, Amsterdam

Eva Jiricna of Eva Jiricna Architects, London

Geoff Jones of Building and Urban Design Associates, Birmingham

Richard Seymour of Seymour/Powell, London

Richard MacCormac of MacCormac, Jamieson, Pritchard, London

John Outram of John Outram Associates, London

Ian Ritchie of Ian Ritchie Associates, London

Robert Venturi and Denise Scott Brown of Venturi, Scott Brown and Associates, Philadelphia

Michael Wilford of Michael Wilford and Partners, and Stirling and Wilford, London

Ken Yeang of T.R. Hamzah and Yeang Sdn Bhd, Kuala Lumpur

I am also grateful to the many students who, through their creative work, have taught me what it is to become a designer. In particular, students from the following universities and colleges:

Aston University, Birmingham, UK

Central Saint Martins, London, UK

Delft University of Technology, Netherlands

De Montfort University, Leicester, UK

Oxford Brookes University, UK

University of Sheffield, UK

Sydney University, Australia

Universiti Sains Malaysia, Penang, Malaysia

Universiti Teknologi, Malaysia

National University of Singapore

Many close colleagues from the Design Research Society and the research community in the field for their publications and personal discussions. In particular, I am indebted to:

Nigel Cross

Kees Dorst

Gabi Goldschmitt

Linda Candy

Ernest Edmonds

Peter Blundell Jones

The many research students who I have been lucky enough to supervise and learn from and who have provided the data and ideas that this book relies upon. They include:

Khairul Khaidzir

Alex Menezes

Marcia Pereira

Alice Pereira

Ishmail Sumsuddin

Joongseok Ryu

Abu Hasan Ismail

Tami Belhadj

Faisal Agabani

Steven Roberts

Loke Shee Ming

Jane Dark

Rashid Embi

Barrie Bowden

George Cotera

Adela Cotera

Abu Bakar

Clive Davies

Robert Ashton

Cristina Cerulli

Paramita Atmotiwirjo

Preface

During my studies at the Oxford School of Architecture I found myself increasingly unhappy at how little we knew about the way our designs impacted on people. I went to study psychology in an attempt at least to correct my deficiency. I got sidetracked. At that time, the study of design was really in its infancy and many of the writers and thinkers were creating methods for designers rather than understanding how they might actually work. Some hugely influential books and papers were written around that time, not least by Christopher Alexander (Alexander 1964), Chris Jones (Jones 1970), Sydney Gregory (Gregory 1966), Bruce Archer (Archer 1969) and Geoffrey Broadbent (Broadbent 1973). Although I owe a huge debt of gratitude to all these authors, my new glimpse of cognitive psychology had left me dissatisfied with their lack of empirical evidence. So I wrote Masters and Doctoral theses based on actual experimental studies of how designers thought.

I published the first version of *How Designers Think* in 1980 and it has been in continuous print ever since, going through four editions. However, the book always had an uncomfortable structure. It was initially written to further stimulate the blossoming research field. The development of the field perhaps owes more to Nigel Cross, not just for his books and papers but also for steering the leading journal *Design Studies* through all those years. However, increasingly, students read the book and many have been kind enough to tell me how helpful they found it.

Having written several other books, I returned to *How Designers Think* in recent years wondering how to bring it up to date. Having worked with Kees Dorst on the way designers acquire their expertise (Lawson and Dorst 2009), it seemed time to restructure this book. This version is therefore specifically meant to accompany the process of learning to design. It is a sort of guide or handbook to take design students through their journey of learning to perform one of the most miraculous of human achievements, the designing of new things and places.

I hope it might also prove useful to those who teach design and even to my fellow researchers. But the structure and style of these pages are specifically crafted with the student in mind.

References

Alexander, C. (1964). *Notes on the Synthesis of Form*. New York, McGraw Hill.

Archer, L. B. (1969). "The structure of the design process". *Design Methods in Architecture*. G. Broadbent and A. Ward. London, Lund Humphries.

Broadbent, G. (1973). *Design in Architecture*. New York, John Wiley.

Gregory, S. A. (1966). *The Design Method*. London, Butterworths.

Jones, J. C. (1970). *Design Methods: Seeds of Human Futures*. New York, John Wiley.

Lawson, B. R. and C. H. Dorst (2009). *Design Expertise*. Oxford, Elsevier/Architectural Press.

Chapter 1

Design as a set of skills you can learn

This book

In writing this book I am making some basic and simple guesses about you the reader. I assume you are either considering starting, or have begun to study, a design course. This course will involve either two- or three-dimensional design or possibly what we might call abstract or conceptual design.

Design courses

Two-dimensional design courses usually involve graphic design of some sort and increasingly web page design. Three-dimensional design courses are concerned with the creation of objects or places. They include product or industrial design and architecture as well as interior, landscape and urban design. Abstract courses include software and systems design.

This book is intended to be a helpful companion on your journey through a design-based course as you gradually become a more competent and, hopefully, creative designer. The sequence of ideas introduced should approximate to the way you meet challenges as you go. It is all based on our current understanding of the design process and how we learn to acquire design expertise. We are all different and there is no one right way to learn, just as there is no one right way to design.

These insets

The material found in these insets gives more detail, examples, quotes and images that should help to amplify understanding. You will often find the words of admired designers or of other students here to help explain.

Learning

Learning to design is not something that you can do just from a book. You must experience and make sense of design for yourself. The kind of learning you are embarking on requires you to acquire and absorb knowledge but it also requires you to develop a whole range of skills. This book is mostly about the skills rather than the knowledge. Some of the knowledge you will need is technical or historical. You will not find that in this book. Other knowledge you will need is about the materials of design including geometry, form, colour, texture, proportion and so on. That is not here either. You will also need to know about lots of designs in your field. This book should help you to understand how to use all this knowledge.

You will also need to acquire a number of what we might call practical skills. Drawing, surveying and measuring and using computers are obvious examples. Again, this book will not help you much with those but it should help you to understand their importance and how to use them in your design process.

Finally, you will need to learn the various mental processes that make up the wonderful act of designing. This book will help you to recognise those skills, learn and practise them and integrate them into a design process that works for you and makes a natural fit with your developing views about what makes good design.

Models of learning

1.1

You might like to choose between two images of possible learning models (Figure 1.1).

1. You are effectively some kind of raw material. Your design school/university is a production line that will take you and mould you into a finished product.
2. Your design school/university is like a secret cave, the walls of which are encrusted with precious jewels. Your degree course gives you the tools that enable you to prise out the jewels.

Essentially the question here is are you a raw material or are you an explorer? If you have chosen the first image in Figure 1.1 this book is unlikely to help you. I have written it with the second model in mind. I doubt design can ever really be learned using the first model. You will also find that this book returns to some ideas several times. This is because the mental tools you need to extract the most precious jewels can only be developed after acquiring some understanding of the simpler tools.

Learning to design

Designing is one of the most exciting, fascinating and rewarding tasks the human mind can perform. We have done it for centuries and yet for most of that time we have understood very little about how we do it. This does not make for a very easy educational experience. Some in design education would argue that design cannot be taught and that you simply have to learn it for yourself. There is something in this argument since, as we shall see, design is a highly individual process. In the end you must find a way of taking responsibility for your own development as a designer. This book should not be seen as teaching you how to design but rather helping you to learn from your experiences. You are likely to be learning by tackling a series of design projects that increase in complexity. My own tutor was fond of saying that 'simplicity is beyond complexity'. Learning to make a complicated problem into a simple solution is one of the most precious design skills.

Learning by designing

Frans de la Haye is an industrial designer who has also worked in furniture and graphic design. He is known for being able to reduce complex sets of functions to simple human-friendly forms (Figure 1.2). He has been highly

(continued)

(continued)

1.2

influential in Dutch design education, particularly through his work at Eindhoven. He has summed up this process of learning by designing perfectly.

> If all goes well you will have changed after every project; you will have developed yourself further. If you manage to deal with change in this manner it energises you. I think this can be taught. If you confront students with this in design school, you are just in time.
>
> (Lawson and Dorst 2009)

This book is intended to help with this timely process.

We strive to achieve the best we can in all our design projects. This is the first of many paradoxes about design education. At the end of your course how good each of your designs were will actually matter very little. What really matters is how much you learn from each project. For many of us learning to design is a lifetime journey and certainly one that will extend to long after you leave university and qualify.

Becoming a designer takes time

It may take longer than you think.

An exhibition celebrating the work of the best upcoming architects in Singapore defined 'young' architects as those under 45 years of age.

And the architectural critic Hugh Pearman said 'in architecture, you are young if you are under 50, an infant if you are under 40 and a babe in arms if you are under 30' (Lawson 2006).

By comparison, Professor John Postgate FRS, writing about the career of scientists, said

> It would be greatly to the advantage of all concerned if they (scientists), like the military, were normally taken on for a career-length term, say 25 years. At age 45 they would, subject to performance, normally be promoted by one grade and retired immediately on half pay.

Some involved in the education of designers may tell you that they cannot teach you to design and you must learn for yourself. This is probably true but, after a lifetime of teaching design students, I am sure we can help that process along a little bit.

This book (again)

The chapters in this book are put in an order that, I hope, follows the learning experience as well as any fixed order can. Learning, and most certainly learning to design, does not follow a linear path. It is probably better to think of it as somehow circling around and getting a deeper understanding each time. There is even a whole set of educational ideas known as the 'spiral curriculum' based on this (though it really is more like a helix than a spiral). This means that we will often come back to ideas mentioned earlier in the book.

I have written the chapters to be as self-contained as possible. They are all fairly short and deal with only a very few main ideas; in many cases a whole chapter only deals with one major idea. I hope you will find you can read a chapter at one sitting as it were. To make this work for you some important illustrations appear more than once. You might notice already that this section has a heading that also appeared at the start of the chapter. It will be helpful if you get into your head this idea of going around in circles but with an increasingly deeper understanding, helped by the learning you have been doing. In that cave I mentioned earlier, you can dig more out of it each time you return to it. Things often make more sense once you have begun work yourself. If, on the other hand, you want to probe a deeper understanding then you might like to try looking at one of the other books mentioned below.

Other books about designing that may help

This book is written specifically for those learning to design. If you are trying to increase your understanding of design or would like to explore that field further then you may find my other books of interest. They include:

> *How Designers Think, 4th Edition* (Lawson 2006);
>
> *What Designers Know* (Lawson 2004);
>
> *Design in Mind* (Lawson 1994);
>
> *Design Expertise*, written jointly with Kees Dorst (Lawson and Dorst 2009).

In addition, similar ground is covered in different ways in:

> *Design Thinking* by Nigel Cross (Cross 2011);
>
> *Understanding Design* by Kees Dorst (Dorst 2006).

Finally, if you want to look at similar issues to those covered here as a teacher rather than a student you might also look at:

> *Design Education* (Lyon 2011);
>
> *Design Pedagogy* (Tovey 2015).

A special way of thinking and unusual places

Design involves a very special way of thinking. We will learn more about this as we proceed but some features are very obvious on design courses. They are different from most other university courses in a number of ways. I have walked into industrial design schools in London and Delft, into architecture schools in Brazil, Sydney and Singapore, interior design schools in Birmingham and Hong Kong and landscape schools in Edinburgh and Philadelphia, and immediately felt at home. I could quickly get a good feeling for what was going on and what they were trying to do. Here is a delightful paradox; I visited the chemistry department in my own university and found myself in what felt a very foreign place.

The studio

You would expect to find a laboratory in a chemistry department. In a department teaching design-based courses you expect to find a studio. This is

one of the studios at the Sheffield University School of Architecture that I have been connected with for nearly 50 years (Figure 1.3). People come and go and the furniture gets replaced but it has looked like this since I first saw it. As we shall see in Chapter 5, the studio is not just a place. It represents a whole sophisticated and highly specialised system of teaching and learning.

Why should this be? First, design is prescriptive rather than descriptive. Instead of describing the world or explaining it in some way, design suggests how the world might be. We designers might have to admit that this sounds rather arrogant. While scientists strive to understand and describe our world and historians tell us how it was in the past, we just tell everybody how it should be in the future. On a design-based course there is no great body of abstract theory to learn, rather it tends to be very practical. While many university courses tend to take things apart and study them in separate components or modules, design courses concentrate more on putting things together and have large blocks of largely unscheduled project work. They are more about synthesis than analysis.

All this results in not just different methods of teaching and learning but even quite different-looking places in which this happens. The most obvious of all these is the 'studio' but even the library in a design school often looks different and it needs to be.

Learning how design works in the studio

Early on in my academic career I invited an urban sociologist to work with me on a studio design project where the students were re-imagining an urban area that had become rundown and full of social problems. She found collaborating with me almost impossible. She would make a suggestion and I would typically say something like 'no you don't understand, design just doesn't work that way'. One day she totally lost patience, saying 'well why don't you just give me the undergraduate textbook and I'll go away and read it'. My answer made her even more confused and angry. I said 'there isn't such a book; design courses just don't have textbooks'.

I was lucky to read architecture first and then study for a Masters degree and Doctorate in psychology. About half the students on my Masters course had undergraduate degrees in psychology and they pointed me in the direction of the standard undergraduate textbooks on psychology. I got one out of the library and read it cover to cover in a few days. It was hard work but absolutely possible. My urban sociologist friend did not have the option of reading such a book about design.

We are lucky to have a helpful paper on this very problem written by Laura Willenbrock, an exceptionally perceptive and articulate student, who transferred onto an architecture course from a more conventional one. The paper describes her puzzlement at the way knowledge was being taught in architecture and you may find her paper helpful if you are struggling too (Willenbrock 1991). We will take a closer look at this curious lack of theory and textbooks in a later chapter, and show that it is totally understandable.

A design student's struggle to understand

I transferred into architecture in my sophomore year. I had enrolled initially in Miami University's nationally known International Studies program . . . I remember feeling very anxious about my early days in the undergraduate architecture program at Miami University. I was unsure about the way we were being directed toward knowledge, although I was willing to trust that there was a particular design in the minds of our professors. Whether I was patient, optimistic, or fighting cynicism I am not sure.

(Willenbrock 1991)

One of the issues that my urban sociologist colleague was confronting was the lack of any boundary around the knowledge that might be useful in a design process. This is one of the most fundamental reasons for the lack of complete textbooks for design-based subjects.

There is no boundary around the knowledge that may be useful in design

1.4

This simple garden shelter is where I sometimes sit to write. It illustrates how difficult it is to predict the knowledge that might be useful during a design process. Not long before I designed this shelter I had visited Bali for the first time. I was fascinated by the extraordinary shelters or 'pondoks' constructed in the rice fields by the workers there. Here they would rest and shelter from the very strong and hot mid-day sun. That magical Indonesian island also has the most wonderful collection of temples with characteristic tiers of roofs. You can clearly see the influence of this trip on my design process. This pavilion is not a copy of any building I saw and has features that combine components both of pondoks and temples. The stark truth here is that had I just visited somewhere else my humble garden pavilion would almost certainly have looked quite different. Later in this book we will explore how such apparently random knowledge is creatively recombined and used in design.

It is not just the knowledge base, the timetabling of the course or the physical spaces that give design schools their distinctive flavour. The most important difference is the culture we find in them. Design schools are places where creativity and originality are highly valued. When I studied for a postgraduate degree in psychology my tutors did not expect me to come up with original or even interesting results but they demanded that my methods and processes were sound and rigorous, thoroughly documented and ultimately replicable by others. This felt very odd after five years in architecture school where the end results of my studio work were examined very closely and critically. My tutors hardly ever bothered to ask how I got there but they did believe I might create something new and worthwhile. Just occasionally perhaps I did.

You are quite likely to find this too, as it is normal in most of the schools of design I have encountered. Your tutors will give you high marks for what they consider to be good designs. You are unlikely to get any credit for a good process unless the final design is also assessed to be good. In a way this is quite understandable and reasonable since, if you eventually become a professional designer, your clients, users or customers are paying for the design outcome not the process. However, in another way this is also a pity. Some will argue, and they have a good case, that clients and other stakeholders can become useful participants in the design process and this can lead to better results. For this to happen we need to make design processes rather more transparent. But we are getting ahead of ourselves and must leave the question of how various stakeholders impact on the design process until a later chapter.

Design, thinking and skill

It must be obvious that, as well as thinking in a special way, designing requires you to have a number of practical skills. The most obvious of these must surely be that of drawing. Designers make and use drawings a great deal. We will explore that in detail in a later chapter. Designers also make physical models and sometimes build full-size prototypes. Nowadays, too, we use computer-aided design sometimes for making drawings and sometimes for making 3-D models. All these and other activities require you to learn and develop a series of skills without which you would hardly be able to design anything of any complexity.

But we can consider thinking to be a skill too. Thinking is something we all do all the time without getting self-conscious about it. But if you depend upon that thinking to conduct the core activity of your professional life, you had better be able to do it well. We will therefore later explore the kinds of thinking that are most often used in design and suggest some ways to practise and improve how you do that thinking.

Designing and thinking as skills

The great philosopher Gilbert Ryle said 'thought is very much a matter of drills and skills' (Ryle 1949).

A decade later the British psychologist Frederick Bartlett wrote a book simply called *Thinking* in which he wrote 'thinking should be treated as a complex and high level kind of skill' (Bartlett 1958).

More recently the popular guru of 'Lateral Thinking', Edward de Bono, wrote 'to regard thinking as a skill rather than a gift is the first step towards doing something to improve that skill' (de Bono 1971).

So, we designers are going to have to learn, develop and practise a tricky skill set. Most design courses expect you to begin designing right from the start, so this book will start trying to help you with this pretty quickly too. In fact, it is quite dangerous to delay learning these skills. One of my most cherished pastimes has been to struggle to learn to play a number of musical instruments, particularly the flute. My teacher is fond of warning me not to practise my mistakes. By this of course she means that repeatedly doing something that is bad practice, sloppy, or plain wrong is a surefire way of reinforcing it. Then eventually you have the much greater pain of undoing your whole approach. So if you are going to start doing a lot of designing you had better get going on these core skills too.

This book is intended to help you through this process of learning to design. However, do not think this period of learning is wholly encompassed by your time in design school. When he was over 80 years old, the great cellist Pablo Casals was asked why, at such an age, he continued to practise every day. 'Because', he replied, 'I think I am making some progress'.[1] Of course designing is not a matter of giving a performance but it remains such a difficult thing to do well consistently that you must expect the learning process to continue well after you have left design school, and probably for the rest of your life.

There is one more thing to be said in general about this before we get down to some serious learning. Developing a simple skill like riding a bicycle or swimming is not a smooth process. Designing is so complex in terms of the range of skills involved that you should be ready for a bumpy rather than an even ride. However, the good news is that you have already begun the ride and are well on the way, as we shall see in the next chapter.

Learning complex skills can be frustrating at first

Skill acquisition is rarely a steady process and is more accurately thought of as a staircase rather than a ramp. This will be discussed in much more detail almost at the end of the book in Chapter 25, once we have discussed all the skills involved. For now it will suffice to say that your development can be thought of as a series of steps. This is because certain ideas and concepts, and the skills that go with using them, can suddenly release a newly found competence. Often you are only likely to move up to the next level after realising the need to improve yet again and having the experience and understanding to do so. We tutors in design schools often see our students make sudden leaps forward as they climb the next step on their staircase. It can sometimes be frustrating for tutors as occasionally we think a student has understood when actually they were just lucky and then they appear to tumble back down the staircase again. While we are all different in some ways there seem to be many generalities about this staircase and this book is specifically intended to help you recognise and understand a new step and to make it confidently. What you are about to do can at times seem hugely frustrating but it is ultimately wonderfully fulfilling and great fun. It is also of great value to society and so worth all the effort. Good luck!

Note

1 Pablo Casals' comment was reported in the May 1959 edition of *Reader's Digest*, Volume 74, Personal Glimpses, start page 29, quote page 30, column 1. Pleasantville, New York, The Reader's Digest Association.

References

Bartlett, F. C. (1958). *Thinking*. London, George Allen and Unwin.

Cross, N. (2011). *Design Thinking: Understanding how Designers Think and Work*. Oxford, Berg.

de Bono, E. (1971). *Practical Thinking*. London, Jonathan Cape.

Dorst, C. H. (2006). *Understanding Design: 175 Reflections on Being a Designer*. Amsterdam, BIS Publishers.

Lawson, B. R. (1994). *Design in Mind*. Oxford, Butterworth Architecture.

Lawson, B. R. (2004). *What Designers Know*. Oxford, Elsevier/Architectural Press.

Lawson, B. R. (2006). *How Designers Think*. Oxford, Elsevier/Architectural Press.

Lawson, B. R. and C. H. Dorst (2009). *Design Expertise*. Oxford, Elsevier/Architectural Press.

Lyon, P. (2011). *Design Education: Learning, Teaching and Researching Through Design*. Oxford, Routledge.

Ryle, G. (1949). *The Concept of Mind*. London, Hutchinson.

Tovey, M. (2015). *Design Pedagogy: Developments in Art and Design Education*. Oxford, Routledge.

Willenbrock, L. L. (1991). "An undergraduate voice in architectural education". *Voices in Architectural Education*. T. A. Dutton. New York, Bergin and Garvey: 97–119.

Chapter 2

Getting going (actually you've already started)

Some good news: we are all designers

Designing demands a pretty complicated set of skills with many more to discover in later chapters. Design is full of paradoxes; here is one that may seem confusing.

On the one hand the best designers perform amazing, almost magical tricks of creative imagination that draw great admiration. The very word 'designer' is often used in modern marketing to lend a special cache to items and lift them above the ordinary. So we can even have that most absurd of all, 'designer jeans'. Here the most everyday ordinary object is apparently made exclusive and special simply because the word 'designer' is attached to it as an adjective.

On the other hand, in practice, virtually all of us are designers and probably design in some way as an everyday event. We dress ourselves, selecting and buying items and combining them, often in original and distinctive ways. We layout documents and create our own computer desktops. We arrange our homes and individualise mass-produced objects like cars. We may even take on more ambitious projects such as landscaping our gardens or refurbishing rooms in our homes, perhaps even the whole house. If you have friends or relatives organising a wedding you might see them perform simple graphic design, fashion design, designing interior or exterior places, creating menus and programmes. All these activities look remarkably like designing. They create new objects, appearances or places that had not existed before and that could not really have been predicted by others.

Most of the time people do all these things without claiming they are designing or even thinking so themselves. They have no particular skills at design and probably could not describe any sort of process in a way that might help others to do the same. We might call this 'naïve' design, because it shows characteristics that are consistent with the normal definition of that word.

But the word 'naïve' can also be used rather pejoratively so instead I prefer to think of this kind of work as 'everyday design'. Since you have almost certainly done a considerable amount of this you might consider yourself already to be a designer, an everyday designer. Someone starting a design-based degree course might reasonably be expected to be a pretty good everyday designer. That is the good news.

On the other hand we want to help you to become a more sophisticated, admired, sought after, professional designer. Most of us are unlikely to achieve this overnight, so how should we embark on this journey?

Professional design

It is useful to begin by looking at the limitations of everyday design, perhaps where you are now or have been until quite recently. The most obvious difference must surely be in the usual end result. Professional designers aspire to achieve something greater than the mundane, ordinary, and purely utilitarian. Good design is meant to improve the lives of people who come into contact with it, not just in a practical way but also somehow to lift their spirits. The distinctions between good design and the achievements of everyday design are often difficult to pin down but, like elephants, we recognise them when we see them. The great philosopher Wittgenstein became very interested in architecture and naturally turned his thoughts to what distinguished great architecture from mere building.

2.1

the human body is a gesture' (Wilson 1986). We are used to the idea that ballet is indeed a form of gestural movement. This Balinese dancer is performing an exquisitely constructed form of visual language to tell a story in an extraordinarily expressive manner (Figure 2.1). For Wittgenstein, then, architecture is to building what ballet is to walking.

The architect Edwin Lutyens described architecture as 'building with wit'.

But we must be careful with this distinction. The architectural historian Nicolas Pevsner claimed that 'a bicycle shed is mere building. Lincoln Cathedral is architecture' (Pevsner 1943). No doubt he is right about Lincoln Cathedral but perhaps we should not dismiss the possibilities of a bicycle shed so easily. Even the simplest object or structure can be created in a manner that we recognise as designed. My garden shelter was inspired by a trip to Bali (Figure 1.4). Had I been somewhere else it might have looked very different. This suggests that designers often make use of ideas and information from quite different fields and places in their processes. In fact, we cannot place a boundary around the knowledge that a design might draw on. This will be an important issue for us later in the book. It distinguishes the professional act of designing from that of the everyday.

Balinese temples

As well as providing shelter these beautiful structures communicate ideas that are central to the culture of Bali. They create places to celebrate the religion practised there.

2.2

Everyday designing

If we examine everyday design activities we find that many of them are actually little more than making a series of simple decisions that are often limited choices. Hatchuel has clarified this nicely using the everyday example of a group of friends planning an evening (Hatchuel 2002).

They might decide to go to the cinema in which case the task just becomes one of choosing between a limited set of alternatives. It might be just a matter of getting on the internet and looking at what films are showing. There may well be some argument and negotiation between the friends but their choices are limited not by them but by other people. Really this is not designing but choosing.

Alternatively they may decide to organise a party. This becomes a rather more open-ended, complex and sophisticated process. First they have to decide what sort of a party they want and this is not a choice between simple alternatives already packaged. These friends must now envisage possibilities. This requires a creative leap into the unknown unless they are simply going to replicate a previous event. Actually they are quite likely to want to combine different features they liked from a whole series of other events. Maybe they might add in something new too, perhaps something they have always wanted to do. This feels much more like designing than simple problem solving. It is creative and could result in something entirely new, original and unpredictable.

More than just problem solving

Unfortunately the distinction between designing and problem solving is not always quite that simple. Few things in the world of design are. To see one way in which the boundaries are blurred, let us imagine an apparently simple set of choices. We are about to add a conservatory at the rear of our house. We look at the catalogues or websites of a number of suppliers. How are we going to choose between them? Well there are some simple dimensions to the problem such as cost. Perhaps we just want the cheapest; in which case the job is simple and almost done. But what if our budget is not quite so restricted or critical? We might use ordinary single glazing or more thermally efficient sealed cavity-glazed units. There will be different finishes and treatments available. There will be different ventilation patterns, systems of blinds and so on.

Now the task becomes a little more complex because we might have to judge each of these features in different ways. How much money are we prepared to pay for a more thermally efficient solution? We might like the appearance of some more than others but find it almost impossible to say by how much. The level of maintenance required for each type will vary and we may find a difficult tradeoff has to be made between appearance and the frequency and cost of maintenance. There is a lot to be taken into account in arriving at our final choice. We have an extra layer of problem. It is no longer just a matter of making a decision; it is also how to make that decision. Of course there is no one right or correct answer here. Different people in different circumstances will arrive at different conclusions. They must do, or there just would not be all this choice available on the market. This begins to look more like designing than simple problem solving. This is because we have introduced a situation in which all the choices cannot be made using the same kinds of criteria or methods of measuring.

Measuring success

Effectively this means that designing usually involves reconciling the incommensurate. If you are just doing this for yourself you do not have to justify how you arrive at an answer, but if you are a professional designer working for a client you may need to explain how all this works. You should certainly be aware of it yourself.

Four ways of measuring success with numbers

There are four accepted sets of numerical scales that we might have to use in design. They are called 'ratio', 'interval', 'ordinal' and 'nominal'.

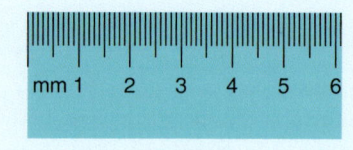

2.3

Ratio scales

We measure distance or money along a 'ratio' scale (Figure 2.3). We can say that 6 centimetres is three times as far as 2 centimetres. The ratio of 3:1 remains constant all the way up the scale. This is so obvious that we might easily be tempted to think all numbers work this way.

Interval scales

We cannot say that 20°C is five times hotter than 4°C. This is because 0°C does not mean an absence of heat. It is just an arbitrary point, which happens to be the freezing point of water. This becomes obvious if you use the Fahrenheit scale where the freezing point of water is not 0°F but 32°F. However, temperature scales do have constant intervals, so the difference between 0 and 10 degrees is the same as the difference between 10 and 20 degrees (Figure 2.4).

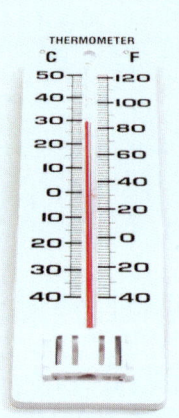

2.4

	Team	GP	W	D	L	GF	GA	GD	Pts
1.	Manchester City	7	6	1	0	21	3	18	19
2.	Liverpool	7	6	1	0	15	3	12	19
3.	Chelsea	7	5	2	0	15	5	10	17
4.	Tottenham Hotspur	7	5	0	2	14	7	7	15
5.	Arsenal	7	5	0	2	14	9	5	15
6.	Watford	7	4	1	2	11	8	3	13
7.	Bournemouth	7	4	1	2	12	12	0	13
8.	Leicester City	7	4	0	3	13	10	3	12
9.	Wolverhampton Wan...	7	3	3	1	8	6	2	12
10.	Manchester United	7	3	1	3	10	12	-2	10

2.5

Ordinal scales

When we show alternative design ideas to our clients they may tell us they prefer one idea to another but are unable to say exactly by how much. We find many such ranking scales in design. We can list our order of preference but the intervals between numbers may vary. It is just their order that remains fixed rather like the league positions of sports teams (Figure 2.5). In a league table the number of points scored is not likely to show identical intervals.

Nominal scales

Here numbers are used in place of names (Figure 2.6). The numbers on the back of football players' shirts do not imply order. No intervals or ratios can meaningfully be applied here. This kind of number is often used in legislation that governs design products.

2.6

When factors in a design situation are measured along different types of scales there can be no correct way of relating them to each other. More often than not design involves some compromise, some trading off of one thing against another. This must inevitably lead us to the conclusion that there cannot be right or wrong answers here, and that each of us may look at the design alternatives and rank them differently. This is going to make your life as a professional designer a little difficult.

The danger of numbers in design

You may have found the previous section rather dull but it is useful to understand numbering systems. There have been attempts to reduce complex decision making down to simple numerical exercises and you should be able to argue for the more sophisticated processes of design. Perhaps the most blatant attempt at this reductionism is the notion of 'cost-benefit analysis'. This mistaken idea turns every decision into the most obvious common currency, money. Then, the argument goes, you simply choose the cheapest. All the subjectivity and varying measurement scales were hidden in the process of converting costs and benefits to sums of money. In our modern scientific age numbers can look authoritative, precise and objective but remember that statistics can be misleading.

In design, numbers can often lead you astray. You will not see them crop up a great deal in the rest of this book. I was giving a talk about this many years ago when a member of the audience, a rather angry architect, said he had a better example of this than any of the ones I gave in my talk. He was right. In this case a misuse of numbers had led a local authority to demand a design that was both more expensive and less effective than the one he had proposed. Even when this was demonstrated to those in power they could not bring themselves to change their decision. After all, the proof was in the numbers, or so they maintained.

The number trap

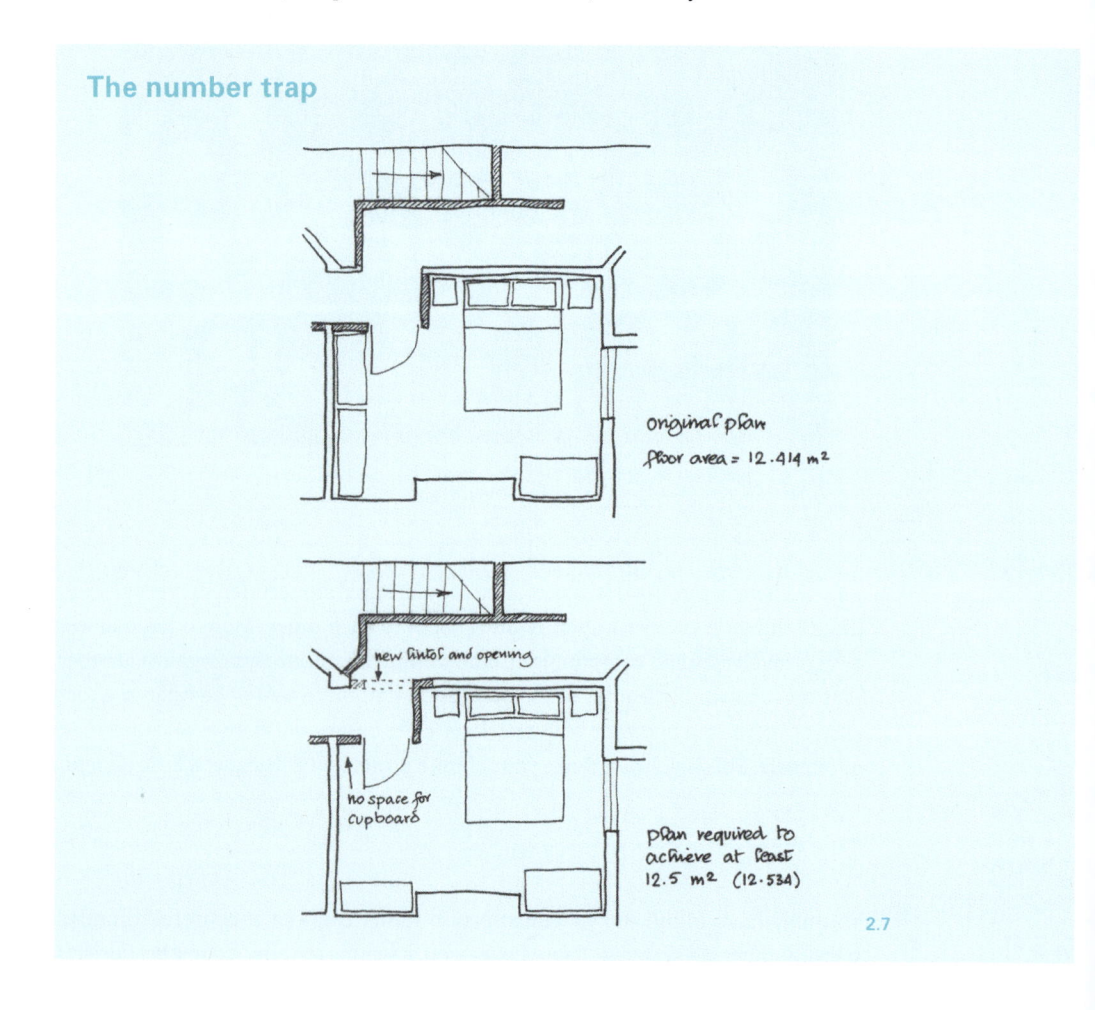

original plan
floor area = 12.414 m²

new lintol and opening

no space for cupboard

plan required to achieve at least 12.5 m² (12.534)

2.7

An architect was converting some Victorian houses to multi-occupancy apartments. The first drawing (Figure 2.7 top) shows a small part of his proposal. It is the newly proposed master bedroom on the upper floor of the house. The hatched walls are necessary for fire compartments around each dwelling. The architect has astutely kept them to the minimum and existing door lintels are used over openings. But the floor area is only 12.414 square metres. The authority required that it should be at least 12.5 square metres. This must be better because the floor area is larger, they maintained. But look carefully at the second drawing (Figure 2.7 bottom) and you will see the design allows for less furniture in the room. It is also more expensive to build, due to the greater extent of alteration of walls and lintels.

I am grateful to Geoff Jones of Building and Urban Design Associates in Birmingham for this example of the danger of numbers in design.

Numbers should really only be used carefully when trying to assess success in design. This requires the sort of expertise and understanding that designers should have but that other stakeholders may not. You may find yourself grappling with clients or regulators who cannot see this, so it is a good idea both to be able to understand it and to be able to explain it.

In professional design it is all in flux

When creating our conservatory we could hire an architect, who might design a totally bespoke solution without being restricted to any manufacturer's catalogue of sizes, shapes or combinations of facilities. In this case we are likely to create solutions that could not be achieved with the 'off the peg' alternatives. This looks much more like a professional design situation, where apparently almost everything is in flux. We would expect our architect to understand all the technicalities of the performance of alternative conservatories and of the way they are connected to the original building. We would expect him or her to know what permissions such as planning might be needed and to be able to complete those processes for us. We would expect our architect to understand such matters as the maintenance of each type of conservatory and to be able to advise us on that.

We also expect our designer to be able to show us what the proposed conservatory would look like in order for us to be sure it is what we want. All this is part of a normal design service. But there is still more to professional design.

We might hope the architect for our conservatory could go further and come up with some possibilities that we had not even imagined and make us think about why we really wanted the conservatory, and help us to arrive at a solution that effectively and beautifully meets all our needs and wishes. Indeed, it is not unusual for a good designer to realise that your original ideas and the brief you produced are actually not what you need at all. Perhaps a conservatory might not really be the best way forward. It might be that a more solid extension to the house might be better, or perhaps a summerhouse at the end of the garden might work better. Maybe you really need to move house altogether and the idea of a conservatory is just papering over the cracks, as it were. A good professional designer should be able to uncover the real problems rather than those expressed and suggest alternatives that had never even crossed the client's mind.

Designing often involves imagining something original

The great British architect Sir Denys Lasdun once said 'it is the architect's job not to give the client what he wanted but what he never even dreamt of' (Lasdun 1965).

There is a wonderful passage in *Das Kapital* (Marx 1867) where Karl Marx says

> A bee puts to shame many an architect in the construction of her cells but what distinguishes the worst of architects from the best of bees is this, that the architect raises his structure in imagination before he erects it in reality. At the end of every labour process we get a result that already existed in the imagination of the labourer at its beginning.

That makes an excellent motto for this book.

So just how do you learn to do all these things and progress from everyday designer to professional designer? We shall get some ideas about that in the next chapter. For now it is important to recognise that designing inevitably involves comparing the incommensurate. If you want to be able to design well you must come to terms with this. Somehow you must be prepared to make decisions that cannot be backed up by any scientific evidence or argument. If this worries you, then design may not be for you. But if you want to rise to that challenge, and to many more that we shall encounter through this book, then be ready for an exciting and rewarding but frequently bumpy ride!

References

Hatchuel, A. (2002). "Towards design theory and expandable rationality: the unfinished program of Herbert Simon". *Journal of Management and Governance* 5(3): 260–273.
Lasdun, D. (1965). "An architect's approach to architecture". *RIBA Journal* 72(4): 184–195.
Marx, K. (1867). *Das Kapital*. Hamberg, Verlag von Otto Meissner.
Pevsner N. (1943). *An Outline of European Architecture*. London, Thames and Hudson.
Wilson, C. S. J. (1986). "The play of use and use of play". *Architectural Review* 180(1073): 15–18.

Chapter 3

From vernacular design to design by drawing

A little history

Just how do you learn to progress from everyday designer to professional designer? Before we can sensibly answer this we need just a small amount of history. Professional design has only really become the norm in relatively recent times and, even now, it would not be meaningful to talk about it in large parts of the developing world. A large proportion of the world's population do not commission a professional designer to create ideas for their homes; they get on and build themselves. The Native Americans did not have architects; they just knew how to make a tepee.

A modern interpretation of the tepee

3.1

(continued)

(continued)

Native Americans made their homes from the materials that were around them and to hand. They were also wonderfully well adapted to the way of life and the climate.

Like the tepee, the igloo is a product of this unselfconscious process. The Inuit do not go to a professional igloo builder, they make their own. These buildings are marvellously well adapted to the special climate their owners must live in and are constructed largely without plans or instructions but follow designs that have evolved and been refined over many generations. These traditional buildings are also firmly embedded in the cultures of their inhabitants.

Design students try their hand at vernacular design

A group of my first year students were involved in a studio project helping them to learn how to design when it suddenly snowed very heavily. They immediately deserted the studio for the local park and built an igloo. There was little debate or argument as they already shared a common image of the traditional igloo.

3.2

Design students make false assumptions

The assumptions made by my students about construction were wrong (Figure 3.2). If you look carefully at the photograph you can see there is still a gap at the top that they were struggling to fill. Not one of them had thought of the traditional and time-honoured technique used by the Inuit. They arrange the blocks of snow along a sloping spiral ramp that gives much better support for the final block.

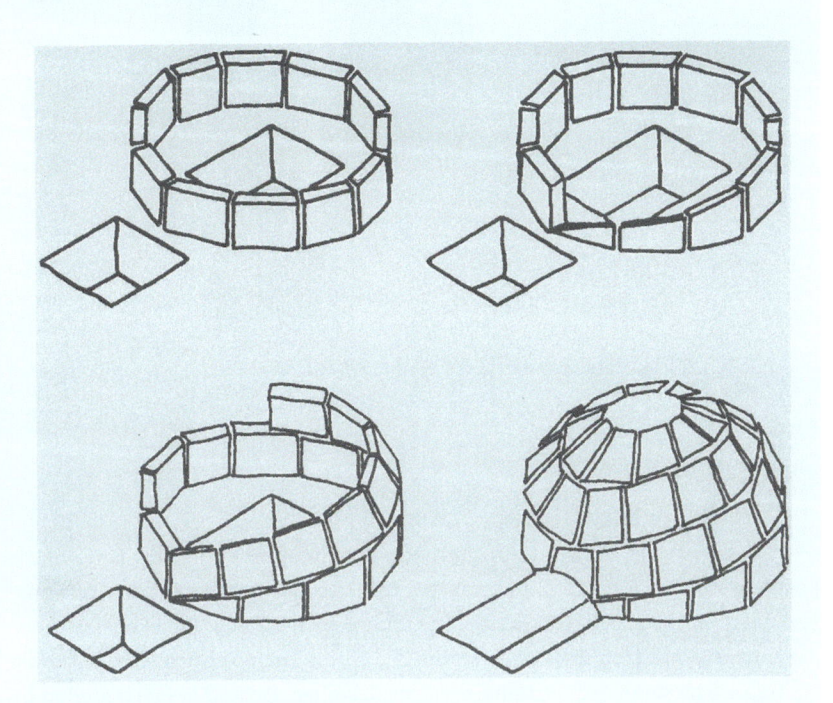

3.3

Some design creativity

Even though they were working in a vernacular fashion my students used a number of creative insights to complete their task. They were struggling to make good blocks of snow. One student had the brilliant idea of using the waste paper bin from my office. It was strong, made of metal and slightly tapered. This was ideal for compacting snow as a foot could easily be rammed down on it. The slight taper meant that when the bin was turned upside down and tapped hard, the block of snow easily slipped out.

(continued)

(continued)

It is not just houses that are made in this unselfconscious way. In the past you went to a tradesman such as a blacksmith to make all sorts of things you needed. His specialism lay not in coming up with new ideas but in knowing how to work iron into well-established forms such as horseshoes or tools. He was a craftsman rather than a creative designer. He had been trained in his craft through an apprenticeship. Typically his father would have taught him in a family business that might have a history going back through many generations. This was generally quite a good way of proceeding since you got objects that were more or less guaranteed to work well enough. They had stood the test of time.

The blacksmith

The blacksmith was a maker who used common patterns for everyday objects. This vernacular or blacksmith way of working integrated designing with making.

This was fine as long as things changed so slowly that these everyday objects could gradually evolve. But the craftsman designer would have been totally lost if asked to design an interface for some new-fangled device called a smart phone that had a touch-sensitive screen. Nowadays we definitely need a professional designer who can work things out afresh to meet entirely new situations.

A good example of this craftsman design can be found in George Sturt's wheelwright's shop (Sturt 1923). Sturt was born into a family that had a long-standing business making cartwheels. He did not follow in the business as an apprentice, instead preferring to travel to widen his education. As a result he developed some analytical skills, but when his father died he inherited the business and came home to run it. He naturally applied his analytical skills to what had hitherto been an unselfconscious craft process. Sturt could not help but notice that the cartwheels made in the workshop were a rather complex pattern that to him looked very difficult to build.

Vernacular design can lead to very sophisticated solutions

The traditional cartwheel is not made in a flat plane but is dished. Laid on their sides, these wheels look like huge saucers. This might seem

(continued)

(continued)

unnecessarily complex. Actually it turns out to be a very clever piece of traditional design. You might like to think why this should be. The answer will be given in a later chapter.

3.6

Not surprisingly Sturt asked his employees why this was since it seemed to him that it would be far simpler and quicker to make them flat (it turns out he was wrong but more of that later). Unfortunately for Sturt the answer he got gave him no reassurance. It was along the lines of 'well we've always made them that way'. It seemed that nobody had ever asked this question before and the wheelwrights themselves had certainly not considered it. Each of them would have started off as an apprentice being shown what to do by the established craftsmen. This distinctive shape had evolved over many generations. Whatever reasons there may have been for this particular design of wheel were lost in the mists of time. This all intrigued Sturt so much that he set out to discover what he called 'the true reason for the dishing of the cartwheel' and, luckily for us, he wrote a book about his enquiries. We might say Sturt was trying to become the first professional design director in the family business. He was also becoming a highly inquisitive researcher, a very modern man in a bygone age. We will come back to this story a bit later and give you the answer that Sturt eventually discovered, but for now let us just say that it turns out that this shape worked wonderfully well for the horse-drawn farm carts of the time. It was, like so many traditional or vernacular designs, beautifully adapted to the situation.

However, we can already see the disadvantage with this craft process of design. It takes a very long time to create and refine these beautiful objects. Often, as in the case of the cartwheels, the process goes on over many generations. We can also hazard a pretty good guess that Sturt's craftsmen would have been totally lost if the internal combustion engine and the pneumatic tyre were suddenly introduced into the equation. As technology and society began to progress and change more rapidly, such a process became too cumbersome. Today the technology used in so many of the artefacts we use and the buildings we live in changes, often dramatically, within a single lifetime. This vernacular craftsman-based process is no longer practical.

The separation of designing from making

So along came the new professional form of designing, which shows two major changes from vernacular designing. First, designing was separated from making. It is common now that designers are not able to make the objects they imagine, and those that make things can seldom design innovative new solutions.

Second, these new designers worked mainly using drawings. Rather than work on the real thing they worked on representations of it and frequently these were drawings. Today, if you are studying one of the major two- or three-dimensional design subjects, you are likely to use drawings and they will probably be the major way you represent an emerging design. However, physical models and computer models are increasingly in use by our contemporary professional designers. If you want to become a designer you are certainly going to have to be able to use all these tools and you had better get going and develop the necessary skills, but we are getting ahead of ourselves a little. We shall return to these representation skills in a short while.

The designer who works not by gradually refining traditional items but rather by working on representations such as drawings has a huge advantage. Many more radical changes can be envisioned in such a process. This means that designs can be adapted to take account of a rapidly developing set of circumstances. The products of traditional design are often delightful. But, no matter how familiar and reassuring the products of traditional design, the idea that we could still use traditional processes is mostly an illusion. Technology has now reached such a rate of change that, for the first time in human development, it occurs significantly within a single lifetime. We can no longer prepare university students for a whole career by just showing how things should be done.

Instead we must teach you to learn and discover how to do things for yourselves. This is what you, dear reader, are trying to do.

Although some commentators and critics, often those in privileged circumstances, have championed a return to traditional forms, especially in architecture, this will no longer offer a certain success. In our current world we often find society lagging behind technology as we struggle to discover how to use new materials and technologies. Those social realities are already showing intergenerational differences. We may now laugh at the absurdity of Alexander Graham Bell's claim about his new telephone when he confidently asserted that, eventually, 'every town in America would have one'. My father spent his life in the telephone industry but I do not believe he ever dreamt that his son would carry one around, take pictures with it, play music and have at his disposal more computing power than the whole university campus possessed during his student years.

George Sturt's wheelwrights could not contemplate the Formula One racing car in terms of the massive torque of its engine or the grip of its pneumatic rubber tyres. More importantly, even if presented with these amazing technical developments, vernacular craftsmen would not have been able to begin designing for them. You, the modern professional designer, can no longer be a traditional craftsman trained for life to be part of a gradual, almost imperceptible, refinement of designs over generations. But you face an almost impossible challenge. You must instead understand the implications of all these changes even though you cannot make the most basic wheel. You must instead create fantastical wheels that no one else has contemplated, and you must do this by representing your designs by drawing in one form or another.

However, the notion of design by drawing is far from perfect. It turns out that it has been responsible for some pretty awful disasters. The fundamental trouble with it is that you cannot always see all the ways the represented design might fail by looking at a drawing. In architecture we could draw and calculate structures for the highest towers for housing the masses. This happened in the crisis generated in Europe by the Second World War when suddenly huge numbers of homes were needed quickly, along with schools and hospitals and other community buildings. We could tell by looking at the drawings and calculations that such buildings, using new materials and structural forms, would not fall down. But it seemed no one could see the social disasters they all too often became. As is the case in modern life, the pace of technological change outstripped our ability to assimilate its products into modern societies.

Sheffield deck access housing

These famous buildings (there were three of them) won all sorts of architectural awards. However, the one shown (Figures 3.7a and 3.7b) rapidly became a major social problem and was demolished. The access decks at every other floor became dangerous places. Apart from the graffiti and muggings, some residents were known to tip disused televisions and other domestic waste items off them causing not only an eyesore but also danger to passers-by. One of the reasons for this was that the decks were not overlooked by windows, which you can see all face south to get the sun and overlook open space. We have a better understanding of these issues now but at the time they were designed, these problems could not be detected or predicted by looking at the drawings.

3.7a and 3.7b

Often today industrial designers must create completely new products not previously seen. Frequently this involves the combination of several previously separate functions into one item. The smart phone is the archetypal integrated product. This kind of design is now an example of what we might call 'technology push' rather than 'market pull'. In other words, we are designing things because we can, rather than because a client or potential user said they needed or even wanted it. Objects that succeed in creating a demand can be hugely successful and even bring significant global change. The smart phone has now been around for some time but we are only just beginning to deal with the behavioural consequences of the social media it has spawned. As I write this book a prominent British politician is warning that the level of anonymous but widely published abuse directed at public figures is beginning to discourage the next generation from becoming politicians.

I cannot predict what forms of representation may become available to you during your career. All I can do is to warn you that all forms of representation so far devised have their weaknesses and dangerous blind spots. You should learn to distrust any representation and to be suspicious of your design process in so far as it may not be showing you some vitally important issues.

Design by drawing

So now we are largely still working with the process first described by Chris Jones as 'design by drawing'. Jones pointed out that the drawing gives the designer a 'greater perceptual span' (Jones 1966). There are of course many other kinds of modelling you may use but, so far, none of them has come close to the power, flexibility and subtlety of the human sketch. Computer and physical models both take a considerable amount of time and skill to produce and computer systems usually demand that you talk their language rather than your own. They are invaluable and powerful aids to design but generally only at the later stages when examining the detail of a largely frozen design. Certainly the drafting and modelling systems of today are far better than the first generation of software. They also offer huge advantages of multiple representations and even interactive immersive experiences for our clients. As Jones might have said, they provide an even greater perceptual span. The view the designer has of the potential solution is increased but, as tools during the early conceptual phases of designing, they remain clunky to use compared with the human sketch.

So if design by drawing has largely replaced the vernacular process then learning the language of design drawings must be your next step. In fact, designers use many quite different kinds of drawings, each having its own purpose, language and structure. They will all be introduced in the next chapter so you can begin to hone your skills and develop your own way of designing.

References

Jones, J. C. (1966). "Design methods reviewed". *The Design Method*, S. A. Gregory. London, Butterworth.
Sturt, G. (1923). *The Wheelwright's Shop*. Cambridge, Cambridge University Press.

Chapter 4

Drawing in design

Something between a thing and a thought

An old saying that a picture is between a thing and a thought could be the motto for this chapter. Designers are almost inseparable from their drawings, which somehow encapsulate their thoughts. However, just as we saw in Chapter 2 that there are many kinds of numbers, so there are many types of drawings that designers commonly employ. Each type of design drawing not only has a specific use but also a particular set of rules and employs its own language. So you need quickly to understand all these graphical languages and begin to use them fluently. A more detailed exploration of design drawing types and their uses can be found in chapters four and five of *What Designers Know* (Lawson 2004).

Presentation drawings

These are the grandest and most well known of design drawings but we do not need to say much about them here. As the name suggests, they are used to present the design and perhaps to convince the viewer of its strengths. We might use them to address clients, users, the general public, investors, manufacturers and a whole host of other stakeholders. These drawings are often polished, may also get exhibited in galleries and are sometimes confused with art. Since they come after the real work of the design process we need not concern ourselves with them much here.

A presentation drawing of an urban design competition submission

This drawing (Figure 4.1) was done for clients who were choosing their design team for a major international urban design competition.

(continued)

(continued)

The competition was to plan the area known as Grangegorman in Dublin (The plan can be seen in Figure 20.4).

4.1

There are many excellent books on how to produce presentation drawings (I particularly like the series by Tom Porter and Sue Goodman (Porter and Goodman 1980; Porter and Goodman 1983; Porter and Goodman 1988) but there are many others). It is also the case that, today, such drawings are probably more likely to be prepared using a computer rather than by hand. Just as I cannot discuss all the skills of manual drawing so I cannot spend time looking at computer-aided drawing systems which will, in any case, become out of date remarkably quickly. Of course both manual presentation drawing and computer-aided drawing are vital skills you must acquire but this book is not intended to help you with that process.

There are two warnings you should take heed of here. First, presentation drawings are prepared by designers who have a vested interest in what is normally a commercial transaction. For this reason, such drawings can often be done in a manner that emphasises certain features or characteristics and also perhaps conceals possible weaknesses. We should therefore approach them with a degree of care and just a touch of suspicion.

Second, should you choose to use computer-aided drawing during the early periods of learning to design, you should also take care to develop your manual drawing skills. Without the latter you are unlikely to be able to produce all the drawing types listed here with easy facility and this may seriously hamper your overall design skills.

Consultation drawings

These are a special and often less grand form of presentation drawings done with the specific objective of eliciting a response from clients, users or other stakeholders.

They are created during the design process and often, as illustrated here, might portray alternatives about which some expression of preference or comment is desired. For this reason, these drawings can often be simplified to show perhaps only a few issues on which consultation is required. Sometimes designers will choose to put a series of alternatives out for consultation. In these cases it may be far quicker to generate these alternatives using computer-aided drawing since each alternative may be drafted more quickly by editing the previous one. In some cases the computer may even be used to create alternatives semi-automatically but discussion of this must wait until Chapter 17. This then suggests you must learn to use computer-drawing systems but never at the cost of developing your manual drawing skills.

Consultation drawings

Consultation drawings of alternative design layouts by James Stirling and Michael Wilford for Temasek Polytechnic in Singapore (Figure 4.2). These drawings and more were shown to the client as part of understanding their wishes in an intriguing design process that we shall look at again in Chapter 17. They show only the overall layout and disposition of major elements on the site. There is deliberately very little information here about the appearance of buildings. Stirling and Wilford wanted to leave those issues until a later stage. This is characteristic of the way they worked.

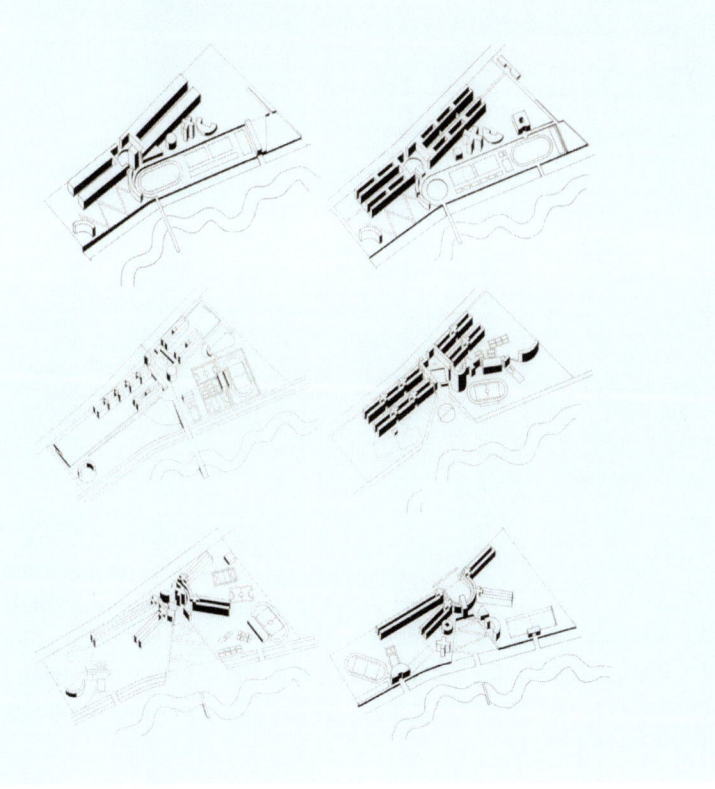

4.2

Instruction drawings

These drawings also occur either very late in the whole process of design or, more often, after it. They are intended as an unambiguous one-way form of communication from the designer to a constructor, manufacturer or supplier. They are used to explain how the design could or should be made. You may even have been at the receiving end of such drawings when trying to assemble some flat-packed furniture. While meant to be clear and unambiguous, these drawings often employ a set of conventions that are unknown to the general public and hence can seem dense and very technical.

Instruction drawings

A typical instruction drawing by the architect Ken Yeang (Figure 4.3). These cross sections through a proposed building would be difficult to understand properly unless you had already trained as either an architect or a builder.

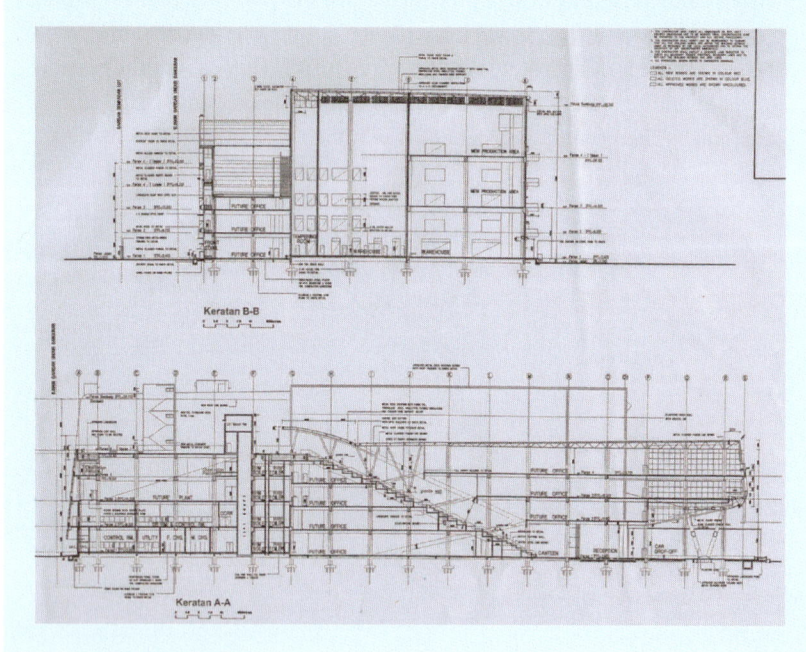

4.3

Actually there is a way in which these drawings can become an important part of the design process. As the designer draws them a certain degree of thinking about the technical realities of the designed object is necessary, perhaps for the first time. It is quite likely that the designer sees in his or her own drawing a problem hitherto unrecognised and then has to make changes or detail the design in ways not anticipated.

In professional practice, such drawings are often generated using computer-aided drawing systems. Such drawings often undergo development during the detailed design stages, and being able to label versions of such drawings and keep earlier versions can be a vital aid to managing the process and removing the uncertainty about whether all members of the design team, the manufacturers or builders and regulation officers are all working with the same information. With some computer systems you may be able to model the whole design in three dimensions and then automatically generate plans, elevations and other projections. Again, this can be a tremendous aid to organisation, as all the projections will be helping to describe the same three-dimensional object.

The detail can be very important

Of course this later process may also involve different personnel in the design practice. This is nicely illustrated by Mark Gross (Gross 1994) quoting an MIT thesis about the great architect Louis Kahn, who often used very thick charcoal in his outline design drawings that were inevitably vague, leaving his staff with problems of resolution as they tried to prepare the more detailed instruction drawings.

> He cheated a lot. That charcoal line was very thick . . . he would make everything work and then he'd go away. You wouldn't see him for maybe the next day, and you were left with these very thick lines that when reduced to realistic wall thicknesses and space – you couldn't put this functional stuff back in.

Experiential drawings

These drawings are usually not done as part of a particular design process but as part of the process of informing design in general. Designers habitually sketch things or places they see and record them for possible future reference. They are part of the essential process of developing a body of reference or potential precedent that we shall discuss in a later chapter. These drawings can take many forms. At one end of the spectrum they might really be as much a form of art as any life drawing, portrait, or landscape. At the other end they are effectively a 'note to self' that only their author is likely to understand. The drawing by the architect John Outram of Le Corbusier's famous Chapel at Ronchamp shown here illustrates exactly this quality.

Experiential drawings

John Outram's experiential drawing of Le Corbusier's Chapel at Ronchamp (Figure 4.4) is a perfect example of the experiential drawing as 'note to self', making extensive use of Outram's own personal notations analysing and recording features of the building for future reference.

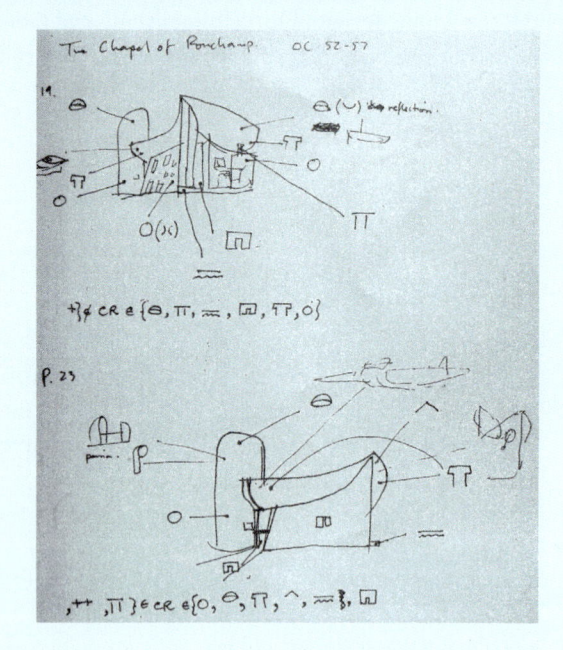

4.4

A word of caution about using modern information technology is appropriate here. Of course the digital camera and its incorporation into the smart phone can apparently save you a huge amount of time when compared with manual sketching. This brings two dangers. The first is that you do not learn to 'see' properly when taking photographs since the process requires little or no mental processing on your part. The second is that you cannot easily add notes to remind yourself what it was about an image that was important. Manual experiential drawings can be selective and annotated and these two features make them more powerful.

Diagrams

Diagrams include charts and graphs and other representations of selective data or information. Unlike most other types of drawings here, they do not represent an attempt to portray a possible solution in any physical sense. More often than not, designers use them to represent some aspects of the problem in an attempt to understand it better. In recent times a good deal of attention has been given to the way careful and imaginative graphical design can portray data more meaningfully. Among the most common design diagrams are the 'bubble diagrams' used by architects to represent desired flow and adjacencies around a building. One of the very first computer-aided architectural design computer programs was created to make these representations from a matrix of numbers and then to go on and attempt some form of simple layout. It was first demonstrated on a hospital unit as in our illustration here (Figure 4.5). Such a use of computers has unsurprisingly never taken off. The process of making the diagram by hand means you process the information in your brain and this gives a much deeper understanding that can be vital in the design process.

Diagrams

Diagrams have rules that should be carefully observed if they are to be powerful and useful. Consistency about what lines and bubbles mean in this example is of paramount importance. Here (Figure 4.5) the lines represent a desired adjacency in the design due to frequent or important direct flow of people. The bubbles represent spaces in the brief. Their area might be used to represent the relative areas of the spaces. The diagram could be elaborated by indicating flow of goods, materials or equipment using a graphically different line. Similarly, patient movements could be included and so on. The very act of composing the diagram can often help form some useful ideas about a possible design configuration in the designer's mind.

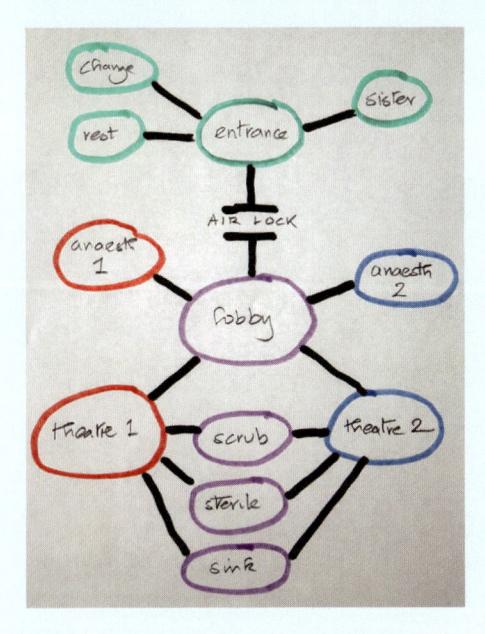

4.5

Calculation drawings

Calculation drawings are used more often at the relatively detailed and technical end of the design formulation. They offer simple graphical ways of determining some aspect or dimension of the design that otherwise might be calculated by arithmetic or geometry. Staircase, roof and other three-dimensional features of buildings are obvious examples of how these simple graphical devices might be used. Elsewhere in this book we see the example of Utzon's famous 'sails' or shells for Sydney Opera House. At the time he designed this ground-breaking piece of architecture Utzon lacked any purely mathematical way of calculating the location of points on the proposed irregular surfaces. This eventually drove Utzon to rationalise his irregular curves into spherical surfaces. Today we have computer-aided design systems that can plot irregular curved surfaces and these are most commonly used in the aeronautical design fields.

A calculation drawing

Eva Jiricna uses this sketch to calculate the size of a ceiling coving detail (Figure 4.6).

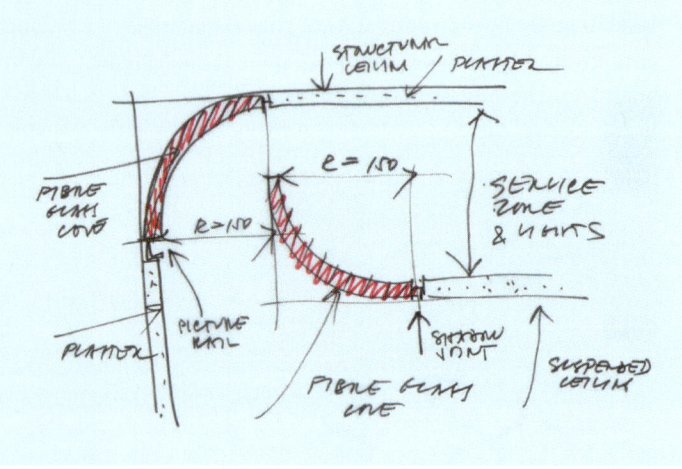

4.6

Fabulous drawings

We now enter the world of drawings done by designers to express some aspects, qualities or features of a proposed design. Designers do these, and our final category, proposition drawings, more or less for their own purposes. Some 'fabulous drawings', especially when done by famous designers, have come to be seen as pieces of art. We will not enter the delicate and difficult debate of when a design drawing is a piece of art. Such an argument could easily take up the remainder of the pages of this book and still not satisfy all the positions taken up by those who seek to define what art is or is not. However, perhaps the most famous fabulous drawings in architecture really were intended as art. These are the works by Piranesi known as Carceri. He created frighteningly huge spaces that had vast proportions and vertiginous vaults and staircases. Lighting, tone and texture were all used to create a feeling of space rather than representing one that could actually exist. Indeed a number of writers have pointed out that several of his images could not ever be produced in normal three-dimensional geometry and that they share similar characteristics with the visual illusions of Escher.

A truly fabulous drawing

This drawing (Figure 4.7) is fabulous in both senses of the word. It conjures up a huge and terrifying interior that could well be a prison. However, the various elements are disposed for effect rather than any attempt to portray a real or buildable place.

4.7

The title used here refers to 'fabulous' in its generic sense of relating to fabled properties. These drawings are often done without too much attention to practical realities or detailed matters of realisation. They are mostly done in order to express qualities in a rather loose sense rather than actual configurations. Indeed it can be useful to you as a designer to become temporarily free of the shackles of reality in order to create a fabulous drawing that can inform the design. Such drawings are often seen in the design of automobile bodies, fashion and theatre design. These conjure up a quality rather than propose a particular realisation. In the motor industry such drawings can become three-dimensional models in the form of 'concept' cars to be exhibited long before a production model has been created.

A 'concept' car drawing by Loewy

This drawing (Figure 4.8) of a 'concept car' by the great industrial designer Raymond Loewy was not meant literally. It was never built, but the sketch showed the essence of a number of ideas that were incorporated, in more refined forms, into cars that were built.

4.8

The suspension of critical thought and disbelief is one of the most widely accepted of what we might call 'creativity techniques'. In fact, a whole series of formal processes are created around this idea. Most famous among these are Gordon's 'Synectics' (Gordon 1961) and de Bono's 'Lateral Thinking' (de Bono 1970).

Fabulous drawings

This fabulous drawing (Figure 4.9) by Frank Gehry is a wonderful example of the genre. It represents the ideas behind the possible geometry of his

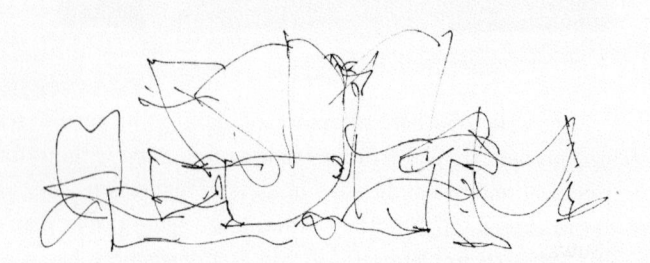

4.9

Disney Hall in a most evocative way. These kinds of images must have been invaluable in a design process that eventually would require the resolution of very complex geometry into a practical realisation. That process can easily be the cause of the design losing the very power and dynamism Gehry clearly wanted. Fabulous drawings can thus bring the design team back to the original idea in a challenging but creative way. They almost represent some form of design Holy Grail, never attainable but always a highly desired and imagined target.

Proposition drawings

Last but far from least we come to the sorts of drawings that designers habitually do and that are often unselfconsciously produced in order to make some proposition about how the design might be. This kind of drawing is right at the very centre, perhaps even the heartbeat, of the design process. A propositional drawing allows you to freeze some aspects of the design almost as a sort of hypothesis. 'What if it looked a bit like this?', is almost what you are saying when doing this drawing. It is an experiment, an investigation. This drawing is not expected to be final or correct but rather a step along a path that at some later time you may retrace. It is this sort of drawing that Donald Schön had in mind when he described the designer as 'having a conversation with the drawing' (Schön 1983). You do this sort of drawing in order to see what you are thinking and what the consequences might be. You externalise some features of the design situation that you have in mind. This may allow you to critically examine them or alternatively freeze them temporarily in order to see what they might mean for some other aspects as yet less well understood. In a sense the drawing talks back to you and allows you to see things you could not when purely using your 'mind's eye'.

'Seeing' through drawing

Suwa and Twersky studied the way designers work with drawings. Their work strongly suggests that designers respond to the geometric properties of their drawings as they develop them and that they may 'see' other ideas than those that were in their mind before they began the drawing (Suwa and Tversky 1997). You can almost see that process happening in

(continued)

(continued)

(continued)

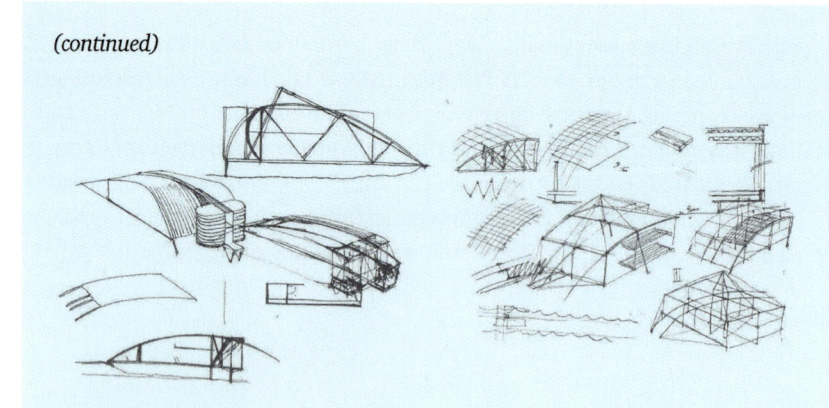

4.10

these design drawings by the architect Ian Ritchie (Figure 4.10). One idea appears to be drawn on top of another responding to an idea it suggests.

Some great designers on drawing during design

I have often sat down at a student's drawing board to help them, only to find that they have not yet drawn out some key aspect of their design. Such students are inclined to say that they know what it would look like, or they have the idea in their head. But even the very best designers tell us that this is not likely to be good enough.

The need to draw

'I want to see things. I don't trust anything else. I place things in front of me on paper so that I can see them. I want to see therefore I draw' (Carlo Scarpa).

'Whenever we have a design session or crit review in the office I cannot say anything until I've got a pencil in my hand' (Richard MacCormac).

'To start with you see the thing in your mind and it doesn't exist on paper and then you start making simple sketches and organizing things and then you start doing layer after layer . . . it is very much a dialogue' (Santiago Calatrava).

(Lawson 1994)

A problem with such drawings is that they become so much part of a conversation that most designers draw over them several times, altering some features each time. They may be extremely difficult to read and understand unless their author is describing the mental processes at the same time. Even the author may struggle later to understand exactly what they represent. There often comes a moment when the drawing is so overlain with alternative ideas that you instinctively feel a new drawing is needed. Developing a feeling for this is one of the skills you need to acquire. Little can be done to help you with this process in a book but this may well come up in design tutorials that we shall discuss in Chapter 11.

A further complication here is that early drawings in a sequence can look more like 'fabulous' drawings than 'propositional' ones. What this tells us is that my categorisation of all these drawing types is done more to help me describe them to you than for absolute accuracy. In the heat of the design process drawings may often slide from one type into another. There is nothing wrong with this if it helps thinking go forward. The sequence of drawings by my friend the architect Ken Yeang shows this nicely.

These categories can blur into one another

4.11

Propositional drawings (early)

The renowned Malaysian architect Ken Yeang is designing a Hard Rock Café Hotel. Is this an early propositional drawing (Figure 4.11) or would it more accurately be described as 'fabulous'? Maybe it is a halfway house here.

(continued)

(continued)

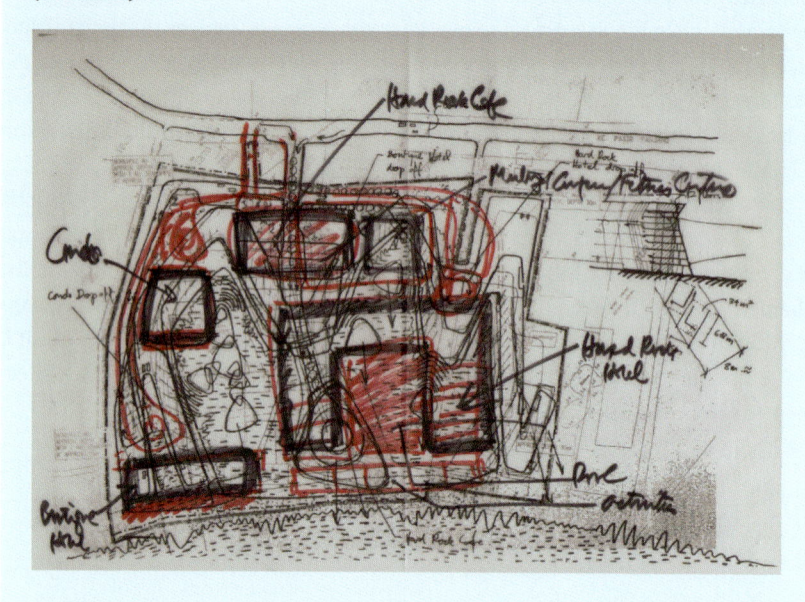

4.12

Propositional drawings (intermediate)

A further drawing (Figure 4.12) done by Ken Yeang for the same project in which he is overlaying his ideas onto a more accurate survey drawing of the site, thus making his proposition more realistic than in the previous case.

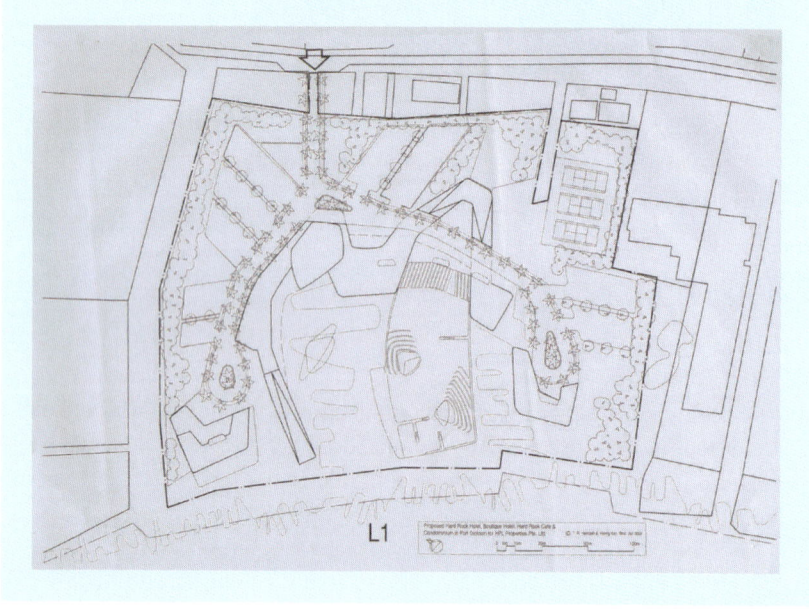

4.13

Propositional drawings (detailed)

Ken Yeang has produced a much firmer and more realistic version of the plan (Figure 4.13) he was developing as an early proposition in the previous two figures. This might almost become a 'presentation' or 'consultation' drawing to show the idea to other interested parties.

The drawings shown here by Ken Yeang show a progressive amount of detail. In the early days of our research studies of the design process, it was often assumed that this is the way design progresses, from the general to the particular, from outline to detail. We shall discuss this notion in much more detail in a later chapter but, just to turn on a little warning light, I have included another illustration here. This is an interpretation of a sequence of propositional drawings by the wonderful Italian architect Carlo Scarpa and it is taken from a book by Stephen Groak with his permission (Groak 1992). It shows the work of an architect who believed in the idea of design emerging from detail and, in particular, being informed by an understanding of the problems that might face the craftsman in constructing the finished design.

Conversation with a drawing

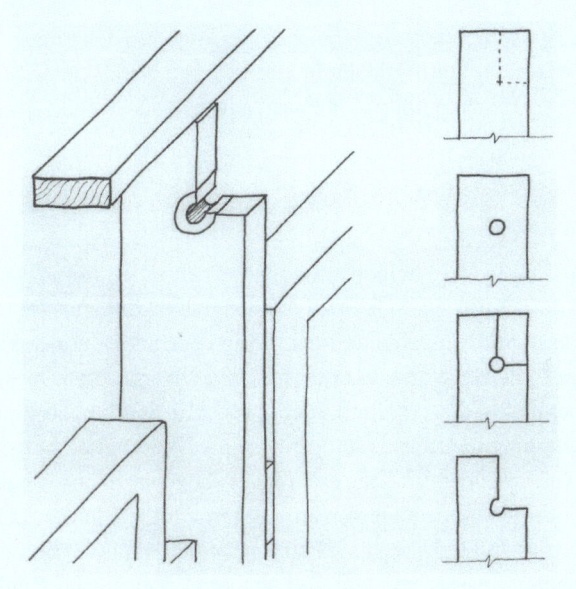

4.14

(continued)

(continued)

Carlo Scarpa having a conversation with his drawing in order to understand how a handrail detail might be constructed (Figure 4.14). He wanted the handrail for a wooden bridge to be the right width to grip. However, the upright posts needed to be deeper for structural reasons. On the right, Scarpa draws the post and the cuts the carpenter would need to make to narrow the post where it meets the handrail. As the drawings continue he imagines the carpenter sawing and the difficulty of making two cuts at right angles that do not overlap. He imagines drilling a hole to which the carpenter could cut and feel when the right point had been reached. Finally, in the main drawing, Scarpa decides to insert a small brass disc to finish off the detail.

So, sometimes design works at least partly from detail to generality. I can think of no neater way of summing this up than the aphorism used by Robert Venturi in conversation with me. But a more thorough investigation of direction in design must wait until a later chapter.

Design does not always go from the general towards the more detailed

'We have a rule that says sometimes the detail wags the dog. We don't necessarily go from the general to the particular but rather often you do detailing at the beginning very much to inform' (Robert Venturi).

(Lawson 1994)

What this chapter should have demonstrated is the centrality and importance of drawing in the design process. It is simply unimaginable that most of us could ever design well without being able to draw. Design becomes a conversation with the drawing at some stage and, in order for this conversation to move along at a speed that does not hold back your thinking, you really need to become proficient in drawing. Learning to draw in all the kinds of ways discussed here is thus essential. It is also vital to understand the differences between all these kinds of drawings. Lines and other marks may mean quite different things in the various drawing types discussed and they need interpreting very carefully. Whether you have drawn much before or not, you will find any good design school will put developing this skill at the very centre of the course. Design schools are very special kinds of places that, to begin with, can sometimes feel strange. We will discover something of how they work and what they expect you to learn in the next chapter.

Making models

Although this is a chapter on drawing, most of what we have discussed is also possible by making models. Models have the advantage of being three-dimensional and thus enable you to more accurately understand your own design. However, it is almost always the case that models take longer to create than drawings. This may slow down your design process at a time when speed is critical. On the other hand, that slowing down may help to impose a period of reflection. You must learn to be able to make this decision for yourself. So, just as you need to learn to draw well and use computers, you also need to learn and practise making physical models. Only then will you have the facility you need not only to move forward creatively in your design process but also to be able to manage that process. Some of these issues about managing speed while designing will be discussed more in Chapter 9.

Of course we are now in the early stages of a potential revolution in computer systems that allow you to build a computer model that can then be 'printed' in three dimensions. This may soon be another skill you need to learn.

Using computers

There is some evidence to suggest that the computer helps to liberate designers in terms of the three-dimensional complexity of the forms they can produce. Frank Gehry and Santiago Calatrava, who have been discussed in this book, are among those regularly creating the most complex forms. Bill Mitchell claims that Gehry has shown that 'architecture can be liberated from its increasingly sclerotic conventions' (Mitchell 1990). It is absolutely certain that Gehry could not have produced buildings such as his Guggenheim Museum in Bilbao or Walt Disney Concert Hall in Los Angeles without very sophisticated computer-aided design. However, there is an irony here. Frank Gehry does not work on computers directly but only through his highly trained and specialised staff who can operate the very sophisticated software needed.

In fact, Gehry works in much more plastic materials as you can see in Figure 4.9. From his conversations with Gehry, Zeara tells us that 'the computer was introduced into Frank Gehry's office in such a way that it would not interfere with a design process that had been evolving over thirty years' (Zeara 1995). Another author who has studied Frank Gehry tells us that 'Gehry does not like the way objects look in the computer and that he avoids looking at the computer screens in the office' (Lindsey 2001).

From my own studies of Santiago Calatrava (Lawson 1994) it is clear that he also relies heavily on computers for structural analysis such as finite element software and production drawings but he does not use computers as part of his creative design process. 'I like to sketch quickly by hand' (Lawson 1994). Perhaps these are examples of designers who would have been using computers had they been introduced earlier into their careers. Herman Hertzberger laconically told me that 'I need all my energy for my design, and I decided not to learn to use CAD like I decided not to learn the violin at my age' (Lawson 1994). However, it is also possible that Nigel Cross has it right (Cross 2001) when he asks 'why isn't using a CAD system a more enjoyable, and perhaps, also more intellectually demanding experience than it has turned out to be'. What Cross is probably referring to here is the need so often to learn to speak the language of the computer system rather than the more direct way of expressing yourself by hand.

There are certainly simple computer sketching systems that enable us to create the sort of sketches that designers use that we have called 'propositional drawings'. Whether these offer any advantages over the human hand working with pens and pencils on paper is far from clear. One of the most unusual and yet creative uses of computer drawing in a design process appears later in this book. Look at Figure 18.7 in Chapter 18 and you will see Robert Venturi sticking computer-drafted columns of the National Gallery in London onto a crude cardboard model of his proposed design (Lawson 2011).

Do computer drawing systems restrict creativity?

There is some research that suggests such systems reduce rather than enhance the creativity of the designer using them. Goel observed graphic designers working by hand or with MacDraw and found the computer-based drawings tended to be less dense and ambiguous than those created by hand (Goel 1995). He also observed that the designers using computers made fewer 'lateral transformations' (new moves) than their manual counterparts. That is to say they tended to persist with an idea for longer, 'vertically transforming' it (developmental moves). The inference here is that the less ambiguous drawing in MacDraw offered the designers fewer interpretations of their own ideas. Several other experiments have supported the idea that using computer graphical systems may restrict creativity (Bilda and Demirkan 2003; Kvan et al. 2003). Of course, in the future, we may well be able to design computer graphic systems that do not have these disadvantages.

One further concern that we have already touched on is that the more you use a computer drawing tool the less you practise drawing by hand. Without a facility of eye–brain–hand you may never learn the skills to analyse what you see as you acquire your databank of design precedents. You will have to make up your mind about all this for yourself. Do think deliberately about how to incorporate computers into your design process in ways that improve rather than restrict your creative powers.

Start sketching

One of the best ways to begin is to develop your skill through experiential drawings. In other words, get a sketchbook and start recording interesting things around you that might just become inspirations at some later date. This will teach you to look and learn. It will help you to develop your under-standing and appreciation of your chosen design field. It will develop your drawing skills and, through this, give you more capability to have design-erly conversations with your drawings when designing.

References

Bilda, Z. and H. Demirkan (2003). "An insight on designers' sketching activities in tradi-tional versus digital media". *Design Studies* 24(1): 27–50.

Cross, N. (2001). "Can a machine design?" *MIT Design Issues* 17(4): 44–50.

de Bono, E. (1970). *Lateral Thinking: A Textbook of Creativity*. London, Ward Lock Educational.

Goel, V. (1995). *Sketches of Thought*. Cambridge, MA, MIT Press.

Gordon, W. J. J. (1961). *Synectics: The Development of Creative Capacity*. New York, Harper and Row.

Groak, S. (1992). *The Idea of Building: Thought and Action in the Design and Production of Buildings*. London, E. & F. N. Spon.

Gross, M. (1994). "The fat pencil, the cocktail napkin, and the slide library". Proceedings, Association for Computer Aided Design in Architecture, National Conference, St Louis.

Kvan, T., J. T. H. Wong and A. H. Vera (2003). "The contribution of structural activities to successful design". *International Journal of Computer Applications in Technology* 16(2/3): 122–126.

Lawson, B. R. (1994). *Design in Mind*. Oxford, Butterworth Architecture.

Lawson, B. R. (2004). *What Designers Know*. Oxford, Elsevier/Architectural Press.

Lawson, B. R. (2011). "Of sails and sieves and sticky tape". *Distributed Intelligence in Design*. T. Kocaturk and B. Mejdoub. Chichester, Wiley-Blackwell: 3–15.

Lindsey, B. (2001). *Digital Gehry: Material Resistance/Digital Construction*. Basel, Birkhauser.

Mitchell, W. (1990). *The Logic of Architecture: Design, Computation, Cognition*. Cambridge MA, MIT Press.

Porter, T. and S. Goodman (1980). *Manual of Graphic Techniques for Architects, Graphic Designers and Artists*. London, Astragal.

Porter, T. and S. Goodman (1983). *Manual of Graphics Techniques 3 for Architects, Graphic Designers and Artists*. London, Astragal.

Porter, T. and S. Goodman (1988). *Designer Primer for Architects, Graphic Designers and Artists*. London, Butterworth Architecture.

Schön, D. A. (1983). *The Reflective Practitioner: How Professionals Think in Action*. London, Temple Smith.

Suwa, M. and B. Tversky (1997). "What do architects and students perceive in their design sketches? A protocol analysis". *Design Studies* 18(4): 385–403.

Zeara, A. (1995). "Frank Gehry 1991–5, conversations with Frank O. Gehry". *El Croquis* 74–5.

Chapter 5

Design schools

A little history

In the first chapter we saw that design-based schools show common characteristics on an international basis and even across the major disciplines such as industrial design, interior design and architecture. The design schools originally grew up more or less as an adjunct to fine art, especially during the highly influential Ecole des Beaux-Arts. The single most influential school in Europe must surely be the Bauhaus in the early part of the twentieth century. Today the general public may see the Bauhaus as a kind of minimalist and essentially modernist style but the original concepts behind it were far more fundamental and they included ideas about process and pedagogy. As a result, our design schools began to find their own identity distinct from fine art while still recognising they had much in common with it. The Bauhaus was interested in virtually all forms of design but developed a set of principles that reconnected making and craftsmanship with design. It was a new form of making including the advanced techniques of mass production that gave it a new highly disciplined edge. The Ulm school took this further in the mid-twentieth century by taking a multidisciplinary approach and adding subjects such as sociology and psychology as well as economics and even philosophy to its syllabus. It shared the position of this book that design processes could be understood and taught. This had a significant influence in the development of industrial and product design schools.

How design schools work

Between them, these schools were responsible for making design, a subject that had previously been mostly learned through apprenticeships, into one that would also be studied in universities and colleges and they shaped the main features of our modern schools. Kees Dorst and I described what we called the 'big four' of these common features; they are the studio, the library, the design tutorial and the crit (Lawson and Dorst 2009). Between them these four concepts offer one of the most accurate and helpful of ways of defining design education. They are all marvellously well adapted to the needs of students learning to design. They are so common that often the schools do not really describe them or explain how they work. Usually this is not intentional but quite simply because they are so well established that they are often taken for granted. A little analysis of them may help. We shall look at the studio in this chapter and the others in later chapters.

The studio

You cannot miss the physical embodiment of the studio when you enter a design-based school. This place is where we are likely not only to learn and practise designing but also where discussions and some pretty heated debates take place, not just about individual designs or projects but more widely about architecture, interior design or product design and so on. The physical equipment of the studio changes with technology. It used to be primarily full of huge drawing boards for students to draw on, and cutting surfaces and even some basic machine tools and so on to make models. Now it is as likely to have computers, printers and access to the internet.

The studio has survived as a place and a concept

5.1a

Design schools

5.1b

These pictures show the studio in the Sheffield University School of Architecture first in the 1930s (Figure 5.1a) and then in 2017 (Figure 5.1b). The haircuts and dress of the students has changed and computers have partly replaced drafting machines but the fundamental pedagogical ideas behind the studio remain the same. Today students might work more in groups and will certainly use computers, but they will be working on design projects for a very substantial proportion of their time at university and in much the same way as they did nearly a century ago.

Design courses obviously vary according to the actual subject being studied, the country and culture, and the interests and expertise of staff. However, we can see some structure and organisation that is pretty common. There are likely to be subjects of a technical, historical, social and even philosophical nature that are chiefly taught in the lecture theatre or seminar room. There will also be skill development subjects taught in a variety of ways. These might include drawing, use of computers, especially computer-aided design, perhaps surveying and measuring and so on. In schools that I am familiar with, this most formal part of the course represents up to half the weekly timetable in year one but would diminish to very little or none at all by the final year. The most common feature of the timetable is likely to be described as 'studio' or something similar, which is usually the largest single item each week. Studio, then, is not just a place, it is also a process with recognisable features.

The studio is practical and unstructured

First and most importantly studio is practical. Students will be set problems and left to work on them, mostly as individuals but also sometimes in groups. Early in the course these problems might be very specific and small in scale. Later they will grow more complex and larger, as well being chosen and defined by the student as much as the tutors.

The studio invariably involves co-location and an unstructured timetable. In essence this means that students usually share the same space, probably, though not always, in their year cohorts. Many have commented on the extent to which students learn from each other. The timetable may have a few key events such as project introductions, visits, talks and crits, but generally it is unstructured and students must learn to manage their own time. While all this can work beautifully, it is also fraught with a number of dangers. Some can find the place so active and buzzing that concentration on their own work becomes difficult. As a young student I never wanted to leave the studio in case I missed some discussion or event and, as a consequence, would then have to make more progress in my own room in the late evening. Learning to organise and pace your work can also present significant challenges for some. This is particularly so with a design task, which invariably expands to fill the time available and often overruns. Even experienced designers have trouble with this and often find they must work late and intensively as a deadline looms.

Studio projects become an obsession and are even invented by students

5.2

The school of architecture I ran occupied the top half dozen floors of a 20-storey tower block, itself situated on a gentle hillside. Late in the evening, if I had been to a concert or the theatre, on my way home the top of the building would shine out like a beacon over the city. This in spite of the university authorities insisting the whole building should close by six pm. Perhaps only design students, so in need of their studio, would be prepared to risk the wrath of the authorities and dodge all the security staff in order to work longer hours. In fact, the students often took advantage of this and designed supergraphics for the windows to help publicise some charity or event (Figure 5.2).

A major disruptive consequence of this all-embracing nature of studio is that students can often run out of time towards the end of projects and be forced to miss lectures and other important and more structured elements of other modules. This can be quite damaging to learning and communicate an unintended lack of value towards essential subjects that are taught outside studio. You will do well to keep your eye on this and try to manage your time. This is not easy, especially early on.

The studio involves learning by doing

Above all, then, the studio is a place where you learn by doing, rather than through any formal instruction. Mostly, students are working on design projects in the studio and there may be no time during their whole degree course when there is not a design project on the go. Not satisfied with this, often design students add their own projects to the studio (see Figure 5.2). You can see, then, how easily students can slip behind in their work without careful and disciplined self-management assisted by their tutors. However, each sees what the other is doing in the studio and somehow or other the collective seems to manage to muddle along and meet most deadlines and keep their other courses going. One uniquely delightful feature of the studio design project is that almost immediately students are generating ideas and following unique directions of their own. There are no right or wrong answers to studio design projects so there is little risk of copying others' work, although students certainly influence each other.

The studio focuses on integration

The next feature of the studio is the very integrative nature of the activity. This makes studio difficult to understand for those not familiar with it. Many other subjects at university will have practical periods. The engineering or science lab class is a prime example. In the arts or social sciences you may be more likely to be asked to write an essay and, later on, a whole dissertation. Usually, however, these periods are not only structured time but also can be found inside a module. Here the practical work helps to develop the understanding of some material delivered in lectures and seminars.

We need to spend a little longer understanding what is meant by integration in design in order to see not only how vital it is but also how intellectually sophisticated. Being able to integrate across different strands of ideas in a single design feature is a skill that requires time and practice. We can find countless examples of this sort of beautiful integration in vernacular design.

The wind tower houses of Dubai

5.3

These remarkable traditional houses in Dubai (Figure 5.3) were designed by a local vernacular process. They are perfectly adapted both to the climate and the culture and provide an integrated solution in which one simple form solves many problems.

A delightful architectural example can be found in the wind tower houses of Dubai. These houses were crammed together closely within easy reach of the creek and therefore work and trade. We can see rising up from the middle of these houses are their distinctive wind towers. In the Gulf there is nearly always a breeze as heat exchanges take place between the air over the water and the air over the land mass. These wind towers allow the breeze to blow through and create a cooling circulation of air in the space below. You can think of this process as the reverse of the chimney found over hot fires in cooler climates. Closer examination shows that these devices have been assimilated into the cultural norms of the region. The precious cool space at the foot of the tower cannot be seen from the door, which is screened and separated by a lobby and reception space that is less comfortable. Thus the privacy of the inner sanctum is guaranteed and closer friends and relatives can be invited further into the house to the cooler and more intimate social space.

The example of the dished cartwheels that we first met in Chapter 3 shows even more integration. This one simple piece of geometry solved problems to do with construction, structural stability and legislation, while giving additional load space without losing manoeuvrability.

The integrated vernacular cartwheel solution

In Chapter 3 we introduced the story of George Sturt and the dished cartwheels. Sturt thought that making the wheels dished would be more complex than making them flat. In fact, he was wrong. It is actually easier to devise a way of dropping the spokes into the rim followed by the hub than it would be to make them all on the flat (Figure 5.4). But there was not just one reason for the dished shape as Sturt had thought. When iron tyres were added to wooden wheels they were heated to expand, allowing them then to cool and contract onto the wheel. This caused tension so, had the wheel been flat, it could have buckled. The now post-tensioned wheel is stronger along the line of the axle than a flat wheel and this strength was needed due to the carthorse's gait, which threw the cart from side to side with each step (Sturt 1923).

(continued)

(continued)

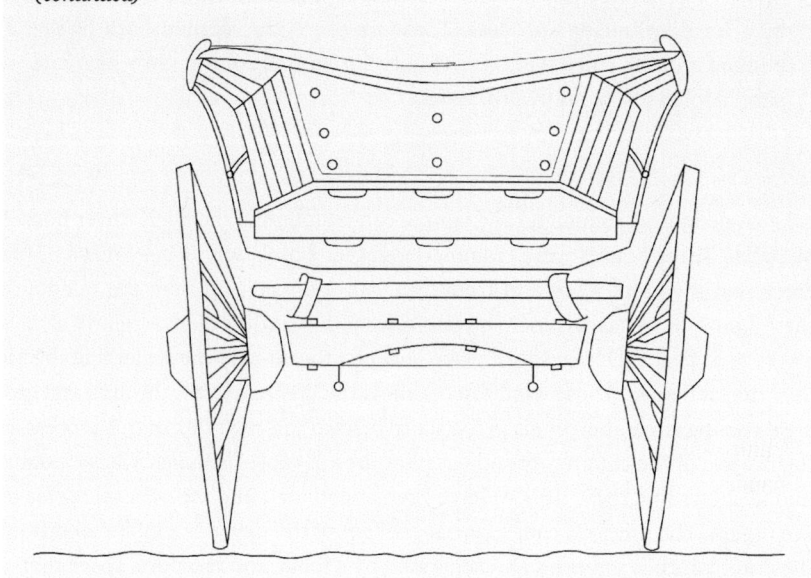

5.4

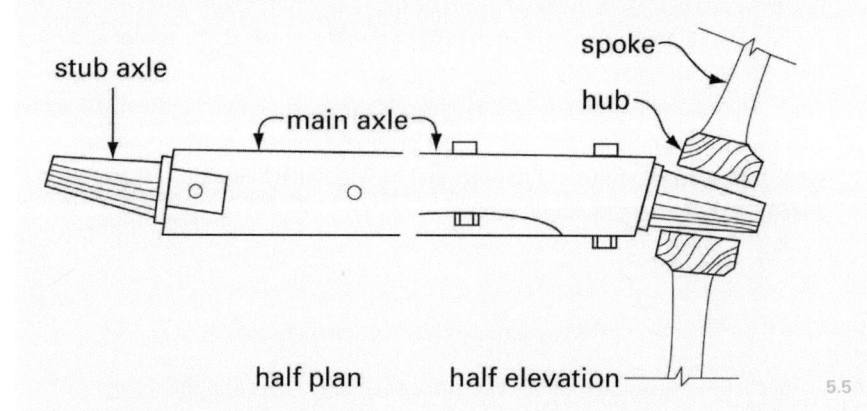

stub axle

main axle

spoke

hub

half plan   half elevation

5.5

The dished cartwheels had to be tilted outwards, thus transferring the load along the line of the spokes at the bottom as the wheel rotated. The axle then had to be angled slightly forward to avoid the wheel dropping off the tilted axle or running against the cotter pin that retained it (there were no sophisticated bearings in those days). You can see that the result of this configuration is a cart able to carry a wider load without increasing the wheel spacing, which would have made the cart less manoeuvrable (Figure 5.5). This also allowed the wheels to run in the ruts in the rough roads caused by the much thicker wheels of passenger coaches. This track spacing was governed by legislation to ensure ruts formed along one line.

But we must not run away with the idea that beautifully integrated solutions can only be realised by the vernacular process. One of London's most well-known buildings is the National Theatre on the South Bank of the river Thames. It was designed by Sir Denys Lasdun in the middle of the twentieth century in a very modernist, perhaps even brutalist, style. Its most iconic external features are strong bands of concrete running horizontally, some right across the river façade, while others are interrupted by the staircase towers set at 45 degrees to the main plan. Lasdun himself described these key design features as having multiple purposes.

Integration

Sir Denys Lasdun, the architect of the British National Theatre on the South Bank of the river Thames, describes the varying functions of the horizontal bands in his building (Figure 5.6).

> They support the interior functions while allowing for flexible planning. They provide coherence to a large scheme, which is nonetheless, broken down to the human scale. They give visual expression to the essentially public nature of the institution: for a theatre must be a place where human contact is enriched and a common experience is shared.
> (Lasdun 1965)

5.6

Some designers have taken the idea of functional integration to extremes when they become almost part of the design dogma. Particularly well known for this is the great Dutch architect Herman Hertzberger (Hertzberger 1971). Hertzberger went even further by trying to create design elements that he hoped the users would find new uses for. When designing a deck-access housing scheme in his native Holland, Hertzberger sited fairly simply detailed concrete blocks on the access deck outside the entrance of each dwelling. These could carry a dwelling number and a light, thus locating and identifying the entrance. They could also be used to sit on or as a simple table for meals. Deliveries could be left inside when the residents were out, and so on. I interviewed Hertzberger at his office and found one of these blocks sitting in the back garden being used by his staff to prop their bicycles against. We cleared a few away and sat down there to conduct our discussion. The block had acquired two more uses.

We can see that this level of integration happens over many years, decades and even centuries in the vernacular. To pull it off successfully in a new and original design demands a mastery over the features and elements available to the designer, which is probably only attained through considerable experience. However, we must leave a discussion of that until a later chapter as we progress further up the levels of design expertise. A major purpose of the studio in schools of design is to encourage students to link together all the parts of their course and to bring all their knowledge into play on a design project. Design is essentially about bringing things together. Perhaps it is at its finest when one single idea integrates many different kinds of functions into one coherent and beautiful solution.

So we have seen that the studio is most often a single place that locates students together in order for them to learn from each other. It is largely based around design problems so uses practical rather than theoretical pedagogy. Students learn by doing in a very practical kind of way. It has an unstructured timetable, making students responsible for planning their time and work. It is quite different from the practical classes that may be found inside the modules of other courses. It largely encourages the student to draw on ideas from across all the modules of their course. This process of bringing ideas together in an integrated way forms one of the most valuable features of the design course.

There is no way that I know of to learn to design without a great deal of practice. However, there are things we can do to help you along the way. In the next chapter we shall begin to explore just what it means to design.

References

Hertzberger, H. (1971). "Looking for the beach under the pavement". *RIBA Journal* 78(8).
Lasdun, D. (1965). "An architect's approach to architecture". *RIBA Journal* 72(4): 184–195.
Lawson, B. R. and C. H. Dorst (2009). *Design Expertise*. Oxford, Elsevier/Architectural Press.
Sturt, G. (1923). *The Wheelwright's Shop*. Cambridge, Cambridge University Press.

Chapter 6

Starting to design

A new research field

Our understanding of design as a process has developed enormously since this became a serious research topic about halfway through the twentieth century. In terms of the history of subjects studied in universities then, this is a very new research field. However, much of the early work was carried out in a spirit of enthusiasm for the scientific method. This did not seem odd at time since the 1960s was a period of belief that science and technology would provide the answer to most problems. In 1963 Harold Wilson, who was to become British Prime Minister the following year, famously addressed the Labour Party conference. He told us that 'a new Britain would need to be forged by the white heat of this scientific revolution'. In this intellectual climate design research work seemed motivated by a desire to make design an open process that was logical and replicable. There was a strong tendency to propose new ways of designing that made it appear more scientific.

More recent research focussed on how designers actually work and on understanding why they often seem to work in ways that initially appear illogical. An important early discovery was that designers characteristically seem to focus on the solution rather than the problem. One experiment studied graduate designers and compared them with graduate scientists as well as with school pupils. A simple description of the experiment is shown here and more thoroughly documented in research papers and books (Lawson 1979). In essence what it showed was that while the scientists began by trying to analyse the problem, the designers began by trying to create solutions. Through the failings of their solutions the designers tended to get a better understanding of the problem. This finding has since been supported by other studies and by observations and interviews with successful and famous designers.

Designers use a solution-focussed approach to problem solving

I ran a simple experiment in which subjects were given a set of blocks coloured red and blue on the vertical faces and white and black on the horizontal faces (Figure 6.1). They were asked to arrange some blocks on a grid to create a surrounding wall that was either as blue or red as possible. But there were some hidden rules about which combinations of blocks would be allowed. The only information available was from a computer that would say whether a submitted design conformed to the rules or not.

We found that science graduates tended to concentrate first on trying to discover the rules and then later attempting to maximise the desired surrounding wall colour. Architecture graduates, by contrast, tended to design an arrangement that gave the maximum desired surround wall colour and, if that was not allowed, they modified it progressively until they found an allowed solution.

6.1

Designers tend to work in a solution-focussed way

This seems perverse and illogical until we delve further into the nature of design problems. It would be like a crossword puzzler simply entering a word of the right length into the boxes and then checking to see if it satisfied the clue or not. Such behaviour would be likely to waste a lot of time since there would be thousands of words to check. We will study design problems in more detail later. For now, let us recognise that design problems are not like puzzles. There is no one right or correct answer to design problems. We shall also discover that design problems are never really fully stated. A lot of requirements and desirable features of solutions are often left unsaid and unrecognised even by a client.

As part of my student experience, I worked with a very experienced architect on some quite complex hospital buildings. He astonished me by instructing that I should do a very quick design without worrying about it too much but to draw it up in a clear and professional way. This was to be done to a ridiculous deadline only a couple of days away. Not surprisingly, I was worried that my design would not be up to scratch but he took one quick look and said it was fine. We showed my drawings to the client committee of doctors, nurses, administrators and so on. As you might expect, they were not very pleased with the design. They talked non-stop for a couple of hours pointing out things they thought were wrong with the design. They were mainly telling us about issues that had not been described in the brief and arguing between themselves about the relative importance or relevance of some major items that were in the brief. We learned a huge amount that day about our problem, and I learned a lesson about designing. A design proposal had elicited more knowledge about the problems than the client had been able to think of when writing the brief.

Briefing can be solution focussed too

So, while others might sometimes ridicule designers for an apparently haphazard approach, we could equally well be critical of clients for quite inadequate and incomplete briefs. Neither criticism is justified. Both courses of action are inevitable given the nature of design problems. The hospital example demonstrates that compiling a brief is extremely difficult, especially when there are many different interests and stakeholders involved. All the things we learned about in Chapter 1 are as true for brief making as for designing. How can a client express preferences and relative importance about so many things that are incommensurate? It is also true that, until a designer starts to work, it is very unlikely that all but the most experienced client can see the inevitable contradictions and conflicts inherent in their brief. It is also only then that most clients may discover just how much their initial brief left out.

I did some work for a well-known high street retail chain that wanted to explore a new standardised range of shop fittings and floor layouts. Two of the objectives in their original brief were as follows:

- Shop fittings should minimise the risk of shoplifting.
- Shop fittings should be designed to maximise sales by enabling customers to feel what it would be like to own items on sale.

These two requirements were several pages apart in the briefing document rather than starkly adjacent as here. I guess you can already see the contradiction.

Retail and consumer psychology tells us that once a customer has held an item in their hands they are far more likely to buy it. Of course, the wrong type of customer is also more likely to steal it. I put the contradiction back to the client and this triggered a major internal conference about their values and objectives. They had simply never seen and faced up to the contradictions in their brief. They started to ask previously unspeakable questions such as how much they were prepared to lose through shoplifting in order to promote their overall sales. So coming into contact with a designer resulted in a re-examination of the fundamental objectives and values of the company.

I have consulted on the design of many hospitals and often found similarly conflicting brief requirements. One perfectly understandable and sensible requirement is to design a layout that minimises walking distance for staff, especially the hard-worked nurses who probably walk many miles in a single shift. However, recent research has demonstrated a significant reduction in recovery times when patients have a view from a window (Ulrich 1984). Research also suggests that, ideally, they should be able to see both the sky and the ground and normal life going on outside the hospital. Most important of all is for their view to enable contact with nature. Now the obvious outcome of minimising walking times in such a complex building is to produce a layout that is very compact and deep planned, which in turn minimises the length of the perimeter wall and reduces the chance of anyone being near enough to any window to get a good view out. How many modern hospitals have been designed without ever really shining a light on this paradox?

A phantom brief

Often inexperienced clients will tell you what they want in terms of finished design rather than clearly expressing the problem. A good friend and colleague, who was an excellent graphic designer, fell into this trap when asking me to design an extension to his house. He told me he needed a study to work in. Unfortunately the house was already rather well designed and the overall form and massing appeared complete. The site was also very tight and his wife loved gardening. Every design I came up with seemed to have as many disadvantages as strengths. One day we were looking at the latest version when a tremendous noise started up as his daughter arrived home from school and started playing the music system in her bedroom. 'There, see, that's the problem' he sighed. For the first time I did see the problem. I suggested he bought a pair of headphones for his daughter instead of extending the house and everyone was happy, except, you might think, me, as I lost a nice project and fee! Of course I kept a friend, which is far more important.

Some students starting a design project

Some years ago I used the brief from an architectural competition as a student project. It was for a large local government office building set in an English town. The students worked in small groups and, after a week, they made public presentations of their progress.

The first group started by describing how they felt that the environmental requirements of the office space were the critical factors. They had studied the literature on office design and showed a sketch of what they proposed would be a typical bay of the building. They thought the building could be assembled by replicating these bays as desired and as the site permitted.

Students start a project

The first student group showed a typical bay of their office (Figure 6.2). It showed the structural and service systems for providing shelter, power, comfort and light while maintaining a relatively uninterrupted floor space to give flexibility of layout.

By contrast the second group had focussed their attention on particular features of the site. The suburban parkland site was a south-facing slope located between two major radial roads connected by a footpath. They hardly spoke at all about the design of office space.

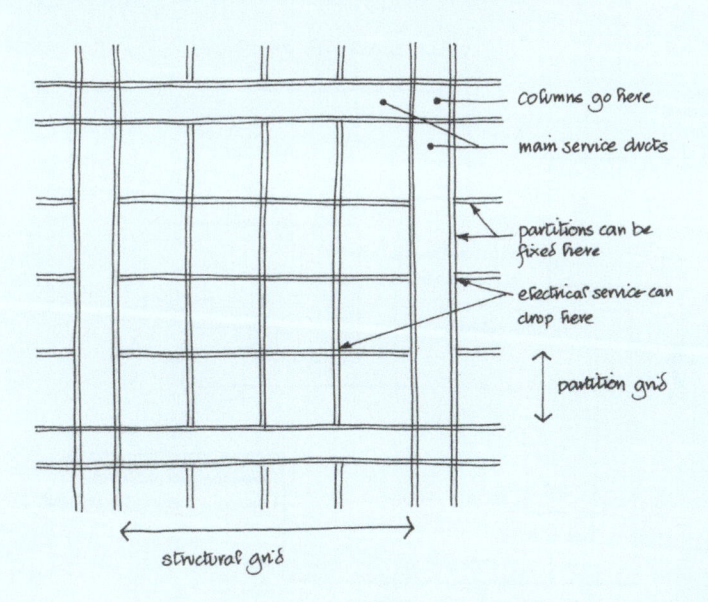

6.2

(continued)

(continued)

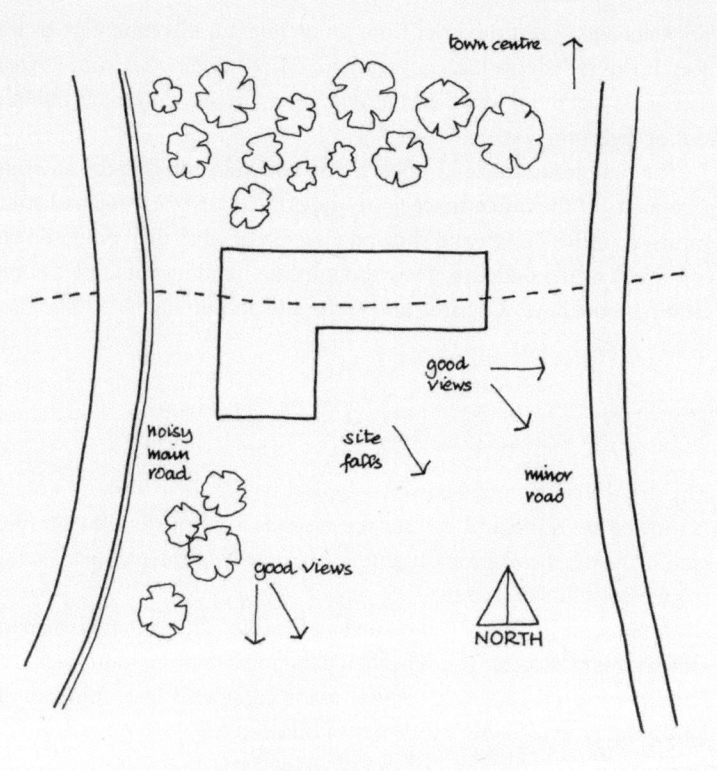

town centre ↑

good views →

Noisy main road

site falls

minor road

good views

NORTH

6.3

office space for employees

main entrance atrium with communal facilities

waiting and interview spaces for each department

foyer for each administrative division with vertical circulation in atrium

6.4

The second student group showed a site plan with the building massed to screen noise from the major road and taking advantage of good views to the south and east (Figure 6.3). They wanted to retain the belt of established trees to the north. They had an idea of creating a local shopping mall on the ground floor following the line of an existing footpath.

The third group had focussed more on the visitors rather than those who worked in the building. This group relied on their own experience of visiting local government offices, which they thought were often rambling and confusing. They were anxious to create a plan that would make the visitor experience less daunting.

The third student group showed a diagrammatic plan of the building indicating how visitors would enter and move around and find their way in the building (Figure 6.4). The plan also showed how visitors and workers were kept apart except where they needed to meet.

You can see that these three groups showed very different work, while actually using the same basic design strategy. They had begun by finding something in the brief, or in their own reading of the problem, that they thought was important. In each case they had begun to design and all showed what we might call a proto-design rather than some abstract analysis. In conversation it was clear that they understood more about the problem and had some ideas about what they might do next.

It is difficult to decide whether any of these approaches are better than the others and it is certainly not possible to declare any to be either right or wrong. By the end of the project all three groups produced a design that was a comprehensive solution to the problem and two of them received a commendation from the competition judges. You might think from this that it does not really matter much where you start a design project but that it seems important to get going and begin creating ideas about the solution.

However, this approach can also lead you into a common design trap. I have tutored countless students in different fields of design and in many countries. No matter what the field, background or location, I find a common problem. Often, when students ask for help, they have simply become too attached to either the first or at least to a very early design idea. The very idea that has helped them to understand the project has now become a block to progress. If you listen to students who are working on the same studio design project chatting to each other, one might tell another that they 'have just started again'. This is of course a complete nonsense and impossible. You can never begin the same project twice since you inevitably know much more about it the second time round. What they mean by this shorthand expression is that they have begun a new line of thought about their solution while using all the experience gained so far. Knowing when to do this is one of the skills you need to acquire in order to become a good designer.

Heuristic thinking can help

So far we have seen that designers seem to like to get going quickly. They rarely begin with a lengthy analysis of the problem but rather prefer to produce some ideas early and quickly. These ideas are propositions. They are expressions of how some aspect or feature of the design might look. They are often incomplete and probably impractical in some way but they move the designer forward. They might sometimes look very systematic, as with the first group of students in the examples above. Sometimes they might seem more emotional and feely.

It might help here to explore the idea of heuristic thinking. The essence of this approach is simultaneously educational and solution seeking. It aims to go in directions that for some reason are thought to have a high probability of finding a good solution. A simple example of this is what are called rules of thumb. These are usually widely known and based on experience rather than theory.

Design can begin with a solution looking for problems

The discussion so far has tended to imply the classical situation of a client commissioning a design, perhaps on behalf of other users. However, this is by no means the only way design can be done. The designer James Dyson is now famous for a whole series of domestic appliances, most notably the cyclone vacuum cleaner. Dyson fitted a cyclone air filter to a paint shop in his factory and noticed that it worked all day without clogging, and so began the design of his highly successful revolutionary vacuum cleaner, which not only maintains constant suction but also removes the need for disposable bags. In fact, Dyson found it impossible to convince any British manufacturers to take on the production of his design and had to market it himself. Thus he eventually had to become his own client. This design process began with a solution looking for problems rather than the other way round.

Sir James Dyson finds a new solution for an old problem

6.5

Sir James Dyson had designed a number of domestic products before the vacuum cleaners for which he is now best known. One of these was his innovative 'ballbarrow' (Figure 6.5). This used a sphere to replace the traditional front wheel. His experience of trying to manoeuvre a normal barrow on muddy ground led him to this idea. Dyson was later to grow impatient with having to climb up to clean the clogged air filters in the roof of the paint shop where the ballbarrows were finished. He devised a cyclone-based air filter to solve this problem and began to wonder why his domestic vacuum cleaner did not also use this principle to maintain suction and eliminate the need for disposable bags. You might also notice that more recent designs of his vacuum cleaners also use the ball idea to make them more easily manoeuvrable.

The minimal brief

The culture of scientific and technological revolution heralded by Harold Wilson had led to a period in which the brief had become a serious business. In architecture, many large buildings were being commissioned by the public sector that was enthusiastic about generating extremely detailed briefs. Nowhere was this more prevalent than in the case of hospitals and schools. This tendency remains to this day, much to the frustration of many architects.

The brief as a mission statement

'Many highly regarded and successful architects share the view that the starting point for design should be as short and terse as possible' (Lawson 1994).

'I'm not interested in the brief so much as finding out what the client's objectives are and in most cases that should be not more than one line, a mission statement' (Ken Yeang).

'We have found over the years that the ideal brief is probably one or two pages, even for the most complex project. Many clients think they have got to produce something that is two inches thick before an architect can even put pen to paper. We prefer it the other way round, we prefer the thinnest possible information so that we can get a grasp on the whole thing and then gradually embellish it with detail later' (Michael Wilford).

'The real problem is often concealed by the way it is written about as a brief . . . we design as a means of coming to terms with the brief and recognize it as a reciprocal relationship between the production of form and the definition of the programme' (Richard MacCormac).

'We never ever get a brief from the client that we can start working on. The client hardly ever knows what they want and sometimes they have got totally rigid ideas about what they want but they are completely wrong, and they don't realize it' (Eva Jiricna).

(Lawson 1994)

What we see emerging from these comments is a wish to get a brief as a very small starting point and that, ideally, the designer and client together can develop the detailed description of the problems alongside the production of ideas about form.

The design school project brief

This interactive view of brief making is not easy to realise in the design school studio. More often than not you will have little or no access to a client in the way these designers want in practice. This is one of the reasons why my school launched a project known as CUDE, which stood for Clients and Users in Design Education. A series of ideas and proposals grew out of that project but there is no evidence that they have become widespread practice in design education. In reality the relationship between clients and designers is an extremely complex and varied one. We shall discuss this far more in later chapters. For now, as a student, you may need to think this through and discuss it with your tutors. However, it is just one way in which the design school studio project can never really be an accurate model of practice.

The design problem and the continuing process

This chapter has suggested a number of things about starting a design project. But these can never be meaningfully discussed in isolation. It is high time we thought about the rest of the process. What exactly do we have to do when designing? This is the topic of Chapter 8. By now, though, you may be wondering why the statement of the problem and the construction of the brief is such a tricky matter when it comes to designing. It turns out that design problems are very special kinds of things and you are unlikely to have run across anything quite like them before. We shall explore all this in the next chapter.

However, before we move on, here are some key lessons from our explorations so far.

- Design problems are rarely comprehensively stated.
- Design is as much about discovering problems as it is about creating solutions.
- Briefing is often best seen as part of the design process.
- Designers tend to work in a solution-focussed way.

References

Lawson, B. R. (1979). "Cognitive strategies in architectural design". *Ergonomics* 22(1): 59–68.

Lawson, B. R. (1994). *Design in Mind*. Oxford, Butterworth Architecture.

Ulrich, R. S. (1984). "View through a window may influence recovery from surgery". *Science* 224(4647): 420–421.

Chapter 7

What's the problem?

Back to front

In the previous chapter we saw that designers tend to work in a solution-focussed manner. During the early phases of the design process, they are more interested in creating designs than understanding problems. Why should this be? Should you be worried about using this approach? Or is there something about design problems that creates this apparently back-to-front process?

The trouble with architects is . . .

Some years ago I was involved in a strategic meeting at the Royal Institute of British Architects about the early forms of computer-aided design. There was some irritation on the part of the architects that this new software was not very user-friendly. An objective was to encourage some standardisation so these systems could be easily learned and the skills transferred from one to another as well as the data.

There were a number of early adopters meeting with representatives of the major software developers. One software systems designer complained about the way architects were using the systems. He began several of his contributions by saying 'the trouble with architects is . . .'. He was really telling us that architects often wanted to use the systems in ways not envisaged by their software designers. Eventually I ran out of patience with this and asked him if he thought that by some amazing coincidence all the stupid people in the world had chosen to become architects. I suggested that an alternative and more likely explanation was that a widely used approach by architects showed they had intelligently adapted to their situation and found a good way of working.

Are design problems special?

Design is often portrayed as a combination of art and science but in reality it belongs in its own category. It is now widely accepted that design problems are indeed rather special and if you study their characteristics the solution-focussed approach makes a good deal of sense.

Design as art and science

Design, in the form of an architect, is seen riding two warring and varied beasts (Figure 7.1). It looks an uncomfortable process. In reality, design is a beast in its own right but of course there are elements that seem artistic and elements that seem scientific.

This cartoon was drawn by the wonderful cartoonist Louis Hellman and first appeared in the catalogue for an exhibition at the RIBA called *The Art of The Process* (Lawson 1993).

7.1

One of these characteristics should already be apparent from some of the material discussed in previous chapters. Take the example of my colleague who thought he wanted a house extension but actually ended up buying his daughter some headphones (Chapter 6). This suggests two things about design problems. The first is that the real problem is often not described. In this case it was the noise made by his daughter's music system while he was trying to work. The second is that people tend to describe the problem by telling you the sort of solution they think they need, in this case a house extension. They are not always right.

What's the problem?

The church tower

I like the silly cautionary tale about a scientist, an engineer and an architect who were standing admiring a church tower and arguing about how tall it was. A passing shopkeeper, seeing a commercial possibility, suggested that they could use one of the new barometers he was selling to measure the height of the tower. He offered a free barometer as a prize for the most accurate result. The scientist carefully measured the atmospheric pressure at the bottom of the tower and again at the top and, from the difference, he calculated the height. The engineer said this would be too approximate so he dropped the barometer from the top and, measuring the time it took to crash to ground below, he calculated the height. Both the scientist and engineer were however surprised that the architect won by coming up with the exact height. He had taken the barometer into the church and given it as a present to the verger who in turn showed him the original architect's drawings stored inside.

7.2

Design problems can often be solved in many quite different ways. Often our training and background determine the approach we take. I was part of a group asked to look creatively at the problem of providing catering on railway trains. The client was concerned that passengers complained about this service and it was also losing money for the train company. Our group included someone from an advertising agency, who said the answer would be to rebrand the catering and create a better image. An industrial designer suggested looking at the design of the buffet car and proposed putting vending machines in each carriage. We also had an operations research consultant who thought it was a matter of being more selective about on which trains and at which times the service should be offered.

Of course I have given you a very simplified account here and the reality was much more complex but it all boiled down to the same basic situation. These consultants were trained not so much in seeing the wider problem as in understanding their own kind of solutions. But design problems are often wide-ranging and difficult to see holistically.

Design problems are 'wicked'

We now generally see design problems as a particular case of what have been described as 'wicked' problems. Of course this does not mean they are in some way evil. Rather they are wicked in the sense of particularly tricky. This group of problems were first identified and described by Horst Rittel who claimed that such problems have a number of identifiable and important characteristics (Rittel and Webber 1973).

No complete description

It is not possible comprehensively to describe a wicked problem. This means that, as you work on them, more aspects or bits of these problems tend to emerge. So starting by creating a solution is not such a strange idea after all. The story of my employer wanting me to produce an ill-considered quick proposal for a hospital shows this. When we showed this to the clients they found it relatively easily to say why it would not work. It was really only then that large chunks of what should have been in the brief began to emerge. But we could still not be certain the whole of the problem had been discovered.

There is no end to a design problem

Wicked problems in general and design problems specifically have no detectable ending. They are not like crossword puzzles that have a complete solution once the last clue has been solved. Actually you stop designing when it somehow feels right, or when you run out of time on a studio project or when a client gets fed up waiting for more iterations.

There are no correct solutions

You cannot ever say that a design solution is right, correct or even optimal. We might be able to say that solutions are good, bad or indifferent. We can sometimes say that one solution is better than another. When multiple stakeholders are involved, and they often are in design, which solutions seem good or bad might well depend on which stakeholder you ask. For example, in industrial design you might have manufacturers, retailers and customers all taking quite different views. The proliferation of reviews of such items on websites like Amazon show how differently people can perceive the same piece of design.

No way of infallibly measuring success

This takes us back to the first chapter when we saw that there are many ways of using numbers and measurements and that these can rarely be combined in a single infallible judgement. So, when you read reviews of designed objects, each reviewer will have used different scales and attributed different levels of importance to them.

There are no infallible methods for solving them.

You cannot tell by looking at a wicked problem which tools might be useful for solving it. Often designers use their experience of previous reasonably similar kinds of problems to help them decide how to work on each one. Design problems can only be understood subjectively.

An inexhaustible number of solutions

Even if you deliberately create alternative solutions there will still be an apparently infinite number of others waiting to be discovered. In a design school we often set the same projects many times, especially for the early years. We never see one design solution completely repeated. It is true that you gradually learn to group solutions together as being fundamentally similar but they are always unique.

Each problem is a symptom of other problems or solutions

Most things that we design are governed by higher-level problems and in turn create lower-level ones. So a motorcar is designed to get people around using a particular system of roads and other facilities. Our need for it comes from many conditions of modern urban life. We need to move often and quickly along unpredictable routes at unpredictable times. In modern life, families rarely live locally and we often have to work away from where we live. So the motorcar is needed because of the nature of modern urban life. However, the car creates other problems. Most obviously these include congestion, pollution, noise and danger to human life.

Each problem is unique

No two design problems are ever quite the same. Such problems are situated in time and sometimes place too. Designing a house in northern Europe is a very different thing to designing one in Malaysia. Designing a domestic device is subject to technical developments, changing economics and cultural backgrounds. Looking at solutions to similar problems can often be helpful but is never an infallible guide.

The designer is always wrong

We cannot shirk our responsibilities here. We can try to do our best but some aspects of every solution are likely to seem pretty bad to some people at some times. We cannot expect to please all the people all of the time. Many design fields are multi-disciplinary and multi-professional. For example, an architect is likely to work with a structural engineer, a services engineer, a quantity surveyor and so on. In my experience each of these colleagues tends to think you are just a poor version of them. If all this worries you then give up trying to become a designer now.

The designer hanging on to the big idea

Design often feels like this. As the designer, you may have a big idea about the way the design should go. However, others around you are snapping

7.3

away trying to introduce their ideas that would inevitably dilute the concept. Of course, they all have something important to say. So it is a battle of wills and ideas that is never easy to get right.

Another drawing by the brilliant cartoonist Louis Hellman (Figure 7.3) first appeared in the catalogue for an exhibition at the RIBA called *The Art of The Process* (Lawson 1993).

What does this all mean for designers?

It actually means quite a lot and we will discover more and more ways in which this impacts on our work as we go through the book. However, I cannot think of a better very short summary than that given by Nigel Cross.

> Designers must have the ability to: produce novel unexpected solutions by applying imagination and constructive forethought to practical problems, using drawings and other modelling media as a means of problem-solving. In doing this, they need to deal with uncertainty and decision-making on the basis of limited information, and resolve ill-defined "wicked" problems. They do this by adopting solution-focussed strategies, applying productive/creative thinking, and using graphic or spatial media.
>
> (Cross 1990)

Don't worry, keep calm

Do not worry! There is no need for you to remember all this to become a designer. People have been designing very successfully and in ways that draw admiration and sometimes contempt, long before we ever started trying to understand how we do it. However, it does help to remember that you are doing something extremely challenging and special because the kinds of problems you will deal with have these special and challenging characteristics. As we go on through this book you should find many suggestions and examples of how to find your way through it all. This book is intended as a sort of companion for you along this tricky road of discovery. It is not intended to be another textbook full of things you must learn and remember.

There is one really important lesson that I hope you will take forward from this chapter. Designing involves finding problems as much as solving them. The process you are trying to learn is fundamentally influenced by this vital and simple fact. My colleague Kees Dorst, with whom I wrote *Design Expertise*, tells a story about a student studying for an engineering degree who was doing design projects jointly with industrial design students. He apparently got exasperated by this during a project and came to his tutor saying 'I am an engineering student. I have a right to know what the problem is' (Lawson and Dorst 2009). Unfortunately designers do not have any such right. It is up to them to find out for themselves. As we shall see later, it is in fact even more complex because clients actually expect that their designers will even create more problems for themselves. If you want a simple building then you can go to a builder but if you want architecture then you need an architect.

Determined problems

This brings us nicely to a helpful analysis of problems by Kees Dorst (Dorst 2006). He pointed out that design problems are mostly neither completely fixed nor completely free. He suggested that problems show one of three states of fixity or determination. First, they can be completely determined by what Kees called 'hard and unalterable needs, requirements and intentions'. We might lump all these together and call them constraints. Taken together, they constrain the range of possible solutions. Determined problems more or less totally determine the solution and thus they can be tackled by problem-solving methods. A crossword puzzle is such a problem. Such perfectly constrained problems are usually artificially created puzzles.

More interestingly for us here, there are two other possibilities. A very large proportion of design problems are under-determined. In other words, the requirements or constraints leave a good deal of room for manoeuvre. You might think that the client who wants a house designing but has few specific requirements leaves you, the designer, free to interpret the problem as you see fit. This of course means that each designer is likely to interpret such problems differently. This interpretation of the problem becomes part of the creative act of designing.

Finally, design problems can sometimes be over-determined. Such problems have so many constraints that it is not possible to satisfy them all. Our house-building client might have so many requirements that, as the designer, you have to negotiate which will be satisfied and which not. Again, there is some freedom of choice here and there will again be no one right answer.

Actually things are probably even more complicated. It seems quite possible to have a design problem that is both under-constrained and over-constrained. Some aspects of it might have few constraints and leave a lot to the designer. In other aspects there are so many constraints that some tough choices need to be made. Some clients may want to be involved in making these choices while others may leave it more or less to you, the designer.

There's more, quite a bit more!

That will do about design problems for now. Actually, there is quite a lot more to say but we will delay further discussion until much later. This is partly because it could all get far too theoretical and abstract here and there are things to learn about the act of designing that are likely to be far more helpful and relevant to your development. When you have got further down this road we will come back to design problems in a way that should help you to manage your design process. That will be almost at the end of the book in Chapters 22 and 23. In the next chapter we shall explore the whole range of activities that together make up the design process.

References

Cross, N. (1990). "The nature and nurture of the design ability". *Design Studies* 11(3):127–140.

Dorst, C. H. (2006). *Understanding Design*. Amsterdam, BIS Publishers.

Lawson, B. R. (1993). "The art of the process". *The Art of the Process: Architectural Design in Practice*. L. Rogers. London, RIBA: 6–11.

Lawson, B. R. and C. H. Dorst (2009). *Design Expertise*. Oxford, Elsevier/Architectural Press.

Rittel, H. W. J. and M. M. Webber (1973). "Dilemmas in a general theory of planning". *Policy Sciences* 4(2): 155–169.

Chapter 8

The components of design thinking

Learning skills

It is about time we explored the things that happen during a design process. It turns out that there are quite a few discernably different activities during design. Once these are identified you can look out for them in your own design process and perhaps identify those that you seem to do well or poorly. This might help you to develop a better process. I must issue a warning before this begins. It is probably not a good idea to be very self-conscious and analytical while trying to design professionally. You are just likely to lose your focus on the outcome of your designing in favour of the process. This is actually just the same for developing most complex skills. Most of us can only really seriously learn to play a sport or a musical instrument without periods of taking things apart and practising them before putting them back together on the field of play or the concert room.

Learning complex skills

This diagram (Figure 8.1) shows how to place the fingers in order to get each of the notes in the lower half of the flute's range. This all has to be learned but you will still not be able to play the flute. There are many other skills involved. Perhaps the most obvious one is developing the right way to shape the mouth and blow.

> Keeping the lips gently closed, extend them a little towards the corners as when half smiling, care being taken not to turn them inwards at all during the process. The "smile", rather a sardonic one perhaps, should draw in the cheeks against the teeth at the sides and the muscular action will produce a firmness of the lips towards the corners. Now, on

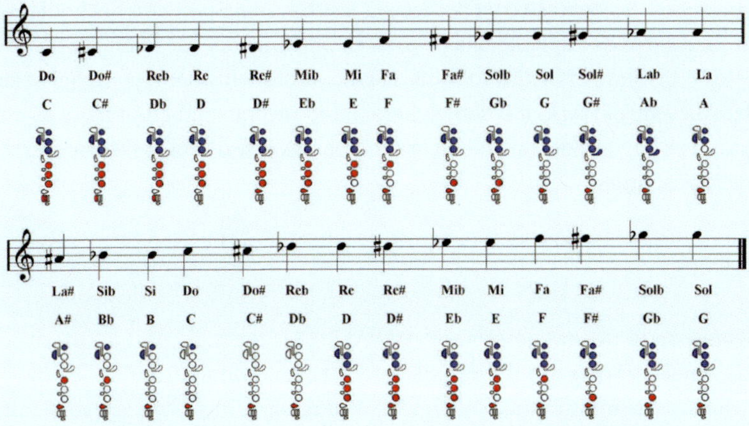

8.1

blowing across the mouthpiece towards its outer edge, the breath will make a small opening in the middle of the lips and, when the jet of air thus formed strikes the outer edge the flute head will sound.

(Chapman 1973)

This may be helpful when learning and developing a good embouchure but you could not expect to interpret music sensitively while thinking about all this advice. James Galway, in his book, actually recommends taking the head joint off the body of the flute to practise this to make sure you are not tempted to worry about fingering and other skills.

In fact, you also have to learn to change the embouchure with the fingers in order to get all the various notes exactly at the correct pitch. Eventually, then, you must integrate all the different skills into one understanding of how to play.

The very first chapter in this book introduced the idea of design as a skill that can be learned, practised and improved. Some teachers in design schools may see designing as a talent that you either have or do not have. It is certainly true that it seems to come more naturally to some than others but that is no different to playing the flute or golf. The reality is that most of us benefit from some analysis and practice. So we must first try to identify all the skills you use when designing.

The design process seen as a sequence of activities

Much of the work of early design researchers centred around finding some map that could be used to navigate through the design process. Effectively these maps implied a list of activities that had to be followed in a proposed sequence.

There were many variants of this and occasionally some still crop up or new ones are proposed. So pervasive were these ideas that some professional bodies even published maps as explanations of what their designers do. Amongst these was the Royal Institute of British Architects, who published what they rather grandly called *The Plan of Work*. It is shown here not to recommend it but more as a cautionary tale. If you look at the diagram it shows a series of tasks apparently in some logical order.

The design process as a sequence of activities

This map of the design process (Figure 8.2) is the basis of the RIBA plan of work. At first sight it looks like a sequence running from left to right. Look more carefully and you will see that the first three boxes are all connected each to the other and could be more honestly represented in a ring. (Incidentally, this illustrates both the power and danger of diagrams, as we discussed in Chapter 4.) In this case, the authors presumably wanted the viewer to see a sequence. This is not based on any scientific evidence, as you might think, but is probably more motivated by the need to show architects moving through a project logically and able to bill the client for parts of their fee at each stage. It would be much harder to convince clients to pay in stages if it looked as if architects were really going round in circles. Actually the RIBA diagram was even further detailed into sub-divisions of activities and reproduced in documents given to clients as part of the agreement of services to be supplied.

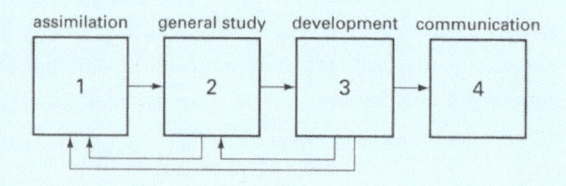

8.2

The RIBA diagram uses its own particular language in order to relate to its plan of work and contractual documents. It does however represent a view of the design process that was fairly widely promulgated in research work at the time.

The general sequential view of designing

A generalised version of the design process as seen by many researchers that implicitly used a problem-solving view of the design process (Figure 8.3). It uses the terms 'analysis', 'synthesis' and 'evaluation' and still has a linear and sequential appearance.

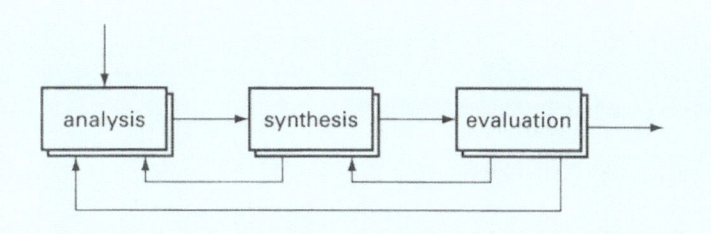

8.3

We have seen how designers are often solution-focussed. They can some-times begin the process with some crude or sketchy proposition rather than assimilating and studying the problem. Such empirical observations bring all these sequential models into question. However, the analysis, synthesis, evaluation diagram has some value. It begins to list some of the things that surely must happen during design. We must eventually come to understand problems by analysing them. We must generate solutions or synthesise them and we must perform some sort of evaluation of these proposed solutions in order to proceed further. But look again very carefully and you will see that there is a return loop back from each activity to the previous one.

A more honest diagram

Figure 8.4 is surely a more honest graphical representation of the design process than the linear version. It shows the three activities of analysis, synthesis and evaluation not in a sequence but in a ring.

During the height of the fashion for seeing design as a sequence of activities an anonymous and heartfelt notice appeared on the wall of the

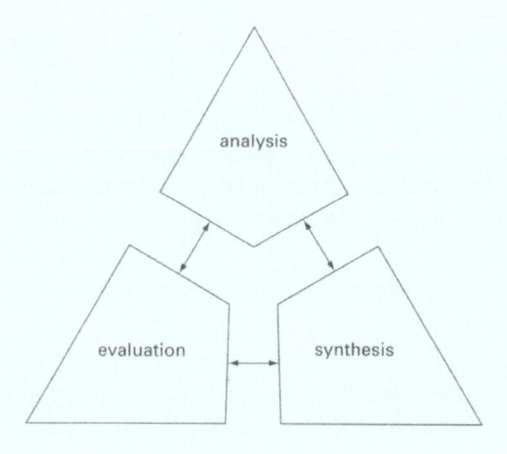

8.4

(continued)

(continued)

Greater London Council Architects Department (as reported by Astragal in *The Architects' Journal*, 22 March 1978):

The six phases of a design project:

1.   Enthusiasm
2.   Disillusionment
3.   Panic
4.   Search for the guilty
5.   Punishment of the innocent
6.   Praise for the non-participants

What happens during design?

In a seminal paper Nigel Cross summarised the scientific knowledge about the activities that make up designing (Cross 1990). He listed many of the things that designers typically do. According to Cross, designers typically 'produce novel unexpected solutions, tolerate uncertainty, work with incomplete information, apply imagination and constructive forethought to practical problems and use drawings and other modelling media as a means of problem solving'.

Cross then goes on to produce an accompanying list of the abilities designers must have to carry out these activities, and to do them well. They need to be able to deal with uncertainty and decision making on the basis of limited information, resolve ill-defined 'wicked' problems by adopting solution-focussed strategies, employ productive/creative thinking and use graphic or spatial modelling media.

In a book called *Design Expertise* that I wrote with Kees Dorst, who is a professor of industrial design in Sydney, we tried to take these ideas a little further and develop a list of the activities that research has shown actually happen during design. We shall use the same structure here, but a more detailed discussion can be found in *Design Expertise* (Lawson and Dorst 2009).

At some stage designers must make design propositions. A design can never exist without this core activity. If designers are employing a solution-focussed strategy this might begin to happen quite early on. So these propositions are sometimes developed and sometimes abandoned as the process continues. We are going to call these propositions 'moves'.

These moves are most often made through some form of representation. The most commonly used early representations are the 'proposition' drawings and 'fabulous' drawings we saw in Chapter 4. Of course, the moves may also be described in words or put into computers. We shall call these skills 'representing'.

Even if they do not begin by studying and analysing the problem, designers clearly have to do some of this activity. We shall refer to these skills as 'formulating'.

As the design proceeds, designers must evaluate the moves they make against some set of criteria, however precisely or vaguely understood. So there is clearly a whole range of skills that we shall refer to as 'evaluating'.

There must be some activities that oversee the whole process and provide support for it. It is all too easy, especially in the early student years, to lose track and find you have gone away from the real problem and wasted a lot of time. A more or less conscious effort is needed to keep the design activity on course towards its target. We shall refer to these skills as 'managing'.

This gives us the bare bones of a model of design skills and activities. We have groups of activities and skills that are all needed and are commonly found in successful design. They are 'formulating', 'representing', 'moving', 'evaluating' and 'managing'. The rest of this chapter will be devoted to putting more flesh on the bones and seeing how these activities are applied in practice. If you are going to be a successful designer you are certainly going to have to do all these things well so you had better learn something about them and how to develop and practise these skills.

Formulating

Although we start with this group of skills during the design process they are inevitably employed on a recurring basis rather than just at the beginning as some of the proposed maps of the design process suggest.

Formulating – identifying

Research projects that include recordings of groups of designers show them naming or identifying parts of the problem that must somehow be accommodated in any solution. This is rather like the introduction of characters early in a play or novel. They are named and their characteristics are listed and how they must be accommodated is described.

Formulating – framing

Back in Chapter 4 we discussed the delightful notion of the designer having a conversation with the situation and doing this primarily through drawing. This idea was first introduced by Donald Schön and another of his important contributions is the idea that designers 'frame' the situation (Schön 1984). This involves describing or 'seeing' the situation in a particular way.

The importance of framing in design

The skill to create and manipulate frames is a central one in determining how the process will unfold . . . the high-level skill of framing is crucial in the development of design expertise, and often the central activity in the working lives of top designers and architects. The quality of design work produced depends as much on the ability of the designer to frame the problem relevantly and productively, as on the ability to arrive at an interesting solution from this standpoint; maybe even more so.

(Lawson and Dorst 2009)

The process is inevitably selective and allows the designer to concentrate on a simplified specific view or frame for a while, and this helps by temporarily reducing complexity. Inevitably, during this process, parts of the problem are temporarily suspended, set aside or ignored. This may allow some moves to be made that later may have to be evaluated against other frames.

An example of the types of identifying leading to a move

Two students of architecture are designing a children's day nursery.

Student A: 'As well as all the indoor accommodation we've got to provide an outdoor play space. It (the brief) says that children should not be able to wander away from it' (*identifying*).

Student B: 'The problem here then is how to create a protected safe outdoor play space' (*framing*).

Student A: 'we could arrange the building in an L shape against this corner of the site where there is already a high wall' (*moving*) he draws (*representing*).

Of course when Student B says 'the problem is', this is strictly speaking nonsense since the brief poses a multitude of problems. This is a framing activity to narrow the problem down in order to make some progress. Student A then takes a solution-focussed approach and immediately suggests and draws a proposed arrangement. In fact this move was later abandoned in favour of a courtyard but it still helped the two students progress with their work.

Representing

We discussed this in Chapter 4. We discussed it early because these skills are so essential that you need to be developing them as early as possible. Now we focus mostly on what we called proposition drawings. These sketches can range from indecipherable scribbles to delightful pieces of artwork. Mostly they are done very quickly as part of the general conversation with the situation. They act as a sort external memory that allows the designer to freeze some aspects of the design while trying other ideas around them. Many designers become so used to the sketch as an aid to thought that they almost instinctively reach for a pencil as they start to talk. Remember, though, that the reason for representing your design is often because you want to evaluate it. So selecting the right sort of representation is vital here. We shall discuss this again later in the chapter.

The central role of drawing

I interviewed the renowned British architect Richard MacCormac about his work and collaborated with him on several exhibitions. At no time in all these conversations did I see him without his pencil. He clearly felt incomplete as a thinker without this graphical aid.

> Whenever we have a kind of design session or crit review session in the office I cannot say anything until I've got a pencil or pen in my hand and one covers acres . . . well we have these rolls of paper and you get through them at a fantastic rate. I feel the pencil to be my spokesman as it were, nowadays I suppose most of what I do is freehand . . . mostly I'm using drawing as a process of criticism and discovery and tweaking and direction finding.
>
> (Lawson 1994)

Normal conversations can sometimes be difficult to start but, once the ice is broken, people are often soon chatting away non-stop. We see something similar with the drawing in the conversation. Designers and artists are notoriously apprehensive about the blank sheet of paper. The two examples of proposition drawings shown here were done by Robert Venturi when he first visited London to begin his commission to design an extension to the National Gallery in Trafalgar Square.

One

Robert Venturi had just visited the National Gallery site for the first time and, that evening, staying in the Savoy Hotel just down the street, he sketched his first thoughts on the menu of the Grill Room (Figure 8.5).

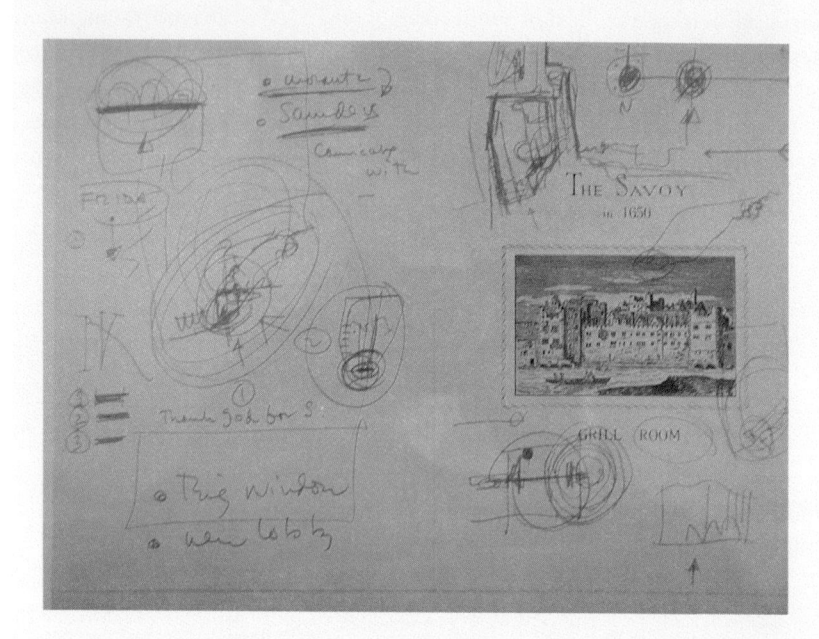

8.5

Two

The next day Robert Venturi flew back to his office just outside Philadelphia on a Pan Am flight and again found the menu to be an effective icebreaker for his conversation with the drawing (Figure 8.6).

Drawing as a conversation with self

These drawings by Venturi were obviously not unusual or exceptions. His partner Denise Scott Brown, who has observed him at work and collaborated with him for many years, described his reliance on the sketch.

> Sometimes the hand does something that the eye then re-interprets and gets an idea from and that kind of drawing for yourself and a few other people around the table is Bob's (Venturi) great specialty and those drawings have a nervousness to them and a tension, some of them are

just wonderful but they are never done as a piece of art, they are done as a communication with self and with people around the table.

(Lawson 1994)

(These two sets of drawings will appear again in Chapter 18 as they turn out to have yet another lesson to teach us there.)

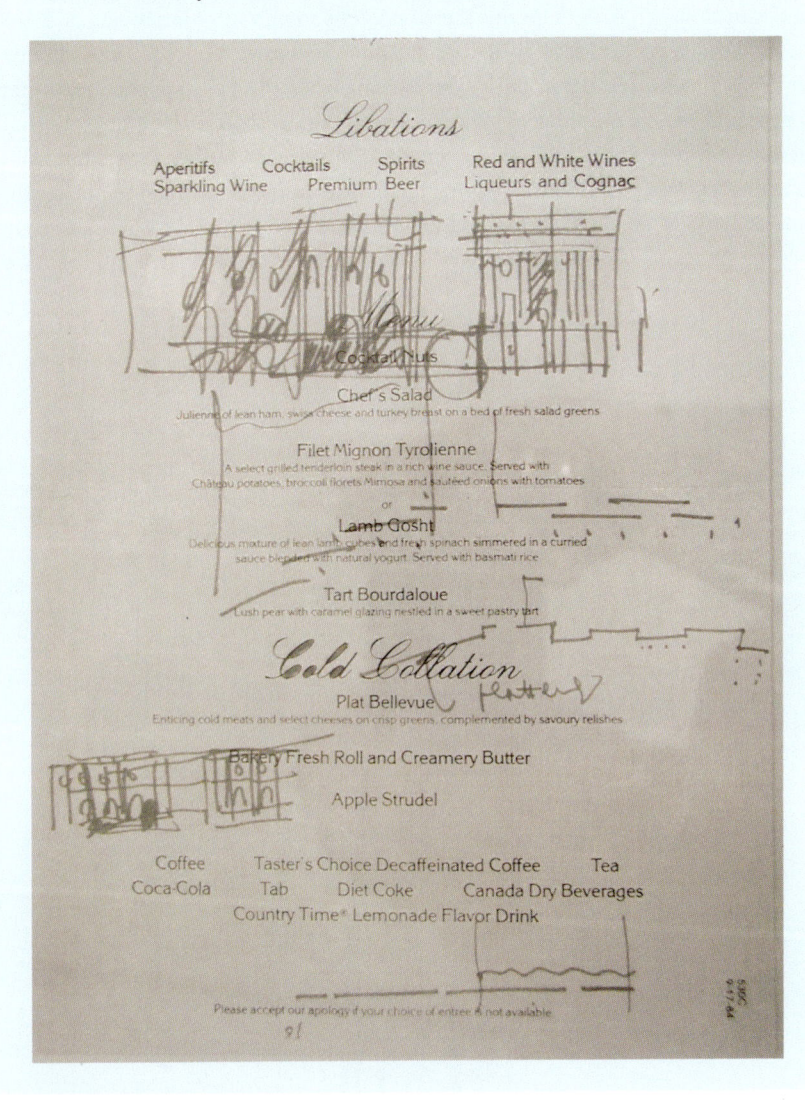

8.6

Moving

By now the idea of moves should be clear. These are propositions about some features, aspects or qualities of the design. Sometimes they are entirely novel but most often they may be only new within this particular design process. Alternatively, they may be developments of, or alterations to, a previous move. We can call these two types of moves 'new' and 'developmental'.

Moves – developmental

Often we see designers making a series of developmental moves. They get an idea and start to sketch it. Perhaps this sketch suggests some way of improving or developing the idea and this may go on for some time. However, sooner or later, this evolutionary process reaches a conclusion. Sensing when this has happened and when you should begin a new idea or variant is one of the key skills in designing. We shall discuss this more in the next chapter on managing design. Suffice to say that, quite often, when I visit a student's drawing board at their request, I can see the current line of thought has been exhausted and that perhaps the student has somehow become attached to it. My job as a tutor is to get them to consider a new kind of move.

Moves both developmental and new

8.7

Some of the literature refers to these as either 'vertical' or 'lateral' transformations. Any move transforms the design in some way but I prefer the nomenclature of 'new' and 'developmental' as shown in these drawings by Robert Venturi (Figure 8.7). He is exploring ideas about the plan. The first drawing is a series of developmental moves as he sketches idea on top of idea. As is normal for such developmental move sketches, it is not possible to be sure what he was actually thinking about here, except that it seems likely he was adjusting the basic idea. However, the top drawing to the right shows a quite new idea for the geometry of the skin. You can see that the remaining drawings, while still dealing with the plan, seem to start new moves each time. While some show a concern about spaces and circulation, others show thoughts about structure and skin.

Moves – new

Developmental moves may often be seen expressed by overdrawing a previous move sketch. There sometimes comes a point when the designer feels the drawing has undergone so many developments that it needs to be refreshed and a new drawing is started. This alone can often be a trigger for a new move. This is clearly a matter of personal style and, when we look at the work of different designers, we can often recognise them from the way drawings are developed and abandoned. The feeling of starting afresh can often be liberating. However, there are many well-established techniques of what is often called 'creative thinking' or 'lateral thinking' and we shall discuss them in later chapters.

Suffice to say here that designers often make use of what is often called 'precedent'. In simple terms this is getting some inspiration from something else that has already been done. This could be work by another designer who is admired, or projects with some common ground. However, it can also be something quite remote like a painting or a film. In Chapter 4 we discussed kinds of drawings and the 'experiential' drawings that designers often keep in sketchbooks can be invaluable for this process. We concluded with a strong recommendation that you begin this process of collecting ideas that might just come in useful one day.

It is worth just making a forward reference here to Chapter 11 where we will discuss the design tutorial. Here a tutor looks at the state of the design or designs at some intermediary stage in the process. This is entirely special to the design student's world and is fraught with many dangers. Some can arise from the tutor not reading proposition drawings and fabulous drawings in the ways that were intended by the student. It may also go wrong when the tutor adopts a role that is misunderstood by the student. We will discuss this more in Chapter 11.

Evaluating

An evaluation may be an absolute or relative matter. The designer usually assesses the current state of the design against some criteria that make sense in relation to some features, quantities or qualities of the design. Alternative solutions or part solutions may be evaluated against each other in a relative sense. This takes us right back to Chapter 2 when we introduced the notion of the various numerical scales. However, many design evaluations can only be subjective. The question that arises here is which stakeholder or stakeholders are being represented by the subjective evaluation. Often, of course, it is entirely a matter for the designer. How such judgements are later, if at all, represented to the paying client or other stakeholders remains a matter of managing the process. Some designers believe strongly in showing alternative solutions for evaluation by the client. Others prefer to present only one solution at a time, which they may modify in the light of criticism. This is clearly a matter of style of process that both designer and client may wish to debate. These issues will be discussed in Chapter 17.

One further point of style or judgement here is just when in a design process you should make evaluations. Often it is easy to demolish a design proposition that has not yet been well developed so delaying evaluation or suspending judgement is clearly an important design skill. On the other hand, you do not want to waste too much time developing a solution that has little prospect of surviving later evaluation. Learning to make these judgments about when to evaluate is one of the most important skills you need to develop. In later chapters we shall examine both the design crit (Chapter 12) and the studio tutorial (Chapter 11). Both of these are occasions when tutors or other external people may make judgements of the student design. Clearly the tutors also need a well-developed sense of whether making a critical evaluation at that stage will be productive for the student.

A key decision you must make is about just what you are evaluating. Is it the whole design or is it some aspect of the design? Of course, sooner or later, you must evaluate the whole design in its integrated form. However, earlier in the process you might want to just look at how it works in a particular way, or how it looks from a particular angle and so on. The point here is that in order to make an evaluation you need the right form of representation. One of the most common failings I find when tutoring design students is that they have in their mind an assessment of some aspect of their design that has been so poorly represented that the evaluation must be questionable. Looking at Chapter 4 again should give you some things to think about here. Should you do a hand sketch, a carefully measured drawing, perhaps on a computer, or do you really need a physical model?

Managing design

In a way the whole of this book is about managing the design process. However, in order to manage effectively and productively, you need to understand what you are trying to do and how and why. Managing sounds rather a dull subject perhaps in a book about an intensely creative process. Perhaps it is, but without it the process can become chaotic and ineffective. You may still come up with some great ideas but, unless you can control them and bring them all into some sort of order that relates to the real-world problem, you are not very likely to be a successful designer. In fact, managing can be very creative too and hopefully you will see that in the next chapter which is devoted to the meta-task of managing design.

A word of caution

We have taken the design process apart in order to understand it, but you should not see it as a halting process of one kind of activity finishing and another starting, all controlled by some management plan. You cannot play the flute by thinking of embouchure and fingering as independent skills. If you look again at Robert Venturi's drawings shown here, he was clearly formulating by selecting some aspect of the plan to work on, probably circulation, making moves both new and developmental and evaluating them as he went. He would almost certainly have some overall reflection on what he was doing to manage the process. Design processes are often a matter of rapidly and unconsciously alternating between all these activities. All this can easily become chaotic and never-ending if you are not careful. In the next chapter we will look at some simple ways of control and of managing yourself through all this complexity.

References

Chapman, F. B. (1973). *Flute Technique*. Oxford, Oxford University Press.
Cross, N. (1990). "The nature and nurture of the design ability". *Design Studies* 11(3): 127–140.
Lawson, B. R. (1994). *Design in Mind*. Oxford, Butterworth Architecture.
Lawson, B. R. and C. H. Dorst (2009). *Design Expertise*. Oxford, Elsevier/Architectural Press.
Schön, D. A. (1984). "Problems, frames and perspectives on designing". *Design Studies* 5(3): 132–136.

Chapter 9

Managing the design process

Management is necessary and need not be dull

Of all the mistakes I most often see student designers making, a lack of overall management is one of the most common. When you are inexperienced in design it is just very easy to get absorbed in a problem. You can become fascinated by how a particular piece of geometry might work, or obsessed with one minor aspect of the brief. All of a sudden you can find yourself running out of time and your project submission ends up looking imbalanced and inadequate. However, the last thing I want to do is to impose on you some managerial straightjacket. We live in times when management speak has become far too popular. Our world has been taken over by those who think 'quality control' is more important than good results. Sadly, the very design school you might be studying in has probably had to jump a whole series of hurdles that impose mindless management systems on it. As dean and head of school, I had to play this very dull game with our authorities. We had management plans coming out of our ears but no one ever really asked if academic staff were brilliantly inspirational when they gave lectures or tutored students.

But you do need to manage what you are doing. It is not a big thing but it could be critical to your success in the studio. In practice, this might mean stopping very briefly every now and then to take stock of where you are and where you are trying to get. So this chapter is intended to give you a few things to look out for that might help you guide your process seamlessly and in a productive direction. It might, for example, mean giving yourself permission to experiment for a while or backtrack to see if you missed anything. But remember that 'self-permission' must be time-limited or you could go off the rails in another way.

A reprise – reflection in action

The processes we explored in the previous chapter can collectively be seen as at the very heart of designing. As a designer you formulate the problem by identifying elements and framing the situation, you make propositional moves, most often representing them in sketches, and you evaluate their likely success and potential. In turn this allows you to see new possibilities, either by making new or developmental moves, or possibly by reframing the problem. From time to time you might identify other elements, new frames and set off a new sequence of moves.

All of this is being what Donald Schön described as a reflective practitioner (Schön 1983). It is a process of conversing with the situation. This is a slightly different concept to that of problem solving. It may seem less directional and more discursive as a process. It is a process in which the problem, which was never very clearly described or stated, gradually comes into focus in parallel with developing possible solutions. It is almost a negotiation between problem and solution as seen by you, the designer. This also clearly implies that briefing, or extracting the problem from the client and others, is a task that must inevitably go on right through the process. It is a continuous process of reflection.

Design as problem solving

If we want to describe all this in the terminology of problem solving we can (Figure 9.1). Some find this easier to understand and more helpful. However, from now on in this book, we shall proceed to develop and use the terminology described in Chapter 8.

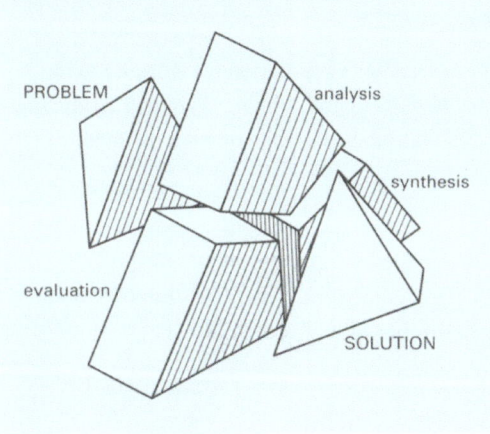

9.1

Reflection on action

Since we have used the term 'reflection in action' to describe the process of designing it is tempting to use the phrase 'reflection on action' for the meta-process of managing. In fact these descriptions already take the process apart by far more than you may feel or recognise when actually designing. There is certainly no need for you to be constantly asking yourself what kind of move you have just made or how you previously framed the problem. In fact, what research shows is that experienced designers are often jumping seamlessly, unconsciously and rapidly between the central design activities we explored in the previous chapter. Making moves and evaluating them is really one continuous process that often leads to some reformulation of the problem. Moreover, all the discoveries that are made during this round of activities also often suggest the need to clarify parts of the brief with whoever might be responsible.

The concept of reflection on action clearly involves the creation of an overview and a stepping out of the 'flow' of the design activity. It involves a mental 'standing back' and asking if the process is going well or might benefit from being steered differently. We shall just introduce this idea here but there will be more help on how to do it much later in the book.

Speed of working

Philippe Starck claims to work extremely quickly. He refers to this speed as being the only way to capture what he calls 'the violence of the idea'. It is interesting that several designers have used similar explanations when talking about this. Just as they want to see the whole picture at a glance, they worry about forgetting one of the complex array of issues they are considering.

Philippe Starck Ghost Chair

The product designer Philippe Starck has a reputation for working extraordinarily quickly. He claims to have designed a chair (Figure 9.2) during the period that the seat belt sign was on during take off on a plane journey.

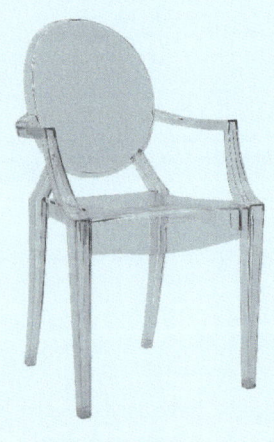

9.2

Actually, when we observe outstanding designers, the process curiously turns out to be both fast and slow. Sometimes they seem to be going so fast that it is almost impossible to keep up a log naming all their actions as they go. Good experienced designers seem to become very fluent in this process and apparently know almost intuitively when to work quickly and when to stand back and slow things down a little. My own personal reflection on this is that I often find an idea emerges quite suddenly out of some confusion and I may work very hard on it for a while. Somehow, and I cannot really tell you how this happens, I reach a point when it feels right to leave it for a while. This is when I might make and drink one of many cups of coffee that design demands I consume. The very process of getting up and going away to put on the coffee seems to allow the mind to work in the background and often the next course of action seems more obvious when I return to the task.

By the way, this feature of both quick and slow, of conscious hard work and unconscious reflection, is not exclusive to designing but can be seen in many other creative tasks. I am now writing novels as well as this sort of book. There are definitely periods when I write furiously as well as periods when a walk around the house or garden allows me to mull over the problem less consciously. I like to do *The Times* cryptic crossword most days as this gets my mind in gear as it were. Sometimes I can struggle fruitlessly for ages with a clue. Perhaps I leave it until a little later in the day and the answer, or a way of getting to the answer, suddenly appears. This apparently inactive period is when you give your mind permission to frame the situation differently.

The designer as juggler

The architect Richard MacCormac uses an analogy of juggling to explain the bursts of intense activity in designing: 'I think it's rather like juggling actually, you know one couldn't juggle slowly over a long period'.

The architect Michael Wilford, James Stirling's partner, agrees and explains why: '[it's like] a juggler who's got six balls in the air . . . and an architect is operating on at least six fronts simultaneously and if you take your eye off one of them and drop it, you're in trouble'.

Richard Burton, from his experience in teaching, thinks that one of the main problems students face when trying to develop their own design process is a failure to work quickly enough. He agrees with Wilford that a major danger of working too slowly is that one or more of the many important issues can get forgotten for too long and then the design becomes too fixed to accommodate these issues when addressed later.

> I like to sketch quickly by hand, sometimes even on the site but not using an orthodox drawing table . . . the first rough sketch is important . . . there are phases sometimes in a project that are extremely intensive but then to allow the project to mature you must give it time and perhaps change it at times.
>
> (Santiago Calatrava)

All quotations from *Design In Mind* (Lawson 1994).

So learning to design quickly and range around over many issues in rapid succession seems to be a skill worth trying to develop. Some design schools intersperse their major design projects with single-day sketch-design projects to help address this problem. This idea probably originated in the Beaux Arts period as the 'esquisse'. I was educated very much in this tradition and my tutors would launch a one-day esquisse without notice right in the middle of another much longer project. It taught you how to suddenly grapple with a new problem and work quickly for a short period. You then returned to the major project the next day, probably exhausted, but also now able to think afresh about it.

I have included here some short excerpts from interviews I did with the architect John Outram. Of course, managing the process in a design practice with a range of staff is a different challenge to managing a solo design studio project. We shall return to John's design management process in a later chapter. He has developed a very distinctive and effective way of working.

The esquisse in the practice of John Outram

John Outram is known for a most unusual approach to designing. As you can see (Figure 9.3), he is a prolific sketcher. What is of interest to us here, however, is his use of the 'studio esquisse' in practice.

> When a project comes in we hold an esquisse, everyone in the office does a design . . . I have always felt that you must extract as much energy as you can out of people and definitely our recent work is a synthesis of everyone's ideas in the practice.

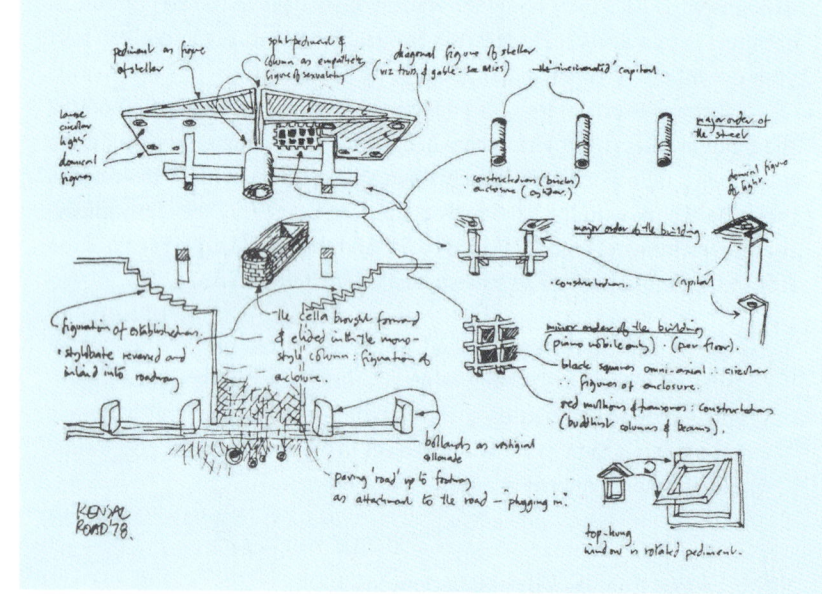

9.3

The richness of John Outram's designs

Figure 9.4 provides a sample of the richness of form, colour and detail created by John Outram's process. This is the interior of the Judge Business School at Cambridge.

9.4

But design can also be slow. The 'coffee moment' is, for me, a way of slowing things down for a while and thinking about something else. This might not sound much like managing the process but it often works. It allows the current design situation to sink into the back of the mind where things still happen but over a longer and more considered time frame. I cannot say if you will feel these moments but I know many designers share this experience. The alternative of carrying on working at this time is often counterproductive. You somehow need to understand your own design idea more fully before letting yourself try to work on detail.

Another way of explaining this might be helpful to those familiar with solving cryptic crosswords. The setters of these delightful but frustrating puzzles often try to create what they call a 'surface'. This is a way of leading you to think about the clue in a certain context. Here we might call this a 'frame'. If you get caught by this trap you will likely puzzle around it endlessly getting nowhere. Eventually you might put the puzzle down in frustrated annoyance and do something else. It is quite uncanny how often, when you return to it some time later, you 'see' a different possible meaning to the clue and solve it almost immediately. In our language here you reframe the situation. While this parallel with crosswords may help some of you, it is also dangerous since crosswords all have one correct answer. Design problems most certainly do not. They require different kinds of thinking. Nevertheless, doing such crosswords may help you to learn to reframe situations that you have become too familiar with. This is one of the key ways of developing creative thought.

The cryptic crossword setter using a 'surface' to create a misleading frame

This clue appeared in *The Times* Cryptic Crossword:

Fine applications programming interface for browser (5)

Cryptic crossword clues almost always have two parts. One is a definition, albeit somewhat vague, and the other is some form of wordplay. One of the tricks needed to solve these clues is to find which part of the clue is which. This clue reads in an uninterrupted fashion, deliberately making this quite difficult. Also, all these key words lead you to believe that it is about computing in some way. This is what in the cryptic crossword world is called a 'surface', but we might call it a 'frame'.

Actually the correct answer is OKAPI. The word play is 'OK' meaning 'fine', and 'API' is the normal abbreviation for applications programming interface. This leaves the word 'browser', which must be the definition. If you are fooled by the surface you start thinking about internet browsers. But in this case it deviously refers to an animal that feeds by browsing, which is a longer standing use of the word. The OKAPI is an antelope related to the giraffe that feeds in just this way, browsing on tree leaves and grasses. It is a browser.

Of course crosswords are not like design problems, not least because they always have one correct answer. However, the ability to see many alternative interpretations of a situation is common to both solving crosswords and designing. Interestingly, neither of these activities have so far been done consistently well by computers. They require a particularly human form of imagination.

One really popular way of trying to organise a new move is to look at what designers call precedent. Maybe you might pick up some books or magazines and skim through them to see if anything there gives you an idea about starting a new train of thought. We will look at this important idea of 'precedent' in the next chapter.

What I have described above are some features of managing the design process that may have been unselfconscious. There is no deliberating and carefully arriving at the notion that it might be better to walk away for a while, it just feels that way. The great American architect Frank Lloyd Wright was obviously a highly intuitive designer but this may be no accident. His mother controlled his education very carefully and was convinced that he should not enquire into his creative processes lest they disappear. She might have had a case. Certainly endless introspection is not often a recipe for good action. But for most of us some deliberation and careful management is probably a good idea. Knowing when to intervene in your own process seems to be one of the skills good designers have and you should probably try to develop it.

Pause and explore the brief

Contrary to the wishes of many who have tried to establish route maps of the design process, briefing appears to be a continuous process. It is certainly not something that happens exclusively at the beginning but rather represents the problem formulation aspects of designing that are often greatly influenced by the emerging potential solutions. In design, problems do not even necessarily precede solutions in the way normally expected in conventional problem solving. Thinking about solutions and thinking about problems seem inextricably interwoven in the design process. This may well offer us one useful way to distinguish between different design fields. Some design fields have very clearly defined problems that can be quite well described and understood at the beginning of the process or very early in it. Others may characteristically have more open-ended problems that can only be very loosely described and only vaguely understood at the outset. Dorst's idea of under-determined and over-determined problems introduced in Chapter 7 may be helpful in understanding this.

So you must learn to allow yourself to recognise moments that suggest you should seek a clarification or extension or investigation of the brief. This might mean pausing the designing activity for a while and you should not be afraid to do this. It may well be that, by exploring design possibilities, you may have thought of something not considered by the client or other stakeholders. You may be surprised how a question, that now seems so obvious and maybe even central to you, was never even asked by those composing the formal brief. We will explore this in more detail in Chapter 19.

Primary generators

Back in Chapter 6 we introduced the idea that designers tend to work in a solution-focussed way. In Chapter 8 we have seen that one aspect of that might be collecting precedent from previous solutions. In fact, this idea of precedent turns out to be so important that we will devote the whole of the next chapter to exploring it. However, here we introduce another concept that has become widely accepted in the design research world. My colleague Jane Darke was working on her doctorate with me back in the 1980s. She interviewed a series of architects and their clients and users about major public-sector housing schemes in London. She noticed a common trait among these architects, who were all highly experienced, skilled and well recognised. Designing major public-sector housing schemes in post-war England was one of the most difficult of design projects. Many different house types had to be developed for different-sized families and the whole site often had to be designed with much higher densities than had been used traditionally due to the significant shortage of housing that had built up during the Second World War and the immediate post-war periods. The legislative framework surrounding such schemes at that time in the UK further complicated the problem.

Jane noticed that the then prevalent view of design being a logical process starting with briefing and passing through problem analysis to solution synthesis bore little resemblance to what these expert architects were doing. She found they habitually and characteristically began with a strong generative idea and started drawing possible solutions very early on. This strong idea might be something like putting all the housing together in a long snaking wall with horizontal access decks, or developing a series of isolated tower blocks, or using compact courtyards, and so on. Often, as the design proceeded, these ideas might get discarded or another one adopted but, in every case, she found the process was one of coming to understand the problem by attempting solutions based on some simple generative idea. Jane Darke was obviously aware of the more empirical work that had suggested a solution-focussed approach was common among designers. We coined the term 'primary generator' for this idea and it has become widely accepted and used in the research world (Darke 1978). In more traditional design circles this is sometimes described as a 'design concept' or a 'parti'. Other words are used but through this book we will use the term 'primary generator'.

The primary generator

If you find diagrams of the design process as a sequence of activities helpful then this little map (Figure 9.5) shows the working of designers using primary generators. They devise some sort of generative idea, then they conjecture how the design or part of it might look using that concept. Finally they come to a better understanding of the problem by analysing this proto-design.

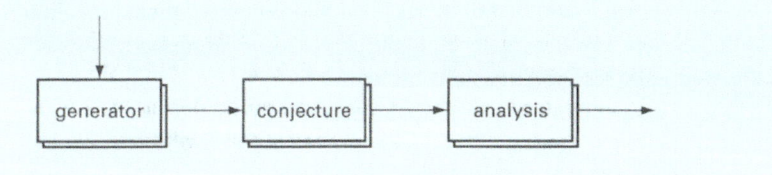

9.5

Not surprisingly, others have either observed the same phenomenon for themselves or have built on Darke's idea. Rowe, in his observations of designers at work, came to similar conclusions. He described design ideas that 'involve the a priori use of an organising principle or model to direct the decision making process' (Rowe 1987). However, he also warned of the dangers of such a device, useful though it obviously is. He records the 'tenacity with which designers will cling to major design ideas and themes in the face of what, at times, might seem insurmountable odds'. It is certainly my experience as a design tutor that relatively inexperienced students can be particularly guilty of this. Often an early idea seemed to allow for progress and a student can become absurdly attached to it, even though it is causing a lot of difficulty. As a tutor I find this is one of the most common problems I encounter at the students' drawing board. They will argue long and hard for something that is creating substantial organisational or technical problems. Learning when to let go of an early idea is another of the most important skills you must develop.

Occasionally I overhear students chatting about their work and this can be quite revealing. Especially early in the morning, one student might ask another how they are getting on. The other might reply to the effect that they 'have just started again'. I have lost count of the number of times that I have heard something like this. Taken literally, it is of course nonsense. It is simply not possible to start a project again because you now know much more about it than you did when you began. It is, however, a useful and well-understood shorthand or abbreviation. The student has probably been working for some time on an idea created by a primary generator. A lot of exploration of how everything would turn out has taken place. Almost certainly the student now realises that this particular primary generator is no longer helping and has probably become one of the significant obstacles. 'Starting again' then really means realising something that you have been in denial about for a while. You need a new direction. The search is on for a new primary generator, or maybe one has already appeared. However, this time around you know a lot more. It may not turn out to be as big a task as it sounds by describing it as 'starting again'.

But here is another of those teasing paradoxes I warned you about. Really good, original and creative designs are often the result of an absolutely dogged persistence in hanging on to the big idea like grim death (remember Figure 7.3). A very famous example must surely be Jorn Utzon's design for the Sydney Opera House. This must easily be one of the most admired and famous buildings of its time and yet the process that gave rise to it was hugely problematic. We saw in Chapter 4 that when Utzon first drew his ideas and submitted them for competition he had no idea how to actually build the complex curved surfaces in his drawings. He eventually resolved them all onto the surface of a single sphere. Many of us might have given up in the face of all the obstacles and we would have lost an astonishing piece of design.

So learning when to put an influential early generative idea aside is not an easy matter. You will just have to come to your own understanding of this as you develop into a professional designer. It turns out that the special kinds of problems that make up design and which give rise to this rather unusual way of working also lead to designers having special kinds of knowledge. As much as anything, this 'designerly way of knowing' gives us the ability to handle the design situation. That is what we will look at in the next chapter.

References

Darke, J. (1978). "The primary generator and the design process". *New Directions in Design Research: Proceedings of EDRA 9*. W. E. Rogers and W. H. Ittleson. Washington, EDRA: 325–337.

Lawson, B. R. (1994). *Design in Mind*. Oxford, Butterworth Architecture.

Rowe, P. G. (1987). *Design Thinking*. Cambridge MA, MIT Press.

Schön, D. A. (1983). *The Reflective Practitioner: How Professionals Think in Action*. London, Temple Smith.

Chapter 10

What designers know

Designers have their own special way of knowing and remembering

In an influential and important paper, Nigel Cross (Cross 1982) asks his readers whether designers know things in a special way and argues that there is some evidence to suggest this is the case. Here we are going to look at a particular aspect of this, one that it is vital to understand when studying design subjects. In Chapter 1 we first saw that design subjects have little theory with which to work to help you get from problem to solution. Engineers must understand and learn some theories in statics and dynamics that they can then use to produce structures or machines. This is not so for the kind of designers this book tries to help. For many years I delivered a course of lectures, seminars and exercises in a module called Architectural Theory. The first thing I had to do was apologise for the title, which I had not chosen. The course discussed how we see and understand architecture; the ways designers of all kinds describe their work and their attitudes, values and philosophies. While this all sounded very theoretical, it was largely quite practical advice. What it did not do was to create some all-embracing theory either of design or architecture. We do not have an Einstein with his 'special theory of relativity' nor do we have basic principles like Newton's Laws of dynamics or more complex concepts such as quantum mechanics.

A lack of theory or even limits

This possibly makes knowing as a designer even more difficult since there is really no boundary around the knowledge you might rely upon when designing. As Nigel Cross also said, 'what you need to know to design depends upon your approach to designing'.

It turns out that we store different kinds of knowledge in different ways in our memory. One of the courses I was taught was called 'Architectural History'. It was presented as a story unfolding through time, starting with the Egyptians, passing through the classical periods of Greece and Rome, and up through European periods to the present day. Our tutor did little to connect this knowledge to our design work in the studio but, nevertheless, he was indeed teaching us about things that would eventually become hugely important in our work as designers. He took a rather old-fashioned pedagogical approach and set us an examination at the end of our third year that was nothing short of torture. We were expected to be able to draw from memory the plans of all the most famous buildings through time as well as many of their major elevations. It required a memory of facts or things that seemed largely unconnected in my mind. I was unable to find any overall structure governing all these facts. I would frequently confuse them and produce hybrid nonsense for my answers or, even worse, completely fail to remember anything about the specified item.

We devised a way to enable us to pass this exam. The trick was to create a set of rules from which you could generate the required drawings, or at least produce something near enough to get away with it. By way of example I am showing you here how we remembered the plan of what is now called Hagia Sophia in Istanbul but was then known as Sancta Sophia in Constantinople.

A remarkable experience – Hagia Sophia in Istanbul

As a student I only knew this incredible building through drawings (Figure 10.1). About 40 years later I visited it for the first time. It has an amazing structure enabling it to span a huge uninterrupted space. With such limited technology this is nothing short of incredible. Goodness knows what impact it must have made when first built.

10.1

Rules versus experiences – theoretical memory

You can see that the rules for getting at least the outline of the plan were easy to follow (Figure 10.2). You start with a square, draw a circle inside it, put two rhomboids on either end and add little semicircles to the sloping sides. Finally you add small rectangles onto the short side and on one of them another semicircle.

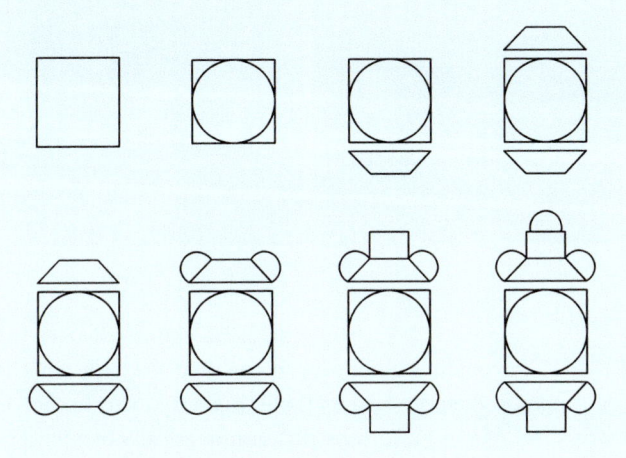

10.2

Now I chose this example for several reasons. I did indeed use this in my history exam and passed. My first visit to this building some 40 years later was also remarkable. I stood there in this wonderful piece of architecture and realised that I could not remember the rules we used to draw the plan. However, even though frustrated by this lack of memory of the rules, other recollections came flooding back unbeckoned into my mind. They were entirely about occasions and not rules.

Rules versus experiences – episodic memory

No matter how hard I tried I could only vaguely remember the rules for generating the plan of Hagia Sophia. But I could easily remember that, some 40 years earlier, I had sat with a group of students in Christ Church meadow in Oxford having a picnic while we tried to write all our memory rules (Figure 10.3). I was amazed to find I could remember that it was a sunny day and that we had a bottle of wine (white). I could recall who was with me, even how they were dressed and many other quite trivial details. I remembered the event clearly but the rules hardly at all.

(continued)

(continued)

10.3

This illustrates the fundamental difference in the way we treat what is called theoretical or semantic memory and episodic memory. The former is largely logical and structural. We use it to construct grammatically correct sentences even though we may have never uttered those words in that order before. We remember how to calculate Pi, or convert from Fahrenheit to Centigrade and do long division. The second type of memory, episodic, we use to store events, people and, of course, places and objects. The extent to which these are dealt with differently in our minds can be illustrated by the tragedy of later-life dementia or trauma-generated amnesia. Often people will forget places and their way around in them, people and their relationships, even perhaps their own name and where they were born, but they can still do sums and speak correctly phrased sentences.

I have told you this story because it teaches us something so vital about the knowledge we use as designers that it frames and structures the whole way we must learn. We designers generally need relatively little theoretical knowledge but a familiarity with designed objects, with places as well as natural phenomena, paintings, and even poetry can all be of fundamental value in the design process.

Inspiration in design

While designers do not have much theory, they can draw plenty of inspiration from previous designs and things around them. The beauty of looking at existing design work is that this knowledge comes ready packed in a designerly way of knowing. Seeing how others have tackled similar problems often tells us more than reading long theoretical and abstract studies about the problem. Similarly, historical work can tell us a great deal about what might be constant over time and what has changed. A design-based course will often include field trips and visits abroad. Design work that is located, such as architecture, somehow becomes more understandable when you see it in different countries. For many years I have held visiting posts in tropical countries and countries with fundamentally different cultures to my own. Seeing traditional buildings in wet tropical climates taught me more about how the architecture works in my own north European climate. Seeing how Chinese rituals are catered for in Singapore or Hong Kong explains the role of architecture in setting the scene for cultural life in a European context too.

Precedent – or, more accurately, reference

So, as a design student, you must begin what will become the work of a lifetime. Collecting and understanding your design world is of incalculable value. As you go on that work becomes a veritable goldmine of ideas. Designers often refer to this as 'precedent'. In fact, as Gabi Goldschmidt has wisely pointed out, this is a misleading term (Goldschmidt 1998). It conjures up images of lawyers who will plead a case by showing precedents that resulted in verdicts they want. In the legal world the skill lies in showing ever more precisely how accurate a precedent is and therefore being able to claim that your case deserves similar treatment. This is not so at all in the design world. Here a precedent may show only passing resemblance to your case or current design project. Indeed, useful design precedents may occur in objects or places designed for quite different conditions or circumstances. As designers we also like to be original so the precedent is often only a starting point from which our own work may develop into something quite different. Design precedent then is often only very loosely copied or imitated. So the word is misleading and Gabi Goldschmidt's preferred word 'reference' would be more accurate. But 'precedent' is common parlance in the design world so we will stick with it in this book.

Time to be old fashioned

It is time to be a little avuncular and issue a warning. The digital camera is now so ubiquitous and even present in many other objects like phones that we think nothing of using it to record what we do and what happens around us. But the camera really does too much to be useful to us here. We only have to glance, point and press a button. In bygone times photography was more tedious, expensive and uncertain in results, which arrived days or even weeks later. So, in the past, designers had little choice but to sketch what they saw. This had a number of advantages. It was, of course, immediate but you could also easily incorporate explanatory notes and you could draw in such a way as to emphasise features of particular interest. If you were a serious designer you invariably carried a pocket sketchbook and took it out at any opportunity to record things. One of many complicating things about design precedent is that at the time you first see it you may have little or no idea when or how it may come in handy. We introduced the concept of experiential drawings in Chapter 4 and I exhorted you then to start sketching. Hopefully this chapter will help you to understand why.

John Outram's analytical sketch of Buckminster Fuller's Dymaxion House

Sketching demands that you process what you see through the eye–brain–hand system. None of this is likely to happen if you just take a digital picture, although that can be dug out for analysis later. The sketch can go much further. This particular experiential sketch is intensely analytical, recording the overall shape as well as many junction details (Figure 10.4). It is also peppered with examples of John's own private analytical notes recording proportions and parallels with other objects.

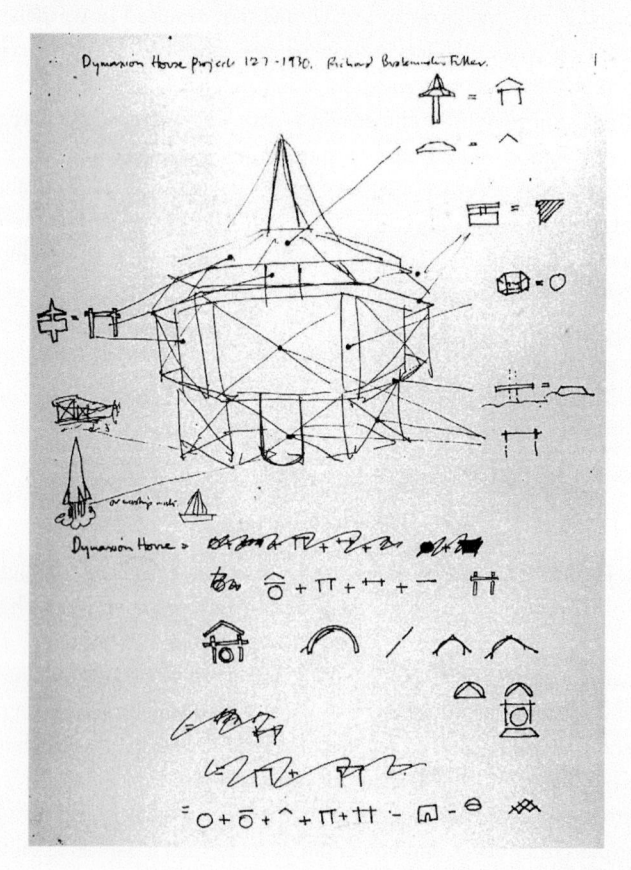

10.4

What designers know

However, the really important advantage that sketching offers over photography is that you must pass the knowledge of what you see through the eye–brain system in order to then instruct the hand what and how to draw. This involves a degree of cognitive processing that ensures the precedent is better understood and remembered. So, to a certain extent, you are analysing it immediately. You then have a conversation with the real world and your sketch that you would be unlikely to achieve when taking a photograph.

An important discipline here is to learn to draw what you see and only what you see. Novice students, who have not been formally taught drawing, can easily draw what they know to be there rather than what they see. This danger is most easily demonstrated by the drawings of young children who are very busy understanding the world around them and understandably get rather pleased with themselves as they gradually work things out.

A simple Miesian tower

This is the Arts Tower at the University of Sheffield where I worked for many years (Figure 10.5). To most local residents it represents a landmark that they navigate by. To architects it is a fairly elegant example of a mid-twentieth-century tower inspired by the traditions arising from the work of Ludwig Mies van der Rohe and his followers and, as such, it has been listed and protected.

10.5

(continued)

(continued)

A child's view

This drawing was done by my daughter when, as a very young girl, she came to work with me one day (Figure 10.6). She had previously been asking questions about some large housing blocks on the route we took into town. She was obviously puzzled by how people in high-rise residential buildings got up to them and where their front doors would be and how they got into the garden. These questions were all framed by her experience of her own home, which was a detached house with a large garden leading to a piece of wild woodland and open landscape on the edge of the Peak District national park. She took this confused knowledge with her into the task of drawing the Arts Tower. You can see that in her mind it is made up of lots of little houses each with a front door and knocker. The elevators are shown with the ropes attached to pull them up and the whole building has a pitched roof. She was of course not drawing what she had seen but what, in her mind, she knew must be there.

Actually the drawing is even more sophisticated. Look closely and you will see the door is in the centre of each house and the knocker is in the centre of the door. My daughter had already learned something about foreground and background and symmetry and axis.

10.6

There is a further advantage to making lots of sketches that you may or may not feel applies to you. You learn how to draw. If you came, as many now do, to university or college without formally studying art, you may not have such a good facility with sketching. This in turn is very likely to hold you up when doing the kinds of design drawings we talked about in Chapter 4. Now that form of conversation needs to be easy and free without having to pay attention to the business of actually making the marks on paper. So, even though you have digital cameras all around you, please try to keep a sketchbook and learn to make sketches of precedent. You never know where and when something useful will crop up so you really need a small sketchbook that is always with you, just like your phone.

The design library

Back in Chapter 5 we discussed the 'big four' special characteristics of a design school. They were the studio, the design library, the design tutorial and the crit. It must by now be apparent that a design library is a slightly different beast from the library found in other academic departments. Design students gain what we might call 'accelerated experience' by looking at and understanding possible precedent. One key source for this must surely be the library. The material in a design department library is likely to be very solution-focussed to match the way of thinking found in design processes. As a design student you will be likely to look at recent and historical design work mostly in solution form. The journals are heavily illustrated and you are likely to browse them as much as to read them in detail.

A very special kind of library

I have spent periods of my career both in design departments and psychology departments. These two kinds of departments need entirely different kinds of libraries. In a psychology department you would not expect undergraduates to read the current issue of all the major journals. You would normally find only postgraduate students and academic research staff consulting these publications. By then these people will have specialised and mostly only read the journals in their chosen specialist field. By contrast, in a design department, we expect the undergraduate student to look at the very latest journals in order to understand the way design in their field is currently going and to get inspiration for their own work. In many universities the journals are located in dusty dungeons, often underground and with little or no daylight, where undergraduates rarely venture. In a design department we really need the journals located with the books, and we need the latest journals on display showing their covers just as magazines appear in bookshops. It might be a picture on the cover of a journal that makes you take it down off the shelf and look at it.

The design library is neither undergraduate nor postgraduate

During my time as Dean, the university librarian came to see me with a puzzling request. The university was going to build a new library. Of course it was to be a place that did not just store books on shelves but would also have fast access to the internet and all sorts of electronic information sources. It was to be open 24 hours a day round the year and was specifically to serve the needs of undergraduates. The existing library was to become a postgraduate library. Our librarian wanted me to go through all the books in the architecture and design sections and specify for each one whether it should be in the undergraduate or postgraduate library.

The lack of theory in design makes it impossible to arrive at such a distinction. There are no undergraduate textbooks that cover all the basics of architecture. There are very few, if indeed any, books that we might say for sure undergraduates would not consult. The librarian had already assumed all the journals and magazines would be left in the postgraduate library. Luckily, we had a subject specialist architecture librarian who had for years looked after the architecture collection. Realising the problem, she asked me to speak to the national association of architecture librarians. This group had been established because of the specialised nature of design libraries (Lawson 2002).

Classifying knowledge in the design library

This in turn leads to another problem for the design library. The Dewey Decimal system of book classification used by most libraries is hopeless for design subjects.

Knowledge classification in libraries

The Dewey Decimal system of knowledge classification imposes an hierarchical tree-like structure on a library. The highest level is shown here:

1. Class 000   Computer science, information and general works
2. Class 100   Philosophy and psychology
3. Class 200   Religion
4. Class 300   Social sciences
5. Class 400   Language
6. Class 500   Science
7. Class 600   Technology
8. Class 700   Arts and recreation
9. Class 800   Literature
10. Class 900   History and geography

Each of these classes is then subdivided using what are called 'Tables'. So, under which class would an architecture or industrial design library come?

While there are other classification systems, most notably in the United States, China and Japan, they all pose similar problems for the librarian seeking to help students of design subjects.

If we just take architecture as an example, there will obviously be books found under 'Arts' and 'Technology'. But we also use 'Science' to understand the way buildings are modifiers of the environment. We also see a good deal of study under 'Social Science' of the impact of buildings on the lives of people in and around them. I know of no school of architecture that does not have a major course on the 'History' of architecture and, of course, on the way historical ideas impact on contemporary design. Much of what is written by those who would call themselves architectural theoreticians would have to be classified under 'Philosophy'. So it goes on. You quickly arrive at the conclusion that if we must use this system of classifying knowledge then the architecture library must have its own set of the complete Dewey system. Without this, the books and journals would be spread across the whole library and could not be located in one place for browsing.

Design libraries and the student pattern of use

But it is not just the way design knowledge is undefined and unbounded that causes problems for the design library. In one of the many economy drives that seem endemic in universities, our architecture library came under pressure. It uses special space and requires its own staff so it becomes an easy target for cuts and savings. A statistic that was used in this argument was the relatively low loans figure compared with the rest of the university library. Students of architecture were not taking books out and therefore, it was argued, they did not need this special library.

By now the reason for this should be apparent. Design students go into the library for a number of reasons. They may be looking for some technical knowledge in order to complete the design they are working on in studio, perhaps how some material behaves or how a structure might support the loads imposed. Perhaps they want to be able to check the performance of a building in terms of energy consumption and so on. However, even more often, design students go into their library for inspiration. They may want to see how a certain designer has tackled similar aspects of problems to the ones they currently have. In fact, they are looking for precedent, for pieces or aspects of previous designs that might be useful in their current project. Indeed it is quite likely that their tutors will send them on such a mission. A design tutorial is a very special and particular pedagogy to which we will devote the next chapter. These events quite often involve the tutor drawing on their greater experience and, seeing some perhaps half-developed ideas in the student work, they will suggest some possibly helpful precedent.

Now this means the student browsing around the library looking at books and journals alike for this helpful precedent. They may sketch ideas they find in this search. They may take photocopies. These days they may well use the camera in their smart phone. But they are relatively unlikely to walk out taking masses of books with them. Such a process does not necessarily lead to heavy loans statistics. Unfortunately, design libraries in universities are often vulnerable to an argument supported on one side by hard statistics and on the other by a long and complex argument about how designers work. The argument sadly often loses further ground when it is realised that these students may not even be reading very much but 'just looking at pictures'.

Now you will find that there comes a moment in a design process when you feel in need of this search for inspirational precedent. It is no good waiting until some remote library elsewhere on the campus is open. You need this, and you need it now! Good design practices all have libraries within their studios or drawing offices. The university student needs the same immediacy. So this design library needs to be located very close to the studios and open for long hours.

The design of the course

The 'designerly way of knowing' seems to be one where knowledge is solution oriented rather than problem oriented, and experiential rather than theoretical. This gives rise to a particular problem for those who create and manage design-based courses. In many cases studio will form a large part of the curriculum and will be accompanied by more traditionally taught theoretical courses. In architecture courses there are often lecture programmes in history, structural mechanics, building science, construction and so on. A perennial problem often debated in course planning and examination meetings concerns how these various elements are put together. For example, in my experience it is not unusual to see some students get high marks in exams for structural mechanics and yet also in design studio they show little sign of innovation or creativity in the way their designs employ structure. It is very easy to fall into a way of teaching and examining a subject like structures that relies on theory and example and that unintentionally puts a boundary around this knowledge, making it largely inaccessible in a designerly format.

You, the student, should probably speak up if this is the case on your course but you can also do a great deal to help yourself. There are some good books out there that can help and you can ask your tutors to analyse designs that interest you in relation to the theory being taught. For the example of structural mechanics in architecture I know of no better books than those written by the remarkable engineer Tony Hunt. Tony has what we would call a designerly way of working on the structure of buildings. That these books are referred to as 'sketchbooks' indicates that they follow the same approach (Hunt 1999; Hunt 2003).

If you continue to find courses, especially those of a technical nature, remote from your design work then you should certainly try to discuss this with your tutors. They are quite likely to have been concerned about this problem. I have been in discussions about it in many schools in many countries. It is not always easily solved. If you want to explore this issue in more detail then one of my earlier books, *What Designers Know*, may help (Lawson 2004). It is worth just noting one final point on the example that has been used here. The problem of technical experts such as engineers not sharing a similar way of knowing and thinking to you as a designer continues on into professional life. It is not the purpose of this book to address that issue. Having someone like Tony Hunt who can join in and indeed even lead the design team makes a tremendous difference.

Knowing about solutions, materials and systems

This brings us to a most interesting feature of the way designers know. An engineer like Tony Hunt can look at a drawing and immediately see possible structural systems that could be employed to hold it up and perhaps even give it expression. This tells us that if an architect and a structural engineer look at the same drawing of a building they may 'see' quite different things. A significant contribution to this difference is the way we understand materials and systems and their properties.

In a wonderfully insightful book, Adrian Stokes has introduced a delightful distinction between what he called 'modellers' and 'carvers' (Stokes 1934). He was actually talking about artists but his argument reveals something interesting for us here. According to Stokes, a 'modeller' would assemble a sculpture from a series of components. By contrast, a 'carver' would craft it from materials. The sculptor who carves in stone or wood works with the grain and nature of the material, understanding what can best be done. The great American architect Louis Kahn told us to 'let a brick be what a brick wants to be'. This 'knowing' about solutions in terms of materials and systems is essential in a good design process and designers acquire it during their education and practice. In fact, an experienced designer can 'see' a drawing or model of a design in many different ways and flip between them seamlessly.

Different ways of knowing about the same simple building

An experienced architect can see a drawing as representing a collection of building elements, spaces, or systems (Figure 10.7). Moving between these ways of knowing and representing is simple and automatic in a conversation between two architects but much more difficult in a conversation with a computer.

(continued)

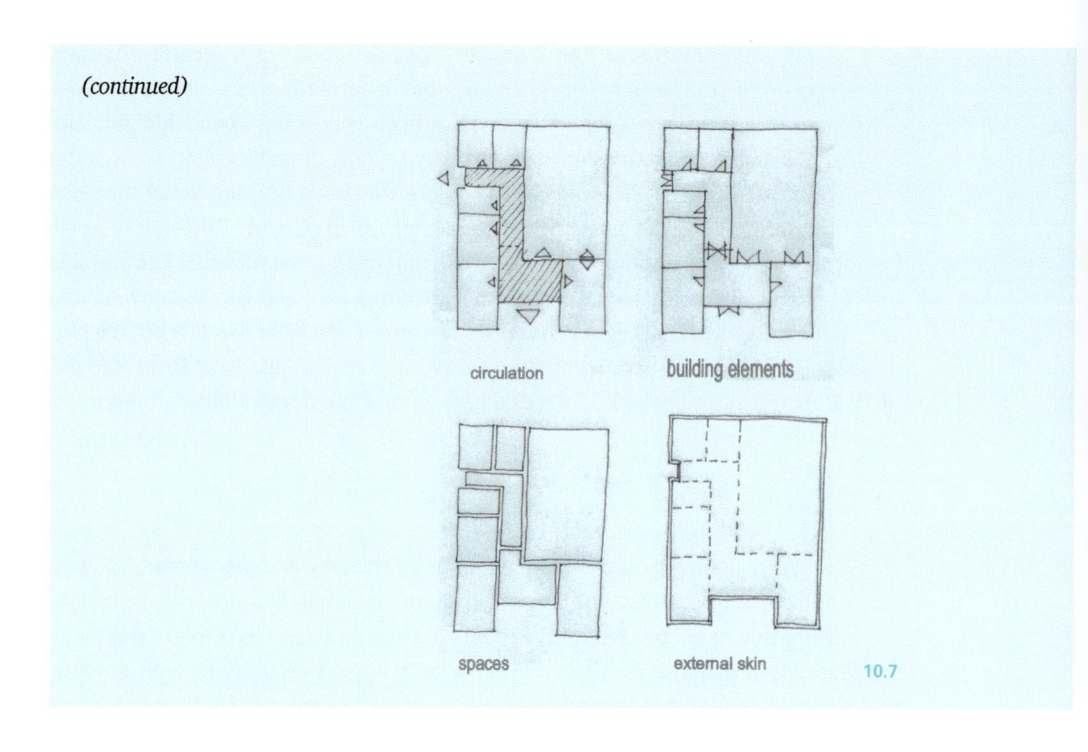

(continued)

circulation   building elements

spaces   external skin   10.7

What designers know

So, the knowledge that designers use when working on projects is often solution-based and seldom theoretical. There is really no boundary we can draw around the knowledge that might be useful. It really depends on your approach to a particular design project. The more you look, visit and learn about your field of design the more knowledge you will have at your disposal when designing. You will continue gathering this material throughout your career. So get going! The main way you will learn to design is through the studio project. The main way in which you will learn to think in a designerly way is through the tutorials and crits you will get on those projects. How these tutorials and crits work and how to get the best out of them are the subjects of the next two chapters.

References

Cross, N. (1982). "Designerly ways of knowing". *Design Studies* 3(4): 221–227.

Goldschmidt, G. (1998). "Creative architectural design: reference versus precedence". *Journal of Architectural and Planning Research* 15(3): 258–270.

Hunt, T. (1999). *Tony Hunt's Sketchbook*. Oxford, Architectural Press.

Hunt, T. (2003). *Tony Hunt's Second Sketchbook*. Oxford, Architectural Press.

Lawson, B. R. (2002). "Architecture libraries from a university perspective". *ARCLIB Bulletin* 11: 1–4.

Lawson, B. R. (2004). *What Designers Know*. Oxford, Elsevier/Architectural Press.

Stokes, A. (1934). *The Stones of Rimini*. London, Faber and Faber.

Chapter 11

The design tutorial

The studio project revisited

In the previous chapter we looked at what designers know and how they know it. In a design school the most common way of acquiring such knowledge is through participation in studio design projects. Associated with such projects are the design tutorial and design crits. We shall look at tutorials in this chapter and crits in the next chapter.

In the design studio, at least in the first couple of years, it is likely that all students will be working on the same brief. In later years a variety of briefs may be issued in parallel with students either assigned to a specific brief or able to choose. In the final year it is often the case that students generate their own briefs for a major project. However, even from the beginning students will take their own creative approach to problems and, for this reason, it is inevitable that the design studio must rely on individual personal tutorials. Most other university courses are unlikely to feature individual tutorials until maybe the final year, so this is another way that the design school is unusual. The combination of providing the studio space, having major amounts of time unscheduled and individual tutorials are defining characteristics of design schools.

In such tutorials a tutor is likely to look at your work in progress. This inevitably means that drawings and probably models and perhaps other representations will be the focus of the tutorial. There will of course be discussion but, on most occasions, many tutors will want to draw as part of their communication. It turns out that this apparently simple encounter between student and tutor can be remarkably sophisticated and complex. One of the complications here is that you are likely to find that your tutor may play several roles during such a tutorial. Moreover, tutors often change roles unconsciously and may move seamlessly between them. This can be confusing to begin with, and it may help to study more explicit descriptions of these roles based on research. We shall explore each in turn and you will find here examples from recordings taken of real tutorials that have been made anonymous.

The teacher role

The most obvious role a tutor can adopt is that of teacher. Your tutor is primarily there to teach you about your subject and this will often happen during a design tutorial. Here a tutor may be genuinely and directly trying to expand your understanding either of skills and processes, or more likely of architecture, industrial design or whatever subject you are studying. The most common things that a tutor is likely to mention here are some ways of distinguishing design that is admired as opposed to being considered weak or poor. A tutor is also likely to discuss matters of emphasis, your use of time and what you should be focussing on, as well as general thoughts about your design field.

The tutor as teacher – a design (architecture) student tutorial

In this example the tutor is suggesting that the student might understand his/her own ideas better by using a different kind of drawing. This is initially done to help the project along but quickly becomes a generic tutorial on ways of drawing sections.

Tutor:	'Well, you can make sections work for you. So that they're not all, you know, it's not just one simple cut line through the building. You can actually manipulate the section so that it's revealing . . ..'
Student:	'You'll go like that and . . .' (*gestures an imaginary line along plan*).
Tutor:	'Yeah, you usually step in parallel. So if you're taking a section through, say, the building here and you get to that point (indicates on the student plan) and you want to show the staircase, you can bring the section back, show it through the lift and stairs and then step it back again and bring it through this space so that you have a series of sections . . . (*draws a stepped section line across the plan*).
	'You can only see that from the section. That's just not available on plan. So, yeah, it's one of the. . . it's a hard drawing to think about because it doesn't come naturally. You've got to kind of practise.'

The consultant role

However, if you request a design tutorial you are most likely to do so for a specific reason. It is likely that you are not asking for some general tutoring about your subject but rather that you simply want some help with your project. Most likely you are not satisfied with the current state of your design and want some advice on how to improve it. Even when your tutor initiates the tutorial you are likely to hear suggestions about how your design could be improved or perhaps how you might direct your work. Here the tutor is really emphasising specific and particular design qualities rather than teaching generic issues. In this role the tutor is probably working more like a senior colleague in a design practice.

Often design schools employ part-time studio tutors who spend their time mainly in practice. This can sometimes be seen by students as helpful in that they are likely to play this consultant role more and thus get the student to produce a design that eventually gets better marks. This also brings in the experience of current practice that full-time tutors may have lost to an extent. Tutoring in this way is often appealing to younger professional designers who may be trying to start their own practice but are not yet able to support themselves financially on a full-time basis. In these cases both student and tutor are gaining something from the arrangement. However, there can also be a downside in that practice-based tutors may also be out of touch with modern teaching methods and can easily leave you confused about generic ideas. Paradoxically, I have also found quite often that such part-time tutors see their 'day in the school' as a way of leaving the harsh practicalities and constraints of the real world behind, so you may not necessarily find these part-time tutors focussing on the current world of practice.

The tutor as consultant – a design student tutorial

In this conversation the tutor is really acting as a consultant offering advice on the basis of experience that is intended to improve the design. There is no generic teaching going on here; it is specific practical advice on how to take this particular project forward.

Tutor: 'So I think I would just examine those spaces and see whether they could be brought down to, say, 2.4 m as a single height, floor to ceiling height . . . which pushes, well it takes a metre and a half off, doesn't it . . . 4.8? And that might just help to bring this down. And simply doing that will have an impact. So, remodeling this bit might push things to a different kind of perspective.'

Student: 'Do you think that the single floor one, 3.3, is too much?'

Tutor: 'I think when it's only one floor and . . . so it's fairly small-scale accommodation, isn't it? I think you can afford to bring that height down so I think the whole thing might shrink. Oh! having said that, I would look at the public spaces at ground level because you've got much larger volumes . . . .. These large kind of, almost auditorium-type spaces; but it could be used as an auditorium. You could have conferences, meetings, all kinds of things happening here. And these are larger spaces, practice rooms, and I think you can afford to push that floor to ceiling height up in at ground floor level.'

The master role

Here the practice-based tutor is typically a major successful and well-known designer. This can be exciting for the student and you may even be flattered to get such people coming to help you. However, in such a role the tutor may be so used to pressing their own ideas that they can often miss something a student is trying to achieve but is not yet able to show strongly or to fully articulate. In research studies we have often also observed the more confident student trying to take on the tutor in this more masterly role and almost inevitably lose and either get frustrated or suffer a loss of confidence. Tutoring by an acknowledged master can be a marvellous experience and lead to much admired results. However, it is not guaranteed to provide a great deal of learning for the student beyond the specific project.

There is sometimes another agenda here. Student work is often submitted for competitions and awards. While, on the one hand, this should bring a huge confidence boost to the lucky and able student, on the other hand it can almost take over the project from a student in order to bring kudos to the school. The odd thing about all this is a paradox that it can be difficult to appreciate for you as a student at the time. In a few years, hopefully, you will have passed your degree and won whatever professional recognition you need. By then, how well you were seen to do in any particular studio project will be almost entirely irrelevant. It is what you learned from the project that will have a lasting effect. This brings into tension the learning versus the need to assess all design work on a continuous basis. We will return to this problem later because it can pose tricky problems for you. Suffice to say now that the design project is simultaneously a learning vehicle and a method of assessment that counts towards your degree or diploma. Often learning is maximised by taking risks and making mistakes. It is rather odd then that the same experimental work is used to arrive at your final assessment.

The tutor as master designer – a design student tutorial

In this conversation the tutor is well known and highly successful. This is a one-off visit to the school and the student is unlikely to get another tutorial from the same source on this project. You will see that the student voice is hardly heard and, even when it is, it is interrupted. The master effectively imposes an approach on the project that the student may or may not be able to develop. Such a tutorial is more likely to focus on the end product than on the process.

Tutor:	'What's this project about?'
Student:	'I'm developing an overall approach to the massing here and . . ..'
Tutor:	'Yes but these rectilinear forms are very restrictive. We've had quite enough of this boring ****. I would free the whole thing up by using more organic and free-flowing form (*takes the student's pencil and draws*). See, like this . . . much more exciting. You can fit the functions in later. We develop a strong conceptual form first and modify it as necessary. Look how this could just flow across here . . ..'

The parrot role

I once interviewed a very good architect, Ian Ritchie, about his design process, and he imagined having a parrot on one shoulder that would look down on his drawings and squawk to remind him of something important (Lawson 1994). In this subtler role the tutor is perhaps trying not to steer you in their direction but to understand what you are trying to achieve and nudging you along that path more quickly or fruitfully. Here the tutor is really a facilitator and this requires considerable skill, not a little humility and a good deal of empathy. Not all tutors can do it all the time. Being a parrot on a student's shoulder is a rather more humble task than being a star designer but it can be incredibly valuable. In turn this can incorporate both generic teaching and consultation to improve the design.

The tutor in 'parrot' mode – a design student tutorial

11.1

(continued)

(continued)

This is an architecture student who is designing a dance school. The tutor tries to discover the student's motivation and then shows ways of developing that idea.

Tutor: 'Have you got any kind of precedent examples, have you looked at the ones that might be relevant?'

Student: 'I looked at Laban [Figure 11.1] and there's one in America by, I can't remember. It's quite new. It was in the journals last month and then, there's the Scottish dance-based and . . ..'

Tutor: 'I mean have you looked at them in depth at all as to what defines their characters in the way they are?'

Student: 'Yeah, well each of them has got their own kind of key, about their sort of façade or maybe like a key sort of idea like the dance space is all about relation to site, lighting and things like that . . . and then Laban is all about sort of the transparency and the material, skin.'

Tutor: 'Right, so what's yours about, you've identified them very clearly. If I said to you what's yours about, what's your project about?'

A thoughtful tutor may appreciate that students can and do learn a great deal from each other. Here the discussion may feature suggestions about how to get together and enable that process more deliberately. Such an idea, of course, deliberately exploits the notion of the studio in which the tutor is really a 'facilitator'. It concentrates on encouraging exploration and learning rather than performing. If this is done well and sympathetically, it may be possible subsequently for students to imagine what this tutor may have said and thus be able to help themselves. Of course the ultimate aim of any tutorial system must be to encourage and enable the student to become self-sufficient. Some of the roles discussed here may help to achieve that more than others.

The complex tutorial

Of course all the example excerpts included here are just that. They are brief snatches of what were considerably longer tutorials. These tutorials lasted between ten minutes and more than half an hour, so in some cases there was extensive discussion. In most cases, by the end of the tutorial, the tutor had moved through several if not all of the modes we have identified here. In fact, it is often quite difficult to see where each role ends and the next begins. This makes the design tutorial an enormously rich and sophisticated piece of pedagogy. However, the lack of clarity and articulation of the roles can also confuse the student. At the end of a design tutorial it may be worth asking yourself what happened, which roles were played and how you should treat each set of material.

It is obviously not possible for me to know how careful, thorough, creative and helpful your tutorials are. You may find that you prefer some tutors to others. However, be wary of always looking for a 'consultant' who may help the project in hand onwards without challenging you to develop. Getting several tutorials from different tutors may be a positive educational experience but it also might leave you confused as to how to proceed with the immediate project. From our studies, there is no doubt that the best tutorials can be wonderfully creative and helpful and even able to generate advice that has long-lasting benefits. However, the same research also shows that some tutorials can be almost entirely unhelpful. Usually this is when the tutor, for whatever reason, takes a strong leadership role rather than trying to understand your motivation and doubts.

A complex and sophisticated design tutorial

In this excerpt from a tutorial with an architecture student the tutor can be observed doing many things. The student presents but is then questioned by the tutor who is trying to understand the student's thought process and objectives. The tutor then questions an obviously unsatisfactory part of the design and the student admits to not being happy with it. The tutor then takes a lead and suggests a simplification of the geometry using an idea based on a well-established notion of spaces that are either served or serving first articulated by Louis Kahn. Even so, the tutor manages to work with the basic ideas developed by the student.

Student: 'The scheme is almost like two cubes at an angle, kind of two separate parts, the bottom level is public, the next is studio and the top is dwellings.'

Tutor: 'And that runs across the two cubes?'

Student: 'Yeah, both of them. Initially I was trying to separate them but when I put one floor on top of another you can't.'

Tutor: 'What's that kink there?'

Student: 'It's been really annoying me but I want the two cubes to relate to the site so it kinda needs to be there.'

Tutor: 'You need to take a decision about this. Actually the idea of putting the two cubes at an angle may introduce something else. Look, you could pull them apart a little and then it becomes the starting point that makes me think.

(continued)

(continued)

> 'You can articulate them and have the circulation drop down there . . . distinguish the public space . . . there's a potential light well developing here . . . bring light into the place in the slot . . . it suggests strongly a place to put the toilets . . . and you've got ventilation. And some privacy . . . at the moment the bathroom is in this prime elevation . . . then it connects better to the bedrooms too . . . in fact the kitchen can come in too . . . you could look at Louis Kahn's idea of served v. servant spaces.'
>
> Student: 'Oh and now we get the clarity back too, we run the slot right across.'

Our analysis suggests that tutoring a student without having some understanding of where you are in terms of your own expertise development may be a dangerous thing to do. And yet it is commonplace in design schools for distinguished visiting critics to be employed from outside the system to play an important tutorial role. Younger part-time design tutors are inevitably nearer to your own level of expertise and experience and may be more sensitive to your difficulties and uncertainties. Such tutors are often employed on a weekly basis and may also offer some continuity through a long project. On the other hand, it can be very exciting to have personal time from a masterly designer of some national or even international repute. Full-time academic staff are more likely to have considerable experience of tutoring and of the common problems and difficulties that arise at your current level of expertise. So, which tutorials are the best? It is of course impossible to say. Try as many as possible and arrive at your own judgement.

An interesting question here is whether tutoring is more helpful from a nearby expertise layer or from one far above the student's current layer. The answer is likely to be that a combination of the two is probably desirable but there does not seem to have been a systematic investigation of this issue.

The agenda

The tutorial conversations used as examples here were systematically collected in a research study that analysed design conversations (Khaidzir and Lawson 2013). When these conversations were between students and a tutor our analysis showed some strong differences in the roles played. Previous work had suggested that interaction in the design studio, and particularly in tutorials, may not always be quite what it seems. Quite often, hidden agendas underpin these conversations (Dutton 1991). Sometimes the hidden agendas of tutor and student might align or converge but not always. When a tutorial proves unhelpful it is likely that the two agendas were not identified and did not converge. It may help you to ask yourself what was happening during such a tutorial. As a student talking to an experienced tutor it is easy to blame yourself for any lack of communication or understanding. However, if you were guilty of anything, it is possible that you failed to ask for clarifications that the tutor had not realised were necessary. This is probably more likely to happen when the tutor is a visitor who does not know you or have experience of your previous work and ambitions. Take the trouble to explain these if you can. Be sure before the tutorial of what you would like to come out of it. It is often the case that good tutors can see other possibilities in your project that flow from their own agendas. Make sure your agenda is clearly understood.

What actually happens in a design tutorial?

Analysis of design tutorials shows that, unsurprisingly, tutors tend to dominate the conversation with a clear hierarchy evident. In fact, on average, tutors speak for about one and a half times as long as students. One way of further analysing this is to relate the comments and actions of the two participants to the design activities we discussed in Chapter 8. We can break the tutorial conversation down into individual comments that can then be classified as being 'formulations', 'moves' or 'evaluations'. Interestingly, both tutors and students spent most time formulating. That is to say that the dominant tone of the conversation is about finding, expressing, structuring and framing problems rather than about suggesting solutions. In our study, tutors spent virtually a third of their time discussing 'moves' but students only did this for about a tenth of their time. The additional expertise of the tutors clearly allowed them to come up with more ideas about solutions and to elaborate and develop them further. In fact, tutors talked about moves for seven times the length of time that students did. This might be thought odd since the whole point of the tutorial was to review the students' progress. However, it is clear from all these results that tutors could read more into the situation from the students' own drawings and models than they were able to themselves.

A further finding may help you to get more from your tutorials. We found a huge discrepancy between students and tutors in terms of what we classified as 'process-based move actions'. A 'process-based move action' is where the comment is about moving towards a solution but in terms of how to do so rather than in terms of the content of the design itself. Tutors spent more than twelve times longer than students making such comments. On reflection this surely suggests one of the great values of the design studio tutorial and it could really only be done in the one-to-one format. Here the tutor is not only suggesting an improvement to the design but also then spending considerably more time helping the student to understand ways of getting there.

Managing the tutorial

Seen from the academic staff perspective, these tutorials are often enjoyable and rewarding experiences. As a design tutor you become actively involved in the design process. In our discussion of the roles tutors play, you can see that in some cases the tutor takes a consultative role, and in the 'parrot' version tries actively to understand and develop the students' line of thought. For this to work well you need to be able to explain and articulate this clearly. In my experience this can often be where things go wrong. A good and experienced tutor may be an expert at drawing this out from you but it is not always easy.

This suggests that you should prepare for the tutorial carefully. Try to have drawings or models available that show the state of your design. Have notes that clearly articulate your process to date and your aims and objectives for the final design. Also make sure to explain where you have uncertainties or ambiguities or perhaps a lack of ideas. All these will help the tutor play valuable roles, not only to push your design forward but also to draw out generic issues for your wider education.

Remember too that this system of personal tutoring is extremely time-consuming and there is likely to be some pressure on the event, so preparation will get the explanations over more quickly allowing more time for constructive suggestions. Good drawings or models are usually more efficient and effective than long-winded vague descriptions. Remember that tutors are likely to be able to imagine their own realities from vague or indistinct representations. In my experience, the tutor misunderstanding the ideas being presented and therefore making suggestions that are built on poor foundations can easily waste a whole tutorial.

Finally, we must realise that the whole conversation in a tutorial depends upon shared concepts and ideas that allow the tutor to introduce and develop suggested actions. We shall discuss how this happens in Chapters 13 and 14, after which you may find your understanding of the tutorial could be revisited. Along with the tutorial, your understanding of design and how you do it will come in the form of studio project crits. Design-based courses are unique in their use of the crit as a teaching device. These can be extremely valuable experiences but they need careful management by both staff and the students. That is the subject of the next chapter.

References

Dutton, T. A. (1991). "The hidden curriculum and the design studio: toward a critical studio pedagogy". *Voices in Architectural Education*. T. A. Dutton. New York, Bergin and Garvey: 165–194.

Khaidzir, K. A. M. and B. R. Lawson (2013). "The cognitive construct of design conversation". *Research in Engineering Design* 24(4): 331–347.

Lawson, B. R. (1994). *Design in Mind*. Oxford, Butterworth Architecture.

Chapter 12

The crit or design jury or review

What's in a name?

The crit carries several names and has variants across both countries and subjects. The idea at the core of this event is simple and fundamental. It is a public event in which student work is displayed and criticised, sometimes by one but more often by a group of critics. This is similar in some ways to the musical master class where a student performs in front of a master who interrupts and comments on the performance, suggesting ways to improve the interpretation. The music student will then usually try to implement the master's recommendations there and then. A group of other students, often from the same cohort, sit around to listen, and hopefully to learn. I have been a victim of this myself in an amateur way, thankfully not as a soloist but as a member of a wind quintet.

A master class

12.1

(continued)

(continued)

This looks like a performance but what gives things away is the random clothing of the group (Figure 12.1). Actually, just behind our camera is a master musician who is going to stop the group and criticise their playing. Behind the master is an audience who learn by hearing others criticised.

In design, however, this changes a little. Whereas in music the master will almost certainly know the piece being played intimately, in design the jury are unlikely to have attempted the particular project. So they are thinking more on their feet, or in reality on the seat of their pants, since they usually sit around in an arc looking at the displayed drawings. If you study architecture, industrial design, landscape design or interior design you are very likely to find this system used widely on your course. The jury may be made up entirely of academic staff but quite often also involves visitors. These visitors are seen to bring an outside view, having not been directly concerned with tutoring the project. They may themselves be designers or they might have other connections with the project, possibly as clients or users. Sometimes more technical expertise is also present on the jury.

A design jury

The design jury, crit, review, or whatever you want to call it, is based on the same pedagogical principles as the musical master class. A student presents a design scheme, a design master comments and criticises and an audience of other students watches on (Figure 12.2).

12.2

The crit as learning experience

For some reason architecture schools seem to be the most enthusiastic of all and often employ outside critics, sometimes including very distinguished and famous architects. There is no doubt that this crit can be a powerful learning experience. In theory the whole student body can see and hear the reaction of experienced and expert designers to not only their own work but also to that of all the other students. Some have argued, and with good reason, that you learn more from hearing criticism of the work of others rather than of your own work. This is a good way to make use of distinguished visiting staff since the whole student body gets to hear their thoughts without them having to prepare a lecture.

How critics think

To get the best out of your crit it is sensible to try to put yourself in the mind of the critic. I have acted as a critic more often than I can possibly remember. I have done it in many countries and on courses ranging from architecture, through landscape design, urban, industrial, interior and graphic design. In my experience, critics find this can be a rewarding but exhausting activity. Often you spend the whole day trying to understand a parade of students who are usually complete strangers. You do your best to get into their mind and find out what they are really trying to do and how you might help them constructively. You inevitably worry about how they will respond if your criticism suggests some serious reappraisal is needed. You also have in mind the other students in attendance and how you can draw out generic lessons for them. So this is a task requiring extraordinary concentration and quite a lot of patience.

When they are visitors, critics inevitably talk to each other during the event itself, possibly during a lunch break and often over dinner. I am certain therefore that I can tell you what irritates critics most. There are two major traps that it is easy for you to fall into and it is quite understandable that you might. These happen to be two things that can be very irritating to a critic.

The first is the long rambling introduction that really goes nowhere but prolongs proceedings pointlessly. This often suggests that the presenting student is nervous about getting to the inadequacies of a design or the lack of work effort. So, get to the point and get there as quickly as you can! The second trap that entangles many students is the failure to accept a weakness that has been pointed out. It is of course understandable that you want to defend your work, and this is especially understandable if the crit is connected with assessment. Your critic is likely to be more experienced than you and may press the case, often leading you deeper into the trap. The consequence of this is that the majority of time is spent discussing your weakest points. When you hear a criticism that in your heart of hearts seems valid then for goodness sake accept it. By all means discuss how you could improve your work, and then move on. Force your critic to move on to discuss the aspects of your work that you feel are stronger. Of course, you should defend your work vigorously if you really believe the criticism is misguided, unfair or the result of a misunderstanding.

Stubbornly defending an obvious weakness not only wastes valuable time in the crit but also makes your critic think that if you cannot see this obvious point you are not likely to make a good designer.

Weaknesses of the crit

This system of crits, juries, or whatever they are called, is extremely widely used in design education. However it is not without its weaknesses and even failings. One can characterise the crit in its worst form rather easily.

The worst crit ever!

This crit goes on for hours in order to review each student. It may even span two or more days. There are so many students present that they find it difficult to maintain their attention. Consequently there is a background hum of chatting to distract the poor victim. Typically the worst juror will sit facing the student work and make comments directly to the presenting student, with no thought about the rest of the student body, who anyway cannot hear what is being said. Some of the visiting critics know each other. They consequently direct some comments to each other rather than the victim or the other students.

Academic staff thought they were being helpful in publishing a timetable. In fact this means that some students presenting towards the end only turn up just before their allotted time and might even steal some extra time to work on the project. Inevitably this crit runs behind the scheduled time and students get even more fidgety. Those students who received quite severe criticism early on understandably leave immediately and fail to learn any of the main lessons.

A major weakness compared with the musical master class is that these crits most usually occur at the end of the project. This means the student is naturally defensive when criticised and usually tries to defend the work against the criticism. Sometimes this is justified but it can occasionally descend into a quite aggressive attack by jurors, especially if they are not experienced teachers. The real weakness here of course is that, unlike the musical master class, as a design student you cannot now improve or adjust your work since it is finished and drawn up. But this problem can be further aggravated by the methods of assessment of studio work in design schools. Often the crit is not just a teaching and learning exercise but also a vehicle for the tutors to arrive at an assessment.

Most design schools use a form of continuous assessment for studio design work and this mark then gets aggregated into the final mark, contributing to the degree classification or score. It is not surprising, then, that students are defensive since they are doing their best to get a good degree. From a learning point of view the mark is rarely announced at the jury. Thankfully it is not like one of those awful television talent show programmes where the jurors hold up scorecards at the end of each performance. The mark is often arrived at in private by the jury, sometimes at the end of each student presentation, or more likely at the end of the day. In such a system you are likely to get to know your mark some time later and, as you can see from Laura Willenbrock's comments below, this can be quite unsatisfactory.

A design student tries to understand her grades

'My struggle with grades was frustrated by the critique or jury review system used to discuss the merits of student work. To me the relationship between the grade and the review is vague and nearly mysterious' (Willenbrock 1991).

The aims of the crit

It is normally assumed that the main reason for the crit is to serve as a learning experience for students. But actually the crit can serve many purposes. In its fully-fledged form it can provide a ceremonial ending for a project and a climax to which you work. Here you can also get general feedback both from staff to students and vice versa. Tutors may be able to describe the learning objectives and say what they hoped students would get from the project. Students can say what they found difficult or unclear and so on. So the crit can enable academic staff to evaluate the design project of which it forms a part. Sometimes an external person who might have acted as a surrogate client might attend, make comments about the practical realities and then take away design ideas that may be of some use later.

However, this also can have its downsides. The quotes shown below from an industrial design student show the tendency of the crit to be followed by an unproductive anti-climax. The next project may start almost immediately and you may find it difficult to get up to speed again quickly.

The all-embracing project – an industrial design student's experience

The period of two weeks before the crit (assessment) until the crit itself I find the most captivating. Everybody is busy, and when you work in a group you find out that now is the time to take decisions. In these moments you really get to know each other and that is when we are, I think, most immersed in design.

(continued)

(continued)

> After having worked with each other intensely for weeks on end, and after everybody has worked the last three days and nights, then you get to the crit. You present, you wait all day and at the end of the day you get the word, whether you made it or not . . .. But then!
>
> Then you get to the really awful period when everybody has had enough of design school and you hardly see each other for three to four weeks. Deadly for your motivation, because of the rush you were in the weeks before means that you lose all energy for a couple of weeks. Back to the sluggish tempo in which you started the semester.
>
> How does this happen? Design should be captivating without the design school assignments and assessments? It would be great to be able to just work on. Why can't we do it?
>
> (Lawson and Dorst 2009)

The crit is such an all-embracing idea and is so pervasive that it has survived and remains valuable even though difficulties and deficiencies have been identified. As far back as the 1990s researchers were asking questions about the crit and the most coherently presented critique of the crit in architecture schools can be found in Anthony's book (Anthony 1991). More recently, educationalists and pedagogical theorists have begun to suggest ways of eliminating some of the problems while retaining the advantages. Many of these suggestions have been tried out and found effective (Doidge et al. 2000). The key idea behind these is the identification and separating out of the various roles the crit can play. In more modern versions of the crit each role can be performed in a more optimal fashion rather than all being compromised as in the traditional version.

The student-led crit

Among the most successful ideas is that students might play a leading role in the running of the crit rather than academic staff and tutors. This sounds revolutionary to some more conservative staff, which might account for such ideas not being universally applied. To be effective, the student-led crit must be very carefully choreographed. That must be done by academic staff who must then consciously place themselves in a less prominent role.

One version of this is shown below and it has proved a valuable tool and could be organised by students during rather than at the end of the project. One key advantage of this system is that all students are involved in some role with specific responsibilities throughout the whole event. The version here was trialled at my school in one year. Students from other years heard about it from their peers and demanded that their tutors implemented it too. We noticed a number of changes taking place. Students were of course talking to their peers here rather than tutors, although the latter may have been present. The most obvious change was that there were fewer excuses given for poor communication and inadequate submission. Once questioned critically, more students seemed prepared to take the criticism on board rather than attack it. In a study we did of these changed behaviours students said they knew that other students would see through their excuses. We also saw cases of admission of errors or deficiencies actually made by students in their presentation, effectively pre-empting comments they realised were likely to be made.

A student-led crit

My favourite way of involving students in a crit works as follows:

- This version of the crit is ideally run during the project rather than at the end. In very long projects it might run more than once.
- The student body is divided up into groups of twelve or as near as possible.
- In each group the twelve students are divided into three panels of four students. All pin up their work. There are then three panels each kept rigidly to time.
- In each panel:

  - The four students present their work to the other eight students for 5 minutes each. One of the other eight students is appointed timekeeper. (Total 20 minutes.)
  - The presenters leave and review what they said, probably over a cup of coffee. During this time the other two panels discuss the presentations and formulate questions. Each of these panels appoints a spokesperson. (20 minutes.)
  - The presenters return and the spokespeople for the other two panels put their questions, give feedback and chair the discussion. (15 minutes.)
  - The four presenters summarise what they feel they have learned and how they might proceed with their designs. (5 minutes.)
  - (Overall total 1 hour.)

- The same procedure is then followed for each of the other two panels. (Overall time of crit is 3 hours.)
- Tutors are allowed to make general concluding observations.

The problem of assessment

One of the advantages of the student-led crit is that it removes the possibility of using it as part of the assessment process. Since this point crops up here it is worth just making a few observations about assessment in design courses.

Inevitably design courses make extensive use of continuous assessment. Compared with many university subjects, there tend to be fewer formal examinations and many more assignments, usually in the form of design projects. This has often made design courses look progressive in educational terms. Psychologically, the concept of knowledge of results is seen as a vital part of learning. This means that you will learn more effectively if you know how well you are doing as soon as possible after completing the task. Imagine trying to learn archery but not being told how near you were to the target bulls-eye until the next day. The proximity of feedback to performance has been shown to improve learning, particularly of skills. So the concept of a design project that is immediately assessed and feedback given seems a strong educational format. However, there are a couple of major problems with this idea.

Creative experimentation

One of the most important and common values that you should find in a design school is that of admiring creativity, originality and the willingness to experiment with new ideas. The problem with the design project here is that it is simultaneously being used for learning and assessment. Experiments by their very nature can sometimes go wrong; perhaps that might even happen more frequently if you are a novice. More experienced practitioners may be able to avoid many of the pitfalls of experiments that are so risky that they are highly likely to fail. They may also know what has already been tried and found wanting. The problem for the early-years student of design is that they do not have this experience so may easily fall flat on their faces when being experimental. Experimenting creatively must be one of the most important ideas behind the design project. However, you are also likely to be assessed and get marks for this project and these will almost certainly been strongly related to the quality of the end product rather than the process.

The Formula One (F1) drivers' championship

For many years, from its inception in 1950 until 1981, Formula One used an interesting scoring system for the drivers' championship. In particular, the driver was assessed on less than the maximum number of races.

The effect of this was to allow a number of failures during the season without this necessarily reducing the driver's overall championship score. This was thought to encourage experimentation by the teams with the technology of the car and the pit stops, and allowed drivers to take calculated risks in races. Interestingly, F1 itself continuously experimented with the scoring system. In some years there was less flexibility in the second half of the season, which allowed for early experimentation but penalised it more towards the end of the season. Usually the number of races scored was at least 75% and often more. This was seen to balance experimentation with reliability and consistency.

For many years I have advocated that design schools should adopt some variant or other of the old Formula One system of scoring. This enables you to discard your worst few marks and thus facilitates risk taking and experimentation.

Two more detailed problems caused by continuous assessment have the potential to impact negatively on design education. The first of these is the notion that not only does every single mark count but that it counts equally in determining some overall classification of performance that might be used by potential employers. By far the worst variant of this is known as GPA, or grade point average. This iniquitous system originated in the United States and has spread to the Middle and Far East in particular. Here every mark from your very first project is logged and all are eventually added up and their mean calculated to give the grade point average. This has two ridiculous consequences.

First, it has a demotivating effect on students entering their final year of study since they have two or more years behind them and shifting their grade point average up significantly is now an almost impossible task. Careful study of television quiz shows will reveal that they almost always use a scoring system that escalates in importance as the competition nears its end. This means the result stays in doubt right through the programme causing more excitement and interest. Even at the last round it is still 'all to play for'. We surely want design students to feel that way about their final year.

The second absurd characteristic of the GPA is that employers surely want to know how good you were at the end of your course not at the beginning. While, in my experience, some students are steady developers, many of the best are relatively late developers. If you are one of the latter then your potential to get employment is misleadingly reduced. I had to battle very hard in my university to be allowed to count final year marks at double value in arriving at the degree classification of a student. We then discovered other subjects such as music and languages were of the same developmental nature and where knowledge is more appropriately assessed this way.

The student role

This book is intended primarily for students and of course you are not in control of the format of the crit, the way it relates to assessment and the whole mark-producing system. However, hopefully this chapter will have made you think about such issues and how you should approach them yourself and the vexed question of learning versus performance in the studio project. You may also be surprised to find that your tutors are willing to engage in such discussions.

The design tutorial and the crit, supported by lectures and seminars, are the main ways you learn to discusss design. These conversations can sometimes seem a little obscure to the uninitiated. The nature and value of design conversations is the subject of our next chapter.

References

Anthony, K. H. (1991). *Design Juries on Trial: The Renaissance of the Design Studio*. New York, Van Nostrand Reinhold.

Doidge, C., R. Sara, R. Parnell and M. Parsons (2000). *The Crit*. Oxford, Architectural Press.

Lawson, B. R. and C. H. Dorst (2009). *Design Expertise*. Oxford, Elsevier/Architectural Press.

Willenbrock, L. L. (1991). "An undergraduate voice in architectural education". *Voices in Architectural Education*. T. A. Dutton. New York, Bergin and Garvey: 97–119.

Chapter 13

Design conversations

Words and pictures

While the design studio inevitably concludes with drawings and models of designs, it proceeds through design tutorials and crits. Essentially both of these are conversations so, in this chapter, we shall look at the nature of design conversations.

A few years ago, one of my research students was investigating how words were used in design processes. In particular, he was interested in whether it might be possible to get a computer to hold a conversation with a designer in a manner that felt human. If this could be achieved, he argued, then the information searching and analysing capabilities of computers might be more fruitfully used in design.

He was giving a seminar on his work when a colleague, who was mainly interested in computer graphics, rudely dismissed the whole idea. 'Go into any design office', he said, 'and all you ever see is drawings. That's where the effort should go'. My student was a little taken aback by his quite forthright stance so I entered the debate. 'Yes', I replied, 'but all you ever hear are words'. This reveals an interesting problem for us. Drawings are, without doubt, one of the most powerful and useful of the media at the designer's disposal, to the extent that it is difficult to imagine how you could design without them. Perhaps they have got relatively more attention because they form a trace of what was done. I have seen countless pieces of research into how designers work with drawings and have done some myself. The words they use while designing disappear into thin air and no record remains of how they were used and what impact they had. So, in this chapter, we shall look at words and conversations in design.

Quite a few researchers have tried to analyse the words that designers use. Often this is in an experimental situation where a designer is asked to describe what they are thinking and doing while being audio- or video-recorded. One of many weaknesses in this approach is that the verbalisation here is entirely artificial (Lloyd et al. 1996). Other design protocols have been analysed while groups of designers are working and the natural conversations between members of this team are analysed. We are getting near some understanding of this and there are some useful and important lessons for the student of design.

The poetry of words

One of the interesting features of using words seems to be their ambiguity; one might almost say their potential for poetry. If our words did not have many overlapping meanings we could not create poetry as we know it. The distinguished Czech architect Eva Jiricna has described the value of this beautifully.

The value of imprecise words in design conversations

Eva Jiricna is famous for her hi-tech interiors (Figure 13.1). One way of achieving this with possibly conservative clients is to reach agreement about design ideas in verbal conversations.

13.1

'I try to express in words what they want, and then I try to twist it into a different statement and then draw it.' Many of her commissions are with repeat clients, suggesting that they are happy with this educative approach. (Lawson 1994.)

While, of course, she is discussing a masterly professional design process with a real client, similar benefits can be found in the design tutorial or the student debate and discussion. One often hears this technique being used in crits in order to negotiate agreement about new ideas.

The vernacular process seemed to use fewer drawings and more words than we might be used to today. An intriguing example of this can be found in a remarkable book by Eric Benfield. He was a stonemason working with Purbeck stone in the south of England. A book about his life, times and work presents very few drawings and he even comments on this. However, what his descriptions do is to convey ideas for form and decoration without being so precise that another mason would have no room for individual craftsmanship.

The life, times and work of a Purbeck stonemason

Eric Benfield comments that drawings were seldom used in his trade. 'Most plans were and are carried in the head, and there are some unlikely looking heads around Swanage which could tell a good deal about the fields that are now being ignorantly built over.' Benfield describes how to make a whole variety of common items. This is his description of the pedestal base for a bird bath or sundial.

> A bird bath or sundial should be about two and a half times as high as it is wide in the base; preferably it should have two or three bases, which give the effect of steps usually seen around village crosses, and a shorter tapering pedestal surmounted by a bath smaller that the bases by at least two inches.
>
> (Benfield 1940)

We can imagine many masons following Benfield each able to create what he wanted and yet to have an individual interpretation.

Leaving something to the imagination and tolerating uncertainty are well recognised as skills that expert designers have and, as a student, you must learn to develop them.

A nice example of this in professional design comes from the renowned English industrial designer Richard Seymour. His design practice, Seymour Powell, was invited to submit to a panel of British Rail in order to win the right to design their new InterCity train, which has since become iconic. Richard told me that their competitors came in with drawings of their ideas. Seymour Powell, however, simply made a short verbal presentation saying that their design would be heroic in the manner of the British Airways Concorde and that it would once again make children want to be train drivers as in earlier times. This brilliantly simple notion allowed each member of the panel to imagine what such a design would be like without showing them distracting drawings that, for some, might have failed in this ambition. There is little doubt that their design achieved this simple but powerful specification. Of course what Richard Seymour really did here was not to propose a design solution but rather to add to the brief in a succinct and appropriate manner.

Seymour's train design

Richard Seymour with his design for a train intended to make children want to become engine drivers again (Figure 13.2).

13.2

Professional design languages

When we study professional designers at work in their own studios or offices, it is immediately apparent that they converse continuously, often by referring to drawings they are looking at or working on. Design conversations take place every day between the members of professional design teams but, unless we go out of our way to study them, such conversations are lost (Stempfle and Badke-Schaub 2002; Austin et al. 2001). Often these design conversations would be difficult to understand if you were not a designer of the same kinds of objects as the team. I first showed some years ago how architects have developed a special language that includes many shorthand expressions for pieces or arrangements of buildings. The simple diagram in Figure 13.3 shows the range of words and concepts that architects conventionally use to describe and discuss pitched roofs. Each of the five terms shown here have a very specific and precise meaning and, between them, they are capable of expressing even the most complex arrangement of flat-plane pitched roofs.

Architects' language for roofs

Architects use a very simple language for describing pitched roofs. They only need very few words with precisely understood definitions, as shown in this diagram (Figure 13.3). The words 'ridge', 'eaves', 'hip', 'valley' and 'verge' cover every possible edge or fold in a roof comprising flat planes. Add the simple word 'pitch', describing the degree of slope, and then a complete roof can be described. A computer program has been written to allow architects to draw a roof plan using this terminology from which the computer can reliably generate the three-dimensional form (Riley and Lawson 1982).

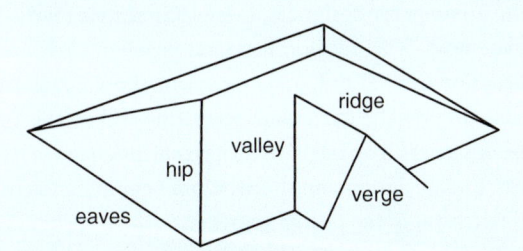

13.3

Complex roofs at Chester Cross

The language shown in Figure 13.3 can describe almost all the roofs in this very complex set of old buildings in the Roman and Medieval city of Chester in the UK (Figure 13.4). The one part that needs special descriptors is the tower over the corner entrance. Not surprisingly, this is a deliberately special piece of architecture to indicate an entrance.

(continued)

(continued)

13.4

Whatever detail there is in the brief or problem statements it is expressed in words. As we have seen, designers tend to think in a solution-focussed manner and begin to express the design in terms of shape and form. The problem statement may contain priorities and matters of detail or of crucial importance. The design is one possible physical embodiment of this and has forms, materials, colours and components. Unfortunately for designers, there is no simple method of translating between the two views. This tension between problem view and solution view of the design situation is what designers must somehow negotiate and find a resolution. The ideas expressed below are an interesting and promising way forward favoured by some designers. You begin in the textual language of the client and the brief and negotiate some agreement there before beginning to create the less nebulous physical portrayal of the design solution.

Design as a negotiation between problem and solution

One way of thinking about the design process is to see it as a negotiation between problem and solution. This negotiation is shown here (Figure 13.5) as conducted by attempts to analyse problems, synthesis solutions and evaluate them. Rather than the apparently one-way diagrams we saw at the beginning of Chapter 8, this model explicitly sees the process as two-way, with an understanding of problem and solution emerging together. It is likely that verbal conversations can be important in this process alongside conversations with drawings.

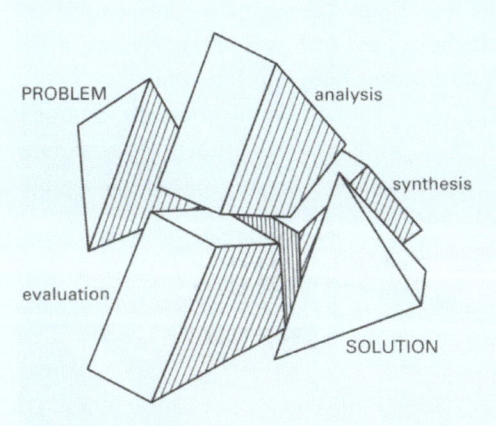

This notion of a simplified shorthand is much more important than you might think. Good experienced designers can draw and sketch very quickly and you need these shorthand ways of talking to enable the conversation to keep up with the thinking and drawing. For the time being, we will just concentrate on the language used to express three-dimensional form of the kind most often developed by each sort of designer. It seems likely, therefore, that designers in other fields will have parallel languages to those employed by the architects. Research in this field has shown this to be the case. The work shown below by Michael Tovey is that used by automobile stylists who use free-form curved forms (Tovey 1992). These are not only more complex than the flat-shaped form of the architectural roof but they are also irregular rather than simple geometric forms such as cones, spheres and so on.

Automobile stylists' conversational language

Michael Tovey suggests that those who he describes as 'automotive stylists' often work in small groups and therefore need to discuss their emerging forms (Figure 13.6). He found that they use what he called a 'typically idiosyncratic form of language' (Tovey 1992). This language is well suited to the highly complex curved forms and irregular shapes seen in so many contemporary car designs. They need, for example, to refer to 'bowed soft

(continued)

(continued)

or hard, shaped surfaces' as well as the folds and creases used in modern vehicles. Their language, however, also enables them to describe how these forms can be generated from simpler forms such as cones, spherical sections and so on. 'Terms might be used such as slippery, exciting, fluid, soap bar, bath tub, tailored, shear, razor look, blitz line, whip lash, sweep spear, tiffany, and wind split' (Tovey 1992). While this obviously facilitates discussions between designers, it probably renders their conversations impenetrable to others.

13.6

Work on fashion and textile designers by Eckert and Stacey showed another variation on this theme. Perhaps because this kind of design is subject to the more rapid change of fashion, they found a language based on describing how new forms or patterns might vary from well-known previous designs.

Fashion and textile designers' conversational language

Eckert and Stacey studied the conversations of fashion and textile designers (Eckert and Stacey 2000). One interesting snippet of conversation found by these researchers was 'a jumper like the blue one last year but a bit longer and with a v-neck'. Not only does this entirely depend upon combinations of standard ideas (v-neck) and previous solutions ('like the blue one last year') but also, in the context of fashion design, 'last year' would conjure up different ideas of length and blue depending on which year you were

Design conversations

talking about. This simple sentence therefore represents a hugely efficient and effective means of communication but can only be shared by experienced designers.

They also found that this communication integrated words and drawings in an extremely powerful manner. 'Mood boards' or 'style sheets' characteristically consist of collections of design examples that exemplify the style of design that is being proposed. One example showed four images of women's clothes with the heading 'understatement' and with the text 'the triumph of essential styles under the profile of understatement and influenced by New Age philosophy. Clear geometric, minimalist lines are emphasised by straight skirts, monochrome suits in neutral or grey colours' (Eckert and Stacey 2000).

Intriguingly, the same researchers found a language of similar structure being used by designers of helicopters, where each innovation was described as the way it varied from a previous model. What we have also observed through other research is that this verbal language can easily become written in documents, papers, books and so on. A study of architects' websites showed that much of the language used was about previous design solutions developed by the architects rather than describing what they did or what a client could expect from them in terms of a service. It seemed as if these websites were designed to be looked at by other architects rather than potential clients.

Conversations with computers

Increasingly computers are being used in design. This is only likely to increase as new technologies develop. As well as modelling and drawing, computers have the power to search for information, to suggest new possibilities and alternatives. We discussed some of the issues here in Chapter 4 on drawing. We also saw in Chapter 10 that the way designers know is not yet easily modelled by computers. We shall return briefly to that again in Chapter 20. However, it should by now be apparent that the way conversations work depends very substantially on what you know and the way you know it. So far, most computer systems used in design require you, the designer, to understand the computer's system of conversing and knowing. So to create a three-dimensional model of your design in a computer may require you to think about your own design in a quite different way. Computer modellers often use a library of fundamental solids such as cuboids, cones, spheres and domes and so on. You have to think how you can assemble a model of your design from these primitives. However, this is probably not the way you would normally think about it. You might think about the way it is actually going to be made or built or about the different materials and components it will be made from. This can be very frustrating. I often see questions from students asking others with more experience how to model a particular form on a particular system. This kind of difficulty is just what you do not need during a creative design process. Nigel Cross (Cross 2001) sums this up perfectly when he asks 'why isn't using a computer system a more enjoyable, and perhaps, also more intellectually demanding experience than it has turned out to be?' We shall return to this problem again in Chapter 20.

Learn your language

So it seems likely that, as a student, you will develop more quickly if you learn and speak the language of your domain, be it architecture, industrial or fashion design, interior or landscape design and so on. Now we know quite a lot about learning languages. First of all, we know that the way you learn your native language is different from the way you learn a foreign language as an adult. In such cases the early use of the language seems to be through constant translation. You almost become a dictionary and grammar reference book. However, eventually your facility in this new language becomes so advanced that you begin to think in it. A good test of this is whether you start to dream in the new language, and perhaps perform the simple arithmetic and counting used when shopping in the new language, rather than through reference back and translation into your native language.

You will probably have already seen that this is not just a simple question of using words. These conversations depend upon the concepts that the words stand for. Such phrases as 'high tech' or 'minimalist lines' are laden with meaning for the designers who use them. We shall discuss what lies behind the acquisition of these design concepts in the next chapter. You are likely to find that design tutorials and crits will often take place in this new language and will depend upon understanding the concepts referred to, so you will have to learn all this pretty quickly.

But here comes the rub. You want to be able to converse, learn and design in your new language but this will then leave you having to translate when talking to other people, such as clients and users, about your work. A common experience reported by my architecture students is that they very quickly find that they cannot talk easily about their work with their parents when they return home from university for vacation. Paying some attention to all these issues is one of the things that will help to move your level of design expertise up from that of a beginner to a more professional level.

Conversations between designers are usually rich in concepts and ideas that are complex and important but they are often expressed in a kind of shorthand. The idea of design concepts and what we shall call schemata are at the very heart of talking about design. They are the subject of our next chapter.

References

Austin, S., J. Steele, S. Macmillan and P. Kirby (2001). "Mapping the conceptual design activity of interdisciplinary design teams". *Design Studies* 22(3): 211–232.

Benfield, E. (1940). *Purbeck Shop: A Stoneworker's Story of Stone*. Cambridge, Cambridge University Press.

Cross, N. (2001). "Can a machine design?" *MIT Design Issues* 17(4): 44–50.

Eckert, C. and M. Stacey (2000). "Sources of inspiration: a language of design". *Design Studies* 21(5): 523–538.

Lawson, B. R. (1994). *Design in Mind*. Oxford, Butterworth Architecture.

Lloyd, P., B. Lawson and P. Scott (1996). "Can concurrent verbalisation reveal design cognition?" *Analysing Design Activity*. N. Cross, H. Christiaans and K. Dorst. Chichester, Wiley: 437–463.

Riley, J. P. and B. R. Lawson (1982). "RODIN: a system of modelling three dimensional roof forms". *CAD82 Conference Proceedings*. Brighton, IPC Press.

Stempfle, J. and P. Badke-Schaub (2002). "Thinking in design teams – an analysis of team communication". *Design Studies* 23(5): 473–496.

Tovey, M. (1992). "Automotive stylists' design thinking". *Research in Design Thinking*. N. Cross, K. Dorst and N. Roozenburg. Delft, Delft University Press: 87–98.

Chapter 14

Design concepts and schemata

Design ideas

We are now ready to discuss rather more sophisticated ideas that will help you to understand your progression to higher levels of design expertise. We have seen how knowledge about design solutions helps to create a store of precedents that are likely to make a significant contribution to your design thinking on future projects. One of the beauties of studying design is that you are always surrounded by examples, both good and bad. Bad examples can almost be as helpful as good ones. Hopefully by now you have become fairly discriminating and can see something of value even in otherwise poor work. As we saw in Chapter 2, measuring and comparing design is not straightforward. It is likely that you are forming views about what sort of design appeals to you or interests you. These views are likely to change over time as you develop. It is the development of this process of discrimination that we are going to examine in this chapter.

In the previous chapter we saw how designers develop special languages through which they can describe designs in their fields. So far we have only seen the use of very simple words such as 'ridge' to help describe a roof or 'tailored' for some car body geometry. Clearly our designers will want to discuss much more detailed and complex sets of ideas and to make evaluative remarks if their conversation is to be productive. In Chapter 10 I included a picture of the building that houses my school of architecture. If you look again at the description you will find it relies on one of the complex sets of ideas we are discussing here. It is what we will now call a schema. A schema is a collection of ideas that, working together, enables us to recognise something in our world. The schema set up here is that of a 'Miesian tower block'. Let us assume we all have schemata that enable us to understand tower blocks and turn our attention to the idea of 'Miesian' ones. They are of course named after the famous and highly influential German architect Mies van de Rohe. All architects, and all but the most naive architectural students, will have their own schema for 'Miesian'. We have our own set of variations on the idea but we share most of our schemata because we have exchanged these ideas with our peers. A schema for Miesian is likely to contain ideas about simple and probably rectilinear geometry, a lack of decoration, largely glazed exterior walls, a degree of separation between the curtain walling and the structural frame, possibly some ideas about colour or lack of it and so on. If you open any good book on Mies you will see many examples of his work that will reinforce these ideas. You build your schema through seeing instances that, to varying degrees, share features that you assimilate into your own schema.

The schema

This concept of the schema is of central significance in terms of the way you will think as a designer, both when designing and when looking at the world. You have seen my very simplified Miesian schema above. Imagine how slow a collaboration with another designer would be if I had to explain all that. So the single word 'Miesian' conveys a huge amount of quite sophisticated information. It facilitates rapid communication of complex ideas and enables us to move forward in our thinking. Design thinking can often proceed extremely rapidly for significant periods so speed of communication is vital so as not to interrupt the creative process.

Developing schemata

Designers think and converse with these schemata in even more sophisticated ways and, as we shall see in the next chapter, they can take even more dramatic shortcuts as a result. However, before discussing that, we must just look at how schemata can be linked and how they develop during education. In order to explain this we are going to imagine we have a student of design who is looking at the picture shown here.

The chaise longue by Le Corbusier

The architect Le Corbusier designed this revolutionary piece of furniture in 1928 (Figure 14.1). It has since become a modern classic and is sufficiently timeless to be used in many settings. The chrome tubular frame sits on the base without any fixing and is so well balanced that it can be simply slid back and forth to create near upright to near horizontal positions.

(continued)

(continued)

It is, of course, the chaise longue by the architect Le Corbusier but, for now, we will assume our student does not yet know that. How would it be described? Well, for a start, the concept of a chaise longue is pretty useful but if you have not yet developed that schema you would have to say something like 'a long sort of chair meant for lounging rather than sitting at a table dining or working. It looks perhaps a little like a sun bed'. Of course even to say this you need even more simple schemata about sitting in chairs. All this is rather tedious so being well enough educated to be familiar with the form known as a chaise longue is rather useful.

14.1

Our student would probably recognise that this was a rather modern design. To do this you might need some schemata about 'modern' in terms of simplicity of form, the use of materials and so on. I would expect to mention the Le Corbusier chaise longue to any designer and assume that all these ideas were automatically understood. So my schema for that includes all the other schemata that I might have that are relevant but can also be used for that period of design or the designer and so on.

All this may seem remarkably obvious and simple but it is in fact a very sophisticated set of mental processes that you become more dependent upon as your expertise develops. In addition, you use these schemata to understand and mentally categorise things you see. As you flick through a magazine or journal all these processes are at work. The more schemata you have that can be applied to design possibilities the more detailed will be your perception and understanding. At the architectural and urban level you may find that you revisit places you saw before this educational process began but now you seem to see far more. Developing this ability to perceive richly is a vital part of your educational process. This is exactly why I strongly recommended that you start sketching as soon as possible. This tends to force a greater degree of understanding and of further schemata development.

From time to time, then, you will modify a schema as you discover new possibilities. So anyone not familiar with the Le Corbusier design may have a schema for a chaise longue that is more traditional, perhaps with a back down one side and end and probably the assumption of a fixed angle of repose. One of the things that creative design often does is to challenge widely accepted schemata in just the way Le Corbusier did. Earlier I referred to this design as a classic. This is another rather sophisticated schema. It is actually quite hard to describe to someone else how they could reliably define a design classic but usually you recognise it when you see it.

In fact, the whole process described above parallels that which you went through as a young child acquiring every-day language skills. As a youngster, you generally begin with very large indiscriminate concepts. Depending on where you live and what you see on a daily basis, you are likely to have started to call all four-legged animals 'cows' or perhaps 'dogs' or 'cats' and so on. As time went on your parents probably pointed out that not all four-legged animals bark. Some moo and others meow. The mental processes are very similar. It may sound rude and unfair but it is sensible to think of yourself as still quite a young child in design terms and you need to work hard at learning more sophisticated concepts.

In fact, the early years of design education are likely to be ones where you try to go beyond personal concepts and where a considerable amount of communication is attempting to develop shared concepts. To understand how this happens it may be helpful to think of such schemata as mainly hierarchical. So the lower-level design ideas are likely to include simple geometric concepts of form such as being symmetrical or axial. However, higher-level ideas may well build on these simple notions. These are much less likely to be easily shared with the general public. Architects, for example, will use schemata that refer to a whole complex of ideas that, taken together, are referenced by the simple notion of a style, or perhaps a period of design, or maybe even the work of a single designer such as Corb or Starck.

So it goes on. While looking at this chair, and maybe sketching it too, you not only use the concepts you already have in your mind but you also modify them and create new ones. Gradually then, over time, you will acquire a much richer set of ideas and concepts that you use to look at the designed world. You can accelerate this process to some extent by seeking out designed objects in your field. You will improve by discussing and debating design with your peers and tutors and this becomes richer as you learn more of the design language we have introduced in Chapter 13. This whole process will benefit from guidance by good teachers and will happen more quickly if you have mental agility and openness to ideas and to changing the way you see the world. Most design-based schools set a high priority on creativity and originality so developing a rich but open set of schemata will be very important to your development.

Schemata as jargon

We see that commonly understood schemata can begin to separate a profession from the rest of society. In common parlance we call this professional jargon. However, schemata can become relevant to many different groupings other than just a whole profession. Such complex schemata enable very quick conversation within design teams but, of course, also run the risk of misunderstanding. I was doing research into a very highly thought of British architectural practice and spent one day interviewing several people in their studio. I was quite surprised to hear the word 'belvedere' used several times and by different people in the practice. Now this is a word that most of the general population might never use in a lifetime. Architects in general would certainly understand it but not normally use it so frequently.

A belvedere schema

A belvedere is generally considered to be either a special building in its own right or a particular part of a building so positioned that it offers a good view, usually of surrounding landscape. They became particularly fashionable in sixteenth-century Italy, probably inspired by an example on a hill overlooking the Vatican Palace.

What is interesting to us here is that the schema, while being quite specific about the prospect from the building, still allows for a very wide range of forms and architectural styles. Consequently, any two belvederes can be recognisable as such and yet hardly share any common features. In fact, the belvedere can overlap with other architectural schemata and take their form, so it is possible, for example, to have a belvedere that is in the form of a loggia.

So strong is this schema that all these examples can be seen as a belvedere, even one that cannot ever actually be built (Figure 14.2).

14.2

Design concepts and schemata

What this suggested was that, at that time, this practice was using the schema in one or more projects as a shortcut to a common set of design principles. Schemata, then, can easily become part of a sub-culture that helps to define a group because outsiders cannot fully understand their discussion. In fact, this particular design practice had given their schema of belvedere some more specific features about the way they meant to use it within new designs.

This process of assimilation into a design practice inevitably carries with it the unconscious development of shared schemata. It may prove very difficult, if not impossible, to be productive in a design practice without the ability to communicate with the shorthands provided by these schemata. Perhaps, in the days before university degree courses in design subjects were so common, this assimilation was a conscious part of the apprenticeship programme. The architect and planner Denise Scott-Brown reflects here on this very idea.

The design practice as a source of schemata

It's very interesting that a young person learns by copying the master . . . and quite often in retrospective exhibitions of an artist you will find that the early paintings look like the artist's master and then this thing of "who am I" begins to grow . . . I don't think it's a bad idea and nor does Bob [Bob Venturi and Denise Scott Brown shared a life and practice partnership] either. It's so funny because it sounds like a contrast of what you say . . . We were taught not to and yet we copy ideologies.

(Lawson 1994)

Design school schemata

This also has its dangers. Wilson showed this happening in schools of architecture (Wilson 1996). As students progressed through the schools she found them using the school schemata progressively more frequently. In the cases she identified, sets of preferences about architecture were embodied in these schemata, which effectively meant the schools were teaching architectural style preferences. Most design schools would deny doing this and would not aspire to do so. It can happen unconsciously and yet still become pervasive and restricting. Other researchers have shown that novice student designers tend to use precedent more literally than experienced students and designers. The more experienced seem more able to extract some generic ideas from precedent quite far away from a problem, while the more junior students are more likely to assimilate and copy the more superficial style. It is difficult to give firm advice on this but it is something worth being aware of as a young student and discussing with peers and tutors. However, the power of such schemata in discussing and developing design is so great that it must on balance be seen as a very positive and necessary part of acquiring design expertise.

The design school as a source of schemata

Margaret Wilson showed shared design schemata developing unwittingly in two quite different schools of architecture (Wilson 1996). In her experiment students from these schools were shown pictures of contemporary architecture carefully selected to exemplify a wide range of work from the most notable architects. Inevitably these showed a considerable variety of styles and influences. The students were asked to assess each image on a 12-point scale of preference. At the end of this task each student was asked to explain what it was they liked about those images attracting the highest scores. This process was repeated for groups of students from each of the six years of the architectural course. The results surprised the academic staff in the two schools. The first-year groups showed a significant overlap in preferences between the two schools. However, as the students progressed up through the years, this disappeared and was replaced by a considerable agreement within each school.

Effectively this shows that a degree of social conformity to stylistic preferences was being developed within each school. The staff at these schools would probably have spoken for all design school staff in believing they were not teaching a style. Shared schemata of course can develop without deliberate intent but through the general process of critique and discussion in tutorials and crits.

MAYA

One example of socialised but powerful design schemata is that of MAYA, most commonly used in industrial design. The influential twentieth-century industrial designer Raymond Loewy has been particularly associated with this idea (Loewy 1979).

Raymond Loewy's idea of MAYA seen at work in his 1934 Hupmobile

The word MAYA was invented from an acronym that stands for Most Advanced Yet Acceptable. Loewy had a huge range of output but was in particular associated with some futuristic environments such as the NASA

Sky lab. However, he was also responsible for many long-lasting designs that have become classics. This motorcar (Figure 14.3) looks unexceptional now but in 1934 when it was designed it pioneered many ideas that are now commonplace in automobile design. However, it was clearly just inside the MAYA boundary and was even then accepted while still looking very futuristic.

14.3

The concept of MAYA is that current design actually has almost undetectable and unknowable boundaries. In commercial design such as fashion and industrial design products may not sell if they stray too far beyond the boundaries of what is currently seen as acceptable. On the other hand, commercial manufacturers may depend on originality and appearing to be at the forefront of design rather than trailing behind it. So identifying these elusive and undefined boundaries of acceptability often becomes a key exercise. In the motor industry what are often called concept cars are announced and launched at motor shows. Their purpose is multi-faceted. The design must be so striking that it attracts attention and gets publicity and perhaps it also defines MAYA in some ways by going beyond it. Of course, by the time the model arrives in the marketplace the design features have been 'toned down', as it were, to bring it just inside the MAYA boundary.

One of the benefits of such a schema as MAYA, however, is that it also helps to define the norm or even the traditional. Not all design needs to be futuristic or even apparently advanced. In particular, objects such as buildings that will stand for many years are often required to embody these more conservative values.

This does not mean design should become sloppy and lazy. Perhaps a nice way of developing a schema for this is illustrated by the architect Bob Maguire who talked of achieving a 'high standard of ordinariness' (Maguire 1971). This may be particularly appropriate when designing buildings for people to occupy and possess for long periods as in mass housing. The great modernist architect Mies van der Rohe, who we have already mentioned in this chapter, once said 'certainly it is not necessary nor possible to invent a new kind of architecture every Monday morning'. One of the skills you must acquire as a designer is to become sensitive to the context of a design project and develop a feeling for what might be desirable in that particular instance. However, some designers who are very successful can become signature architects or designers and are able to impose a set of values specific to their interests on any design project. Thus signature designers are a wonderful source of precedent but may themselves be poor role models for young design students. We shall return to this conundrum in another chapter.

Precedent revisited

Armed with our understanding of schemata it is time to revisit the concept of precedent and thus to understand its role in the design process just a little more deeply. We first saw this idea in Chapter 10 and during that discussion the work of Gabi Goldschmidt is of particular interest here. To remind you, she argued against using the term 'precedent' and preferred the term 'reference' (Goldschmidt 1998). This was because, while in the legal profession lawyers try to demonstrate how accurately a predecent is set up, in design we use the precedent loosely as part of the creative process. This begs another question. Just how loose can a reference be to a precedent before it ceases to have any value in our process? The answer seems to be as loose as the designer wants. However, using precedent in this way is not as easy as it may sound and is yet another skill you need to develop if you have not already done so.

Learning to use precedent

An interesting experiment by Heylighen and Verstijnen shows that students do not necessarily have the ability to use precedent in a creative manner. They made a series of example case studies available to students working on two different design projects. Effectively this was a special and restricted store of potentially useful precedents. One project involved the provision of a library and the other a school. The case studies were made available through a simple computer tool that could record what happened during the browsing process by each student. The computer was provided with nine case studies of which eight were libraries and only one a school.

Design concepts and schemata

After completion of the design project, independent expert judges assessed the resultant designs. These assessed design qualities were then correlated with the extent to which the student had made reference to the case studies. Only students working on the library project showed significant positive correlations. This showed that, at their stage of development, the students were unable to discover and extract generic schemata and transfer them to a different kind of project. This is in contrast with expert architects who frequently and explicitly claim to use precedent from projects that are apparently entirely unrelated (Heylighen and Verstijnen 2003).

Not only is this another reason to begin accumulating precedent as early as possible, but it also suggests the need to develop schemata that allow you to see generic examples of design ideas that are found in projects that appear quite unrelated to the project in hand. Some work one of my students did rather less formally suggested that early-year students browsed the library in a much more restricted manner than later-year students. This tends to show that this is indeed an important design skill that is worth identifying and practising consciously. But this is only really likely to happen as you begin to aquire more sophisticated design schemata.

A cautionary word of realism

All this can sound like a very conscious and deliberate learning strategy. In reality, life is not like that. However, the advice here might well be useful to look back on from time to time to check if your process of design development needs a little attention and tweaking. We are about to discover that more experienced designers and design teams develop design schemata in a very special way. That is what we shall look at in the next chapter.

References

Goldschmidt, G. (1998). "Creative architectural design: reference versus precedence". *Journal of Architectural and Planning Research* 15(3): 258–270.

Heylighen, A. and I. M. Verstijnen (2003). "Close encounters of the architectural kind". *Design Studies* 24(4): 313–326.

Loewy, R. (1979). *Industrial Design*. London, Laurence King.

Maguire, R. (1971). "Architects' approach to architecture: nearness to need". *RIBA Journal* 78(4): 140–148.

Wilson, M. A. (1996). "The socialization of architectural preference". *Journal of Environmental Psychology* 16(1): 33–44.

Chapter 15

Guiding principles

Underpinning ideas

We are now ready to study a common and central feature of a higher level of design expertise. Expert designers do not approach each new problem with a *tabula rasa*, or blank mind. While we might sometimes forget things, none of us can wilfully unlearn our experience. Designers have their own value systems, experience and interests. All these are ideas that underpin the designer's work. Actually, a client expects a good designer not just to solve problems but to invent more. What we might call signature designers are known for their interests and clients go to them aware of this and expecting a solution that is recognisably by the selected designer. All designers bring this intellectual baggage to each problem and apply it sometimes very consciously and, on other occasions, rather less so. For some designers this collection of attitudes, beliefs, values and ideas are ill-formed, vague and difficult to express clearly. For others they might be much more clearly structured and can become almost like a personal philosophy. Indeed, some designers may choose to set them out almost like a theory of practice in books, articles or lectures.

As a student, you may not yet have sufficient experience or have studied your design field deeply enough to have a well-formed approach. Indeed, it might even be desirable to delay this in order to give yourself a wider experience. That must be a decision you take for yourself. Either way, this chapter might help you understand this process. It is primarily about the mental luggage that experienced and mature designers bring into a design process. Before we develop this, however, the argument needs to be put not only in the context of historical development but also of the various design fields.

The vexed question of style

I was taught as a young naive designer at the Oxford School of Architecture. This was at a time when the modern movement was a river of thought in full spate.

This was a period of little doubt, both in our wider society and more specifically in the design professions. We were still in a phase of recovery from the Second World War and a new period of technological innovation and scientific discovery was giving a war-weary Western society new confidence. There were huge new ideas that shook the world. Early in the twentieth century we had begun to understand the atom, thanks in particular to Ernest Rutherford and Niels Bohr. Einstein had dared to question the Newtonian world and develop his theories of relativity. Space and time had been linked. Technological innovation had created the possibility of nuclear energy. It seemed like a new future, a break with the past. We were decades away from worrying about pollution and climate change. The most popular subjects in our universities were science and engineering. Alan Turing had foretold of the modern computer and new subjects were born in the science and engineering faculties of our great universities.

In design we had Gropius with the Bauhaus and the architectural modernist giant of Mies van de Rohe stripping away decoration and announcing a new functionalism, and Le Corbusier even foreseeing globalism with the international style. The view where I studied in Oxford was crystal clear. Modernism was not yet another style; it was something far greater and more important. It was a full stop at the end of architectural history. Architecture was to express its human functions and its technological structures; all else was to be stripped away. In architecture and industrial design there was largely a consensus about where we were going. Style was a dirty word.

Of course this was all nonsense; it just did not seem so at the time. Style persisted but was most associated with fashion. Modern communications meant it could and would change more quickly than society could adapt to it. But that was to come later. Eventually, even industrial design and architecture were to be infected by the latest style of post-modernism. There was no full stop after all.

This is not meant as a serious history lesson. There are many writers far better qualified to deliver that. What is important for us here is the changed world of the designer. Whether you worked in fashion and textiles, or automotive design, you saw fashion as something to drive and change as much as to follow. We saw how MAYA institutionalised that in the previous chapter. If you worked in architecture or industrial design you had no comfort bubble of a predominating style that guided your actions. For the first time in our history, design ideas would change many times over within one lifespan. Designers were free of the shackles of an all-embracing style that they must learn and would use for most, if not all, of their career. But this freedom carried with it an absurdly wide range of possibilities. So you now live in a world that has no general consensus about design and with ideas changing almost daily. How can you approach a design problem in such conditions?

The individual within a set

Today, if you are a student in a school of architecture or industrial design, you are likely to get occasional lectures from visiting speakers. Most often they will be architects or designers who come and show images of buildings or objects they have created. They will likely speak passionately and fervently about their work. Mostly they will not use the word 'style', which, they would argue, trivialises what they do. They may use the term 'philosophy'. They may talk as if their way of approaching design is somehow right. This set of beliefs, interests and approaches is of course special to them and gives them an identity and a selling point. But, of course, their ideas will overlap with those of others to whom they may pay some homage. This gives them an intellectual place to belong and demonstrates that they are not just eccentrics. What will often pervade these talks is an underlying tone of principle. These ideas, they will argue, are not just any old set of thoughts but are derived from fundamental principles.

Walter Gropius, the father of the Bauhaus, claimed that 'the ethical necessity of the New Architecture can no longer be called into doubt' (Gropius 1935). Perhaps this can be seen as an ultimately futile attempt to insert that full stop on design history. Some three decades later, the highly influential James Stirling was to reflect that, as a student, he 'was left with a deep conviction of the moral rightness of the New Architecture' (Stirling 1965). A more recent reflection on the work of Stirling would surely show that his practice went through at least three distinct periods, which not only shows huge inventiveness but an ability to develop new 'convictions'. His long-time partner Michael Wilford, though, was later to tell me that they were both angry at having their middle period described as post-modern by the critics (Lawson 1994).

A moral tone

Actually, this is not so very new after all. Back in the nineteenth century the Victorians had resurrected the gothic style, modified and enriched to suit the times. It was seen as a reaction to the preceding revival of the classics. Pugin argued that the Victorian revival of the gothic style was not only structurally honest but an accurate architectural reflection of the Catholic faith. Writing about the pointed arch, he claimed 'if we view pointed architecture in its true light as Christian art, as the faith itself is perfect, so are the principles upon which it is founded' (Pugin 1973). This moral position must surely be seen as the ultimate defence of a form of design. After all, there can be no higher authority than God.

But we must be careful, since, four centuries before Pugin, no lesser figure than Alberti based his argument on an analysis of Vitruvius. In *De Re Aedificatoria* he had presented Pope Nicolas V with the very opposite conclusion. This rejected the authority of gothic stonemasons and their pointed arches and commended the renaissance ideals and consequently the round arch. This argument also claimed some higher authority since the proportions of the renaissance were seen to relate to the human form. The very same argument was creatively reheated by Le Corbusier in the twentieth century to claim authority for his Modulor, based on the proportions of the golden section.

Le Corbusier using his proportioning system

This house by Le Corbusier makes extensive use of his proportioning system that he called Le Modulor (Figure 15.1). These proportions were based on a series of iterations of the so-called 'golden section', which is roughly the ratio of the diagonal to the side of a square. These proportions could be seen used in the renaissance but Le Corbusier freed himself from the stylistic rules of predetermined architectural elements and created a system of measures from a Fibonacci scale. Such a scale means that each element is the sum of the previous two elements. This can be seen today in the A series of paper sizes. Two A4 pages taken together make an A3 page and so on. All the various A size pages therefore share identical proportions.

15.1

The backlash

As can be seen so often throughout history, there has been something of a reaction against this claiming of moral authority for design. As early as the sixties, the architect Eric Lyons was to argue that 'There is far too much moralising by architects about their work and too often we justify our ineptitudes by moral postures . . . buildings should not exist to demonstrate principles' (Lyons 1968).

Designers arguing against the idea of a design philosophy

The American architect and thinker Robert Venturi agreed with Lyons.

> The architect is not someone who designs in order to prove his or her theory, and certainly not to suit an ideology . . . any building that tries merely to express a theory or any building that starts with a theory works very deductively, so we say we work inductively.

The Czech architect Eva Jiricna, known for her high-tech interiors, certainly does not describe her approach as philosophical.

> I really think that philosophy is a false interpretation of what really happens. You get an idea but that idea is not really of a very philosophical or conceptual thought. It is really something which is an expression of the level of your experience, which is initiated by the question. I don't think great buildings have got great symbolic thinking behind them. I leave it to journalists and architectural critics to find a deep symbolic meaning because I don't think that anybody who looks at buildings can actually read the thinking behind them, and to me it's just totally useless.
>
> (Lawson 1994)

However, there are still many designers who cling to the hope of finding some universal justification for the principle upon which they design. Richard Rogers tell us 'one is constantly seeking universal rules so that one's design decisions do not stem from purely arbitrary preferences' (Suckle 1980).

So, back to the present

The contemporary designer, then, has none of these certainties and few, if any, today would claim a higher moral authority. Precisely because there is no real consensus, each of us finds and develops our own set of principles. Certainly, many will share large parts of their governing ideas with others and we may identify ourselves with major groupings such as those who believe strongly that, given our current world position, all design should be sustainable. So what are we to make of the way design is practised today? What is normal practice in the professional design world you are studying to join?

Guiding principles

Guiding principles is how I have chosen to refer to the underlying ideas that govern the approach a designer takes to each project. I have been privileged to have access to and study many leading designers, some of whom are architects. I have yet to find one practice that is generally acknowledged to be of at least national, if not international standing, that does not have a set of guiding principles that can be articulated. Mostly these principles still have some higher authority within a design practice and may sometimes be argued to come from issues in contemporary society. However, they are seldom held as immutable, but rather tend to develop with time and experience. Sometimes they seem to belong to some even greater notion such as sustainability, but often they are more a pragmatic collection of issues that the designer or practice is interested in and has some experience of. In either case, their existence is not just an aid to the designer working on a project, but a way by which clients may chose designers.

An excellent example of pragmatic guiding principles is shown here. Stirling and Wilford announced these ideas in their major exhibition at the Royal Institute of Architects in London in 1996. In the exhibition catalogue Michael Wilford wrote lucidly and explicitly of what he called a 'series of interlocking strategies'. These had not been mysteriously handed down on tablets of stone but rather developed over three decades of work.

The guiding principles of Stirling and Wilford in 1996

- The expression of primary functional activities of the building through a rich, hierarchical composition of formal geometries.
- Incorporation of coherent circulation patterns to provide clear routes and connections in and around the building.
- Development of spatial sequences to reinforce the circulation patterns and functional activities.
- Articulation of spaces in and around the building to enhance the public realm.
- Subordination of structure and systems to formal and spatial objectives.
- Use of solid and void, light and shade, colour, texture, a limited palette of materials and landscaping in support of formal and spatial objectives.

If you are familiar with the work of Stirling and Wilford it is possible not only to see their own development here but also references to more general principles from the modern movement and even the Beaux Arts with its emphasis on the route and spatial sequence. It is also clear that this practice was not interested in expressing the technology but see it as subservient to the notion of the building expressing its functions. There is, however, no reference here to a visual style. It is therefore possible to see how Stirling and Wilford could move through periods of change in the superficialities of the appearance of their buildings without departing from their guiding principles. This, however, seems to have eluded some of the architectural journalists and critics who have concentrated on these very aspects of the work.

Guiding principles taken from wider contemporary issues

Almost at the other end of the scale, one can see examples of guiding principles that can be expressed equally simply but related to wider issues. A clear example of this, to contrast with Stirling and Wilford's architectural pragmatism, is that of the Malaysian architect Ken Yeang. Yeang had studied at the Architectural Association in London followed by the Department of Landscape at the University of Pennsylvania. He then wrote a doctoral thesis at Cambridge on the ecological issues involved in architectural design. It is not difficult to see that these periods of study had a strong influence on him, as well as providing tools for his chosen set of guiding principles. Not surprisingly, this work must have been heavily influenced by the north-west European climate of the UK. Indeed, at the time, most research in this field had focussed on our temperate climate that can be too cold in winter and occasionally too warm in summer.

Ken Yeang's guiding principles (an early version)

Although Ken Yeang has written many books for the wider public (Yeang and Leong 2017) and for the design professions (Yeang 2016), he still found the time to produce a series of diagrams showing his guiding principles for members of his own practice. Those shown here come from an early version (Figure 15.2). This is surely a valiant attempt to provide a whole set of principles, but described in what we have called a 'designerly way of knowing'. One can imagine a young graduate architect joining Yeang's practice and being able very quickly to start designing in a way that satisfied these guiding principles.

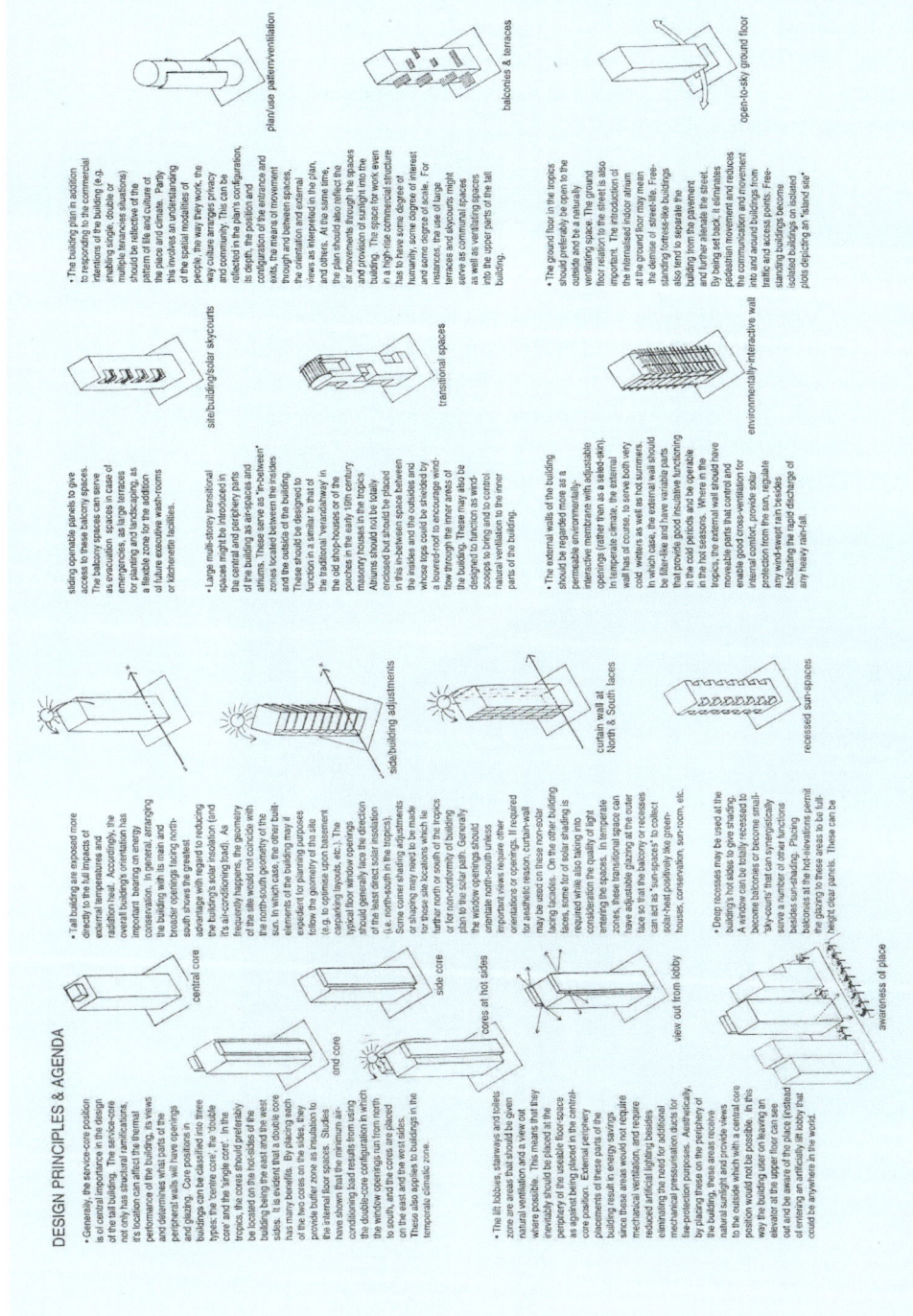

DESIGN PRINCIPLES & AGENDA

• Generally, the service-core position is of central importance in the design of the tall building. The service-core not only has structural ramifications, its location can affect the thermal performance of the tall building, its views and determines what parts of the peripheral walls will have openings and glazing. Core positions in buildings can be classified into three types: the 'centre core', the 'single core' and the 'single core'. In the tropics, the cores should preferably be located on the hot sides of the building being the east and the west sides. It is evident that a double core has many benefits. By placing each of the two cores on the sides, they provide buffer zone on the sides. Studies have shown that the minimum air-conditioning load results from using the double-core configuration in which the window openings run from north to south, and the cores are placed on the east and the west sides. These also applies to buildings in the temporate climatic zone.

• The lift lobbies, stairways and toilets zone are areas that should be given natural ventilation and a view out where possible. This means that they inevitably should be placed at the periphery of the useable floor space as against being placed in the central-core position. External periphery placements of these parts of the building result in energy savings, since these areas would not require mechanical ventilation, and require reduced artificial lighting besides eliminating the need for additional mechanical pressurisation ducts for fire-protection purposes. Aesthetically, by placing these on the periphery of the building, these areas receive natural sunlight and provide views to the outside which with a central-core position would not be possible. In this way the building user on leaving an elevator at the upper floor can see out and be aware of the place (instead of entering an artificially lit lobby that could be anywhere in the world.

central core

side core

end core

cores at hot sides

view out from lobby

awareness of place

• Tall building are exposed more directly to the full impacts of external temperatures and radiation heat. Accordingly, the overall building's orientation has important bearing on energy conservation. In general, arranging the building with its main and broader openings facing north-south shows the greatest advantage with regard to reducing the building's solar insolation (and its air-conditioning load). As frequently happens, the geometry of the site would not coincide with the north-south geometry of the sun. In which case, the other built-elements of the building may if expedient for planning purposes follow the geometry of this site (e.g. to optimise upon basement carparking layouts, etc.). The typical floor window openings should generally face the direction of the least direct solar insolation (i.e. north-south in the tropics). Some corner shading adjustments or shaping may need be made for those site locations which lie further north or south of the tropics or for non-conformity of building plan to the solar path. Generally the window openings should orientate north-south unless important views require other orientations or openings. If required for aesthetic reason, curtain-wall may be used on these non-solar facing facades. On the other building faces, some for of solar shading is required while also taking into consideration the quality of light entering the spaces. In temperate zones, these transitional space can have adjustable glazing at the outer face so that the balcony or recesses can act as 'sun-spaces' to collect solar-heat passively like green-houses, conservation, sun-room, etc.

• Deep recesses may be used at the building's hot sides to give shading. A window can be totally recessed to become balconies or become small-'sky-courts' that can synergistically serve a number of other functions besides sun-shading. Placing balconies at the hot-elevations permit the glazing to these areas to be full-height clear panels. These can be

side/building adjustments

curtain wall at North & South faces

recessed sun-spaces

sliding openable panels to give access to these balcony spaces. The balcony spaces can serve as evacuation spaces in case of emergencies, as large terraces for planting and landscaping, as a flexible zone for the addition of future executive wash-rooms or kitchenette facilities.

• Large multi-storey transitional spaces might be introduced in the central and periphery parts of the building as air-spaces and atriums. These serve as 'in-between' zones located between the insides and the outside of the building. These should be designed to function in a similar to the the traditional 'verandah-way' in the old shop-houses or of the porches in the early 19th century masonry houses in the tropics. Atriums should not be totally enclosed but should be placed in this in-between space between the inside and the outside and whose tops could be shielded by a louvred-roof to encourage wind-flow through the inner areas of the building. These may also be designed to function as wind-scoops to bring and to control natural ventilation to the inner parts of the building.

• The external walls of the building should be regarded more as a permeable environmentally-interactive membrane with adjustable openings (rather than as a sealed-skin). In temperate climate, the external wall has of course, to serve both very cold winters as well as hot summers. In which case, the external wall should be filter-like and have variable parts that provide good insulative functioning in the cold periods and be operable in the hot seasons. Where in the tropics, the external wall should have moveable parts that control and enable good cross-ventilation for internal comfort, provide solar protection from the sun, regulate any wind-swept rain besides facilitating the rapid discharge of any heavy rain-fall.

site/building/solar skycourts

transitional spaces

environmentally-interactive wall

• The building plan in addition to responding to these commercial intentions of the building (e.g. enabling single, double or multiple terraces situations) should be reflective of the pattern of life and culture of the place and climate. Partly this involves an understanding of the spatial modalities of people, the way they work, the way culture arranges privacy and community. This can be reflected in the plan's configuration, its depth, the position and configuration of the entrance and exits, the means of movement through and between spaces, the orientation and external views as interpreted in the plan, and others. At the same time, the plan should also reflect the air movements through the spaces and provision of sunlight into the building. The space for work even in a high-rise commercial structure has to have some degree of humanity, some degree of interest and some degree of scale. For instances, the use of large terraces and skycourts might serve as communal spaces as well as ventilating spaces into the upper parts of the tall building.

• The ground floor in the tropics should preferably be open to the outside and be a naturally ventilating space. The ground floor relation to the street is also important. The introduction of the internalised indoor atrium at the ground floor may mean the demise of street-life. Free-standing fortress-like buildings also tend to separate the building from the pavement and further alienate the street. By being set back, it eliminates pedestrian movement and reduces the communication and movement into and around buildings from traffic and access points. Free-standing buildings become isolated buildings on isolated plots depicting an 'island site'.

plan/use pattern/ventilation

balconies & terraces

open-to-sky ground floor

15.2

Yeang had inevitably acquired another passion. He was tired of seeing his beautiful Malaysian cities invaded by Western architecture that ignored the traditional styles of south-east Asia and Malaysia in particular. It turns out that these traditional forms of architecture were extraordinarily well suited to their climate. Rather like the cartwheel studied by Sturt in Chapters 3 and 5, these forms had grown up over generations rather than having been thought about theoretically. Yeang analysed the way their forms provided shading and cooling ventilation as well as protection from tropical storms.

A traditional Chinese/Malaysian house

The wonderful Blue Mansion in Penang, restored by the local architect Laurence Loh, shows many of the traditional forms and devices developed over centuries to respond to the wet tropical climate. In this picture (Figure 15.3) they include deep overhangs, shaded walkways, and cross ventilation. Interestingly, in this example, since the owner was Chinese, these traditional Malaysian forms and devices have taken on many of the more detailed traditions derived from Chinese culture.

15.3

Yeang published a series of books on how to apply these principles but using contemporary materials and technologies. In particular, he also developed these ideas in relation to the high-rise structures now needed in crowded cities like Kuala Lumpur. Unlike London, Malaysian cities did not develop at high density and the traditional building forms tended to suit separate pavilions rather than closely attached structures. Yeang's guiding principles, then, applied over many years of practice, maintained a steady hand behind his work.

Some of Ken Yeang's sketches for the design of a particular tower

The drawings shown here (Figure 15.4) apply Yeang's guiding principles to a particular project. It is one of Yeang's earlier highly successful series of high-rise buildings in and around the Malaysian capital city of Kula Lumpur. Here we see his idea of continuing the landscape up into the façade of the tower (the final design can be seen in Figure 21.1 in Chapter 21).

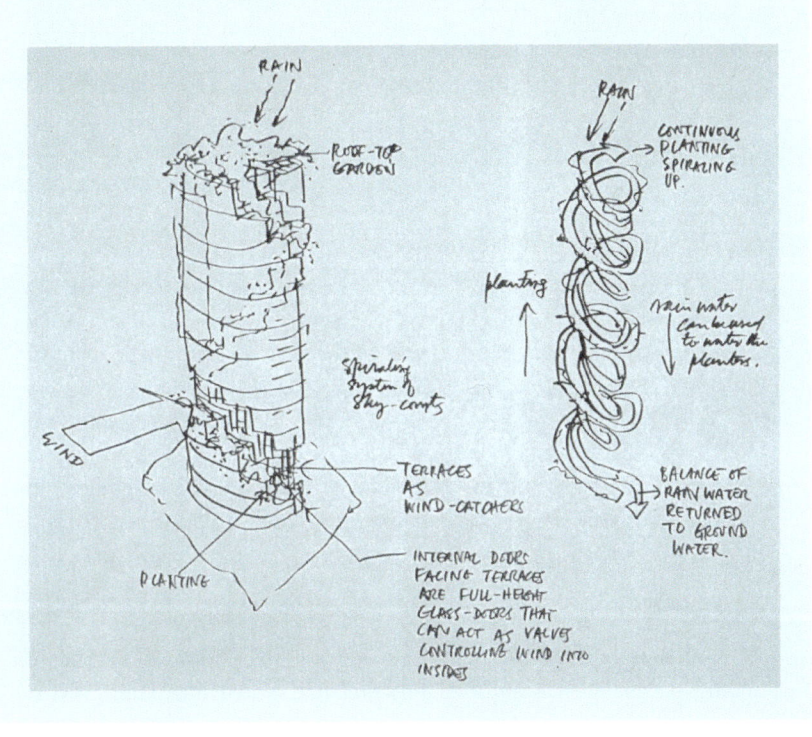

15.4

Guiding principles and schemata

Guiding principles are sets of ideas that are, in effect, a series of design schemata. Not just their expression but also their significance and implications for design will be extensively explored and shared with the design practice. We see clear evidence for this from the study of Ken Yeang shown here. We shall explore these guiding principles later and discover the extent to which they form shared experiences within design practices.

Guiding principles can change over time

The notion that guiding principles could change over time was reinforced from a seemingly unlikely source. Richard Burton, a partner in the highly successful British practice of Ahrends Koralek and Burton, was for some time a champion of sustainable architecture and, in particular, designing to reduce energy consumption. He held a formal role at the Royal Institute of British Architects to promote this approach and was a regular speaker and writer on developing appropriate design strategies. However, his vision of architecture was sufficiently mature for him to appreciate that priorities might change over time.

St Mary's Hospital by Ahrends Koralek and Burton

The principal in charge of this project was Richard Burton and his underpinning guiding principles included a very strong wish to reduce energy consumption. This building (Figure 15.5) succeeded in that objective by consuming less than 50% of the energy of the average hospital being built in the UK at that time. However, Burton was also to say

> Energy in building has had something of a fanfare lately and maybe it will have to continue for some time but soon I hope the subject will take its place among the twenty other major issues a designer of buildings has to consider.
>
> (Lawson 1994)

Some years later, the field of evidence-based design of healthcare buildings became well established. Research had shown that, if designed in ways to reflect research evidence, hospitals could achieve significant reductions in the length of time patients took to recover as well as providing them with a better quality of life during their stay. Much of this evidence also showed improved working conditions for staff (Lawson and Parnell 2016). Burton continued to design hospitals and incorporated these ideas into his guiding principles.

Guiding principles and primary generators

Not surprisingly, designers with strong guiding principles have a ready source of primary generators. Among architects we can see an enormously wide range of guiding principles. One area that could be seen to have emerged from the modern movement is that of building structure. I am lucky to have the sequence of drawings we see here from the design process of Bill Howell.

Building structure as guiding principles

The architect Bill Howell was not only a significant figure in post-war British architecture. With his practice of Howell, Killick, Partridge Amis, he created many acclaimed projects, especially in the housing and higher education sectors. He was also a deep thinker about the design process and took up the chair of the school of architecture at Cambridge. It was likely that, through this opportunity, we would have had much more analysis from him about the nature of designing but, sadly, he was killed in a motor accident only a year later. Howell's guiding principles were firmly established around the structure of his buildings and were invariably expressed both inside and out.

This sequence of drawings (Figure 15.6) show an exchange between Howell and his structural engineer about an increasingly well-understood

(continued)

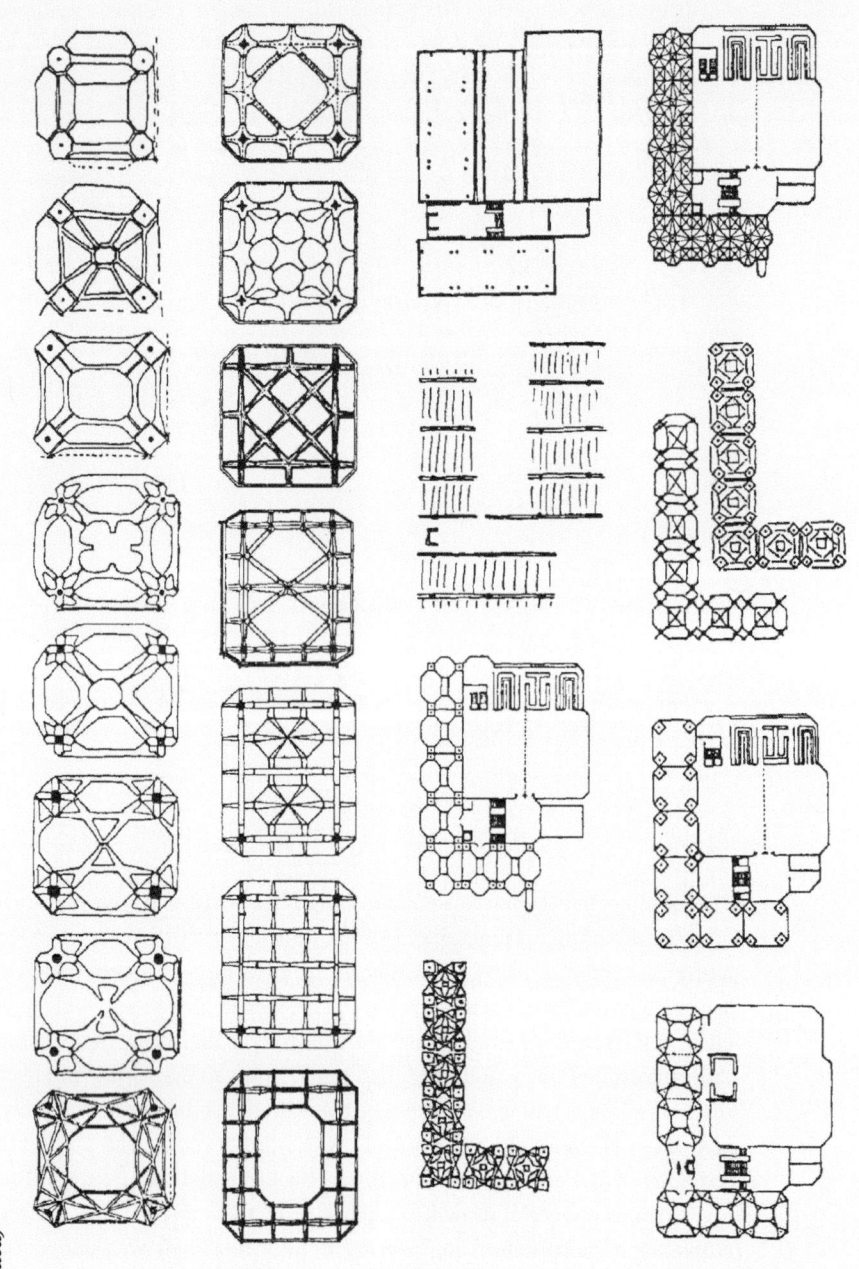

(continued)

15.6

Guiding principles

structure for the University Centre at Cambridge, and are probably best described in Howell's own words.

> While thinking about structural economy, the relationship of internal partitioning to downstanding beams, the relationship of cladding to the structure, and so on, you are taking decisions which affect the relationship of the anatomy of the building to its site and to its neighbours.
>
> (Howell 1970)

Howell thought deeply about this approach and understood it sufficiently to give it the name 'vertebrate architecture'. In this post-war era he worked mainly in reinforced concrete, which allowed sculptural forms for the structural members. 'The interior volume is defined and articulated by actual, visible structure' (Howell 1970).

The final structural arrangement of the building

There can be no doubt that Howell's guiding principles provided a clear and strong primary generator that was relentlessly resolved into the final design (Figure 15.7). It is interesting to note that they include almost the opposite attitude towards structure as seen in Stirling and Wilford's guiding principles listed earlier.

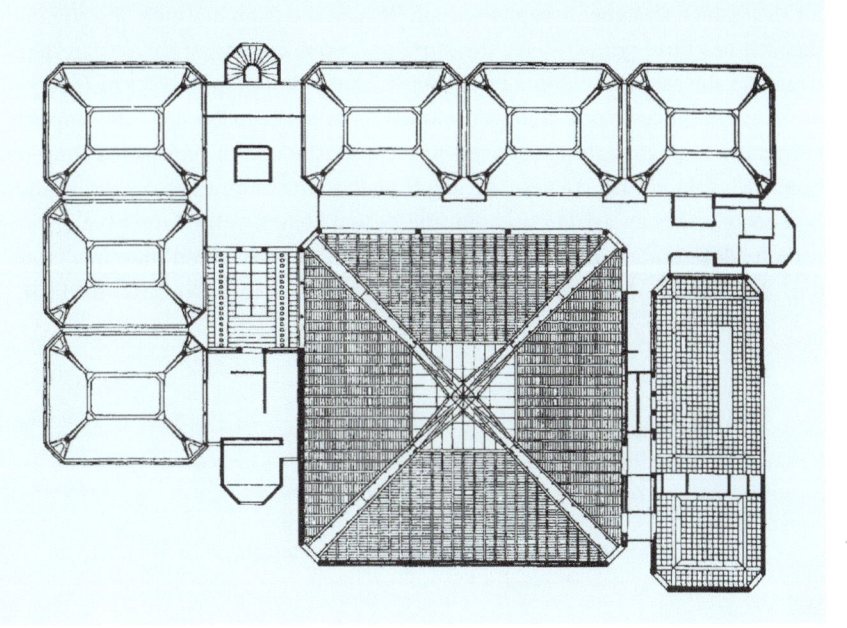

15.7

Let us be absolutely clear about the value of guiding principles here. If they are at least relevant in some way, and are sufficiently well developed, they can make an extraordinarily powerful contribution to starting a design project. We saw in Chapter 6 that drawings can be seen as a conversation with the situation. However, we also saw how sometimes conversations are much more difficult to start than to continue. The drawings on pieces of paper that already have marks on them seem at least to break the ice. The guiding principle can help to do that too. In the language of Schön, they enable the designer to frame the problem in such a way that work can begin without necessarily understanding, or taking into account, the total complexity of the situation. Sometimes you may be lucky or perhaps stubborn enough to pursue a design as relentlessly tightly framed as the Howell example shown here.

It is also important to remember that the starting point provided by a primary generator, especially perhaps one framed by guiding principles, is itself not either right or wrong. It is simply a process by which you can lever yourself into the design process. Howell himself made this point eloquently. He worked all through his career using the same basic approach that he defended very humbly, 'We do it, because we like it' (Howell 1970). There is no claim of a higher authority here. The practice liked the approach, got to understand it well and used it successfully. They then became recognised for the kind of design that resulted and must have been chosen by clients who were well aware of this.

Guiding principles can be about small detail too

The Czech architect Eva Jiricna is particularly well known for her high-tech interiors. Many of these are in retail and especially well known are a series of shops for the fashion designer Joseph Etedgui. We can see from her own descriptions that she has little sympathy for the more philosophical end of the design spectrum and she sees her guiding principles as simple but helpful ways of navigating a design process. This highly developed sense of the technology she employs allows her to begin a design process at the opposite end to that which conventional wisdom would suggest. In much of the early literature on the design process one sees an assumption that the design begins at the larger scale with overall configuration or simple outlines of form. It is assumed that only later, once decisions about these matters are made, do designers move on to the detail.

Eva Jiricna has guiding principles about materials and junctions

In our office we usually start with full-size details . . . if we have, for example, some ideas of what we are going to create with different junctions, then we can create a layout which would be good because certain materials only join in a certain way comfortably. (Figure 15.8.)

(Lawson 1994)

15.8

We are at the end of this chapter but there is still more, much more, to say about guiding principles. It turns out that they play an important role in bridging the gap between theory and practice, between academia and professional consultation; in fact, they are often at the very heart of the development of our understanding of design. Those discussions, however, must wait until a later chapter. We shall return to them in Chapter 19. For now it is important to recognise that a well-established set of guiding principles seems to mark out those designers we might recognise as influential in their profession. We are about to discover some more important characteristics of what we might call the expert designer. That is the subject of the next chapter.

References

Gropius, W. (1935). *The New Architecture and the Bauhaus*. London, Faber and Faber.

Howell, W. G. (1970). "Vertebrate buildings". *RIBA Journal* 77(3).

Lawson, B. and R. Parnell (2016). "Quality of place and wellbeing". *Oxford Textbook of Creative Arts, Health, and Wellbeing*. S. Clift and P. Camic. Oxford, Oxford University Press: 299–308.

Lawson, B. R. (1994). *Design in Mind*. Oxford, Butterworth Architecture.

Lyons, E. (1968). "Too often we justify our ineptitudes by moral postures". *RIBA Journal* 75(5).

Pugin, A.W.N. (1973). *The True Principles of Pointed or Christian Architecture*. New York, Academy Editions Ltd.

Stirling, J. (1965). "An architect's approach to architecture". *RIBA Journal* 72(5).

Suckle, A., Ed. (1980). *By Their Own Design*. New York, Whitney.

Yeang, K. (2016). *The Skyscraper Bioclimatically Considered*. New York, Oro Editions.

Yeang, K. and T. Leong (2017). *It's Not Easy Being Green*. New York, Oro Editions.

Chapter 16

Recognising situations, gambits and affordances

In the previous chapter we saw some ways in which highly experienced, we might call them expert, designers work. You may feel you are already in some ways expert and have some experience of designing, albeit in the rather artificial world of the design school studio. There are two reasons for us pausing here to understand more expert designers. First, it is good to know what really lies ahead of you; how you might want to stretch yourself into this more developed state. The second reason is that you may already have had contact with highly thought of expert designers. Some of them may have talked to your school. Others certainly will have written books or papers that you read. Of course, you will also have seen the final end product of much of their work. So how should you understand this?

Design expertise

There is now a considerable field of research into the acquisition of expertise. Kees Dorst and I tried to apply this understanding for the first time to the world of designing (Lawson and Dorst 2009). Learning to become expert at anything involves a lot of hard work. As I was writing this chapter, I was also reading a book on the life of Wolfgang Amadeus Mozart (Suchet 2016). His was indeed a remarkable life. He wrote some of the world's most loved music and, over 300 years after his death, this music is as popular as ever. However, Mozart was no typical expert. By the age of six he was already performing to rave reviews and could show off a whole series of amazing tricks at the keyboard. He was taken by his father on a tour of the great cities and palaces of Europe along with his almost equally talented sister. This tour lasted for several years and by the end of it he was already composing symphonies and concertos that are still played in concert halls around the world. He composed over 600 serious works, including more than 80 symphonies and concertos, over 20 stageworks, as well as masses and countless pieces of chamber music. He played keyboard, string and wind instruments to performance standard. All this he achieved before a tragically young death at age 35.

Most designers who are considered expert and who I have had the privilege to study were still developing their expertise at the age at which Mozart died. In Chapter 1 we saw that design seems to be a field that needs years of experience in order to mature. There are precious few Mozarts in this world and hardly any of anything like his achievement that I know of in design. Back in the very first chapter of this book we saw some evidence of this in a section entitled 'it may take some time'. The general theories about acquiring expertise suggest a number of important ideas. First, it takes time. The rather simplistic general figure is that, in most fields, becoming truly expert may take at least 10,000 hours of practice and, for many of us, much more. So, unlike Mozart, the average concert pianist must have spent something in the region of this amount of time practising. The other figure that has been bandied around is that, overall, such practice takes about ten years. These are ridiculously simplistic figures and they are contested by some researchers. However, many studies on musicians and sportspeople lend support to them as being in roughly the right order of magnitude.

Expertise is not usually acquired steadily. Most studies show that progress tends to be more like climbing stairs than walking steadily up a ramp. Moreover, it seems that experts do not just do the same things as others but more quickly or better. They actually do different things. Hubert Dreyfus is one of the acknowledged authorities on generic expertise and he has proposed a model in which six major stages, or steps on the staircase, can be identified (Dreyfus and Dreyfus 2005). In our book, Kees Dorst and I tried to identify what these stages might mean in learning to design. This rather hypothetical argument is probably too early in its development to be studied in detail here. However, it does suggest that moving to the higher levels of design expertise is likely to depend on seeing situations differently. There is some evidence to support exactly that conclusion.

Recognising situations

Because design involves such a complex array of skills and knowledge it is sometimes easier to see the arguments in more straightforward fields. These are necessarily not good models of design but they help us to appreciate some features replicated by expert designers. To begin our next step on the staircase of design expertise we shall first look at expertise in chess.

A chess master plays many club members simultaneously

This delightful old picture (Figure 16.1) shows a grand chess master playing all the members of a chess club simultaneously. He wanders up and down between all the tables and appears to make moves without much thought.

16.1

You may have seen these apparently amazing chess masters who can play a whole room full of ordinary club players simultaneously and beat them all. There are reports of this and even videos on the internet. If you watch carefully you will see that often they make moves almost instantly; they hardly ever hesitate. How do they do this? The rest of us probably start each move in a game of chess with some critical examination of the situation on the board. If we are sensible, we first analyse it for dangers that need immediate or planned defence and, only if the coast seems reasonably clear, do we look for attacking opportunities. We might look at a series of possible moves, check each of them for dangers perhaps one or two moves ahead, select the best option and make our move. These great chess masters seem to do all this extremely quickly when playing ordinary club members. If they are performing this feat of playing many games simultaneously, they have played a dozen or more other moves on other boards since the last move on the current board. Can they really remember the situation on all these boards? To most of us this seems almost impossible.

In reality they hardly do any of this at all. They simply recognise the board situation from a substantial store of what, in this book, we have been calling precedent. Chess masters, like expert designers, have deliberately studied huge numbers of situations and can recall them easily. In most board situations they can mentally strip away the unimportant pieces, see the situation core and recognise a sufficiently similar precedent. So, in effect, they are simply recognising a situation rather than analysing it (De Groot 1965). You might say that all the really hard work has been done in years of study. This idea will be explored in more detail in later chapters.

Of course chess is a poor imitation of design, which is usually far more open-ended, but the principles of recognising situations is a distinguishing feature of high levels of expertise in many areas. Musicians, for example, faced with a complex score for the first time and having to sight read, will often be able to recognise patterns from their study of musical theory and from their knowledge of the composer. This means they do not have to read every note but can 'see' a major, minor or chromatic scale or a set of arpeggios, and perhaps recognise the characteristic way in which, say, Mozart might break away from that classical pattern in a phrase and so on. If you are a reasonably proficient player of a musical instrument you might have developed this skill to a certain extent.

However, you do not have to be an excellent musician to prove this step change in perception for yourself.

Perceiving and recognising

Look very quickly at the first of these images and you are quite likely to be able to tell how many dots there are (Figure 16.2). It is of course five. Look at the second in the same way and you are much less likely to be able to perform this simple recognition test. There are nine dots here. Although you can count them one by one, you are unlikely to recognise 'nineness'. However, you can almost certainly do this with the third image. What actually happens here, of course, is that you recognise 'threeness' and do a simple little piece of mental arithmetic. Research on this has suggested that the break point here is about seven. Above seven we find it hard to recognise number and have to count.

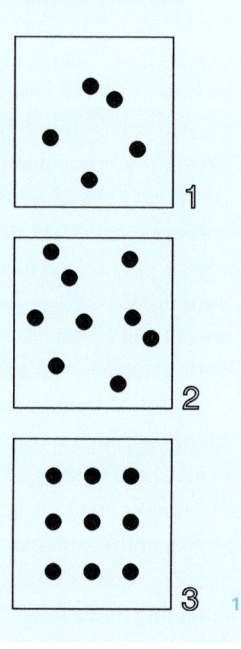

16.2

The next illustration is even more surprising. You are very likely to be an expert at reading English, certainly if you are a native speaker. The illustration here allows

Situations, gambits and affordances

you to test this. It is rather charming since it also gives the explanation, which I do not need to repeat.

You might be quite surprised to discover how little information you rely on to recognise and read words. Of course you also use context when doing this. That is to say, you know that some words are far more likely than others given the preceding words. By honing these skills to a very sophisticated level, some people can achieve extraordinary feats of speed-reading. As you must have always suspected, these people are not reading every letter, not even every word, and certainly not whole sentences or paragraphs.

How little we actually read

Try reading the apparently nonsensical paragraph below.

It's all so obivuos

Aoccdrrnig to rscheearch at an Elingsh uinervtisy, it deosn't mttaer in waht oerdr the ltteers in a wrod are, the olny iprmoetent thing is taht the frist and lsat ltteers are at the rghit pclae. The rset can be a toatl mses. And you can sitll raed it wouthit porbelm. Tihs is bcuseae we do not raed ervey ltetler by istlef but the wrod as a wlohe.

As an amusing aside to this phenomenon I had the very devil of a job typing this as the spill chucker kept correcting it! This phenomenon is the reason that proofreading books like this proves to be such a tricky task. Quite simply your mind corrects all the minor spelling errors and you do not really recognise them. You must slow down and read every word, indeed every letter, in order to manage this.

A young child learning to read would certainly not be able to make sense of this trick paragraph but, by now, you are a real master of reading and can apply this expertise without even realising you are doing it.

If we briefly return to the Chapter 11 on the design tutorial, you will see that tutors behave in some respects in a similar way. I have often been involved in or overheard conversations between studio tutors about their students' progress. In such conversations you can hear them using the names of well-established typical student responses to situations.

Gambits

If we continue the chess analogy one step further, we can introduce the notion of 'gambits'. These are well-known set patterns of play that can be used in certain situations. In chess a gambit is generally seen as an opening move and sequence of subsequent moves in relation to various responses available to your opponent. The word actually comes from the Italian *Dare il gambetta*, which can be translated as 'stick out a leg'. This refers to wrestling and represents a way of moving the bout forward from simple grappling.

In design, however, we use this term to mean any set of design moves that are well understood and can be used in a particular situation. As with so much else, designers characteristically learn and come to recognise these by studying precedent. Architects, for example, may have a whole series of moves in their mind about entrances and how to organise the approach and way in to buildings of varying types. For example, the classical use of a central axis of symmetry along which a major entrance might be sited; patterns such as placing a doorway in a recessive corner, which naturally draws people in but in a much less formal manner, and so on. Similarly, industrial designers might know gambits that help to define a display or a control according to the form of an object.

Earlier in this book I have several times referred to the idea that designers tend to be solution focussed. They concentrate on what a solution might look like and how to get there rather than making some detailed analysis of the problem. So now we can get a glimpse of how this happens for the expert designer. Such experienced designers are likely to have seen many design situations before. In fact they will have schemata of countless such possible situations. These schemata not only allow them to recognise the situation but also include possible gambits for dealing with it.

When I was discussing his design process with Richard MacCormac, he made reference to the chapel they designed for Fitzwilliam College at Cambridge. At one point Richard started to sketch, something he did compulsively while talking, and pointing to his simple diagram he effectively named the situation. A dominating idea, indeed a primary generator for this project, was that of the worship space being on an upper floor as an organic space inside a rectangular enclosure. He said 'for a while we played with the circle in a square idea, you know?' At this point he stopped very deliberately and looked me in the eye. There was no doubt in my mind that he was checking that I shared this schema with him sufficiently for him to go on without further explanation. I nodded and his conversation moved immediately to the next phase of his process. We shall explore the design process behind this project in much more detail in Chapter 19.

My one-time research student Khairul Khaidzir studied design tutorials and frequently found cases where the tutor would look at the student work so far, recognise a situation and immediately rehearse some gambits (Khaidzir and Lawson 2013). 'This is a situation where you could do . . .', or very similar phrases, were found many times in recordings of design tutorials. Furthermore, tutors would also frequently suggest backtracking a little in order to create a situation in which a particularly helpful gambit could be employed. Here the tutor says things such as 'you could bend this a little and then you would be able to do . . .'. This data also showed another particular skill of the tutors. On average they would spend about a third of their time suggesting and developing possible gambits. This enabled them to be constructive and solution focussed. Students, however, spent less than a tenth of their time doing this.

Thinking ahead

There is another skill that we can see in expert chess players which is effectively the extension of the gambit. They will not only know all the sensible moves appropriate to a situation but also the possible responses that might be expected from their opponent. Of course, this then extends into the future. There is some evidence that expert designers have this ability too, although it must be a looser and more open-ended set of possibilities (Ahmed et al. 2003). This research suggests that such designers can see sufficiently far ahead in terms of the implications of the moves they might make in order to evaluate them before spending time working out the detail. Typically, in the recordings of studio design tutors, we hear a sequence that can be characterised as 'you could use this idea but in this case you might need to alter it like that. Then you might also have to change something else, in this case it might have created more problems than it solves . . .', and so on.

Affordances

In analysing design conversations and protocols of design processes, one more skill stands out as being a characteristic of the expert way of thinking. This is to do with how experts classify and structure all the knowledge that they have. We have referred to this as precedent and here we have seen an ability to recognise situations and gambits. This extra skill is to do with what the psychologist James Gibson famously described as 'affordance' (Gibson 1986).

We have already seen that the designer is not like the lawyer trying to prove the closeness of fit of a precedent, but rather uses it creatively and imaginatively. How is this done? An important contribution to this process must certainly be through recognised affordances. The notion of affordance, as introduced by Gibson, is the ability to see the possibilities that some thing, place, person or some argument might offer. Gibson, along with a whole school of cognitive psychology, argues that perception is an active process that looks forward as much as backward. In short, it anticipates action.

An everyday example of this might be the task of changing a light bulb. We might look around the room for something to stand on in order to reach the ceiling. We might see large and small tables, various chairs, sofas, a pile of books, some boxes and so on. We might of course know we have a stepladder in the garage, which is designed specifically for this purpose. We know the task is a short one not involving any particularly heavy weights or difficult actions. In this case we are likely to choose a dining chair with a fairly flat seat and stable legs with no castors. The point here, however, is that such a chair 'affords' the possibility of being stood on. Probably long ago, then, we had learned to store this affordance as part of the schema for such a chair.

Affordances in everyday life

These two pictures (Figures 16.3a and 16.3b) were taken in Kuala Lumpur but they could easily have been taken in countless other cities. They show that people habitually see affordances for personal behaviour in public space. Good places to sit do not have to be designed as seats.

16.3a and 16.3b

Discouraging affordances

These two pictures (Figures 16.4a and 16.4b) were taken in Singapore but they could easily have been taken in countless other cities. Here the designer has unwittingly created places that offer the affordance of sitting but where such behaviour is either thought to be damaging or very dangerous. Usually a sign like this is an indicator of a design failure.

16.4a and 16.4b

In design, things are of course much more complex than this rather banal example. In particular, we may want some affordance of actions that are new or at least unfamiliar. In reverse, we might also want to anticipate how users of our design may see possibilities for actions that might cause problems. Expert designers seem to be able to look at new pieces of precedent and include the range of affordances in their schema. This enables them to use ideas from quite functionally remote purposes as precedent in new designs. Yet again, this is an example of an expert not doing what the novice might do quicker or better but actually doing something different.

While on this subject, it seems appropriate to introduce the ideas of two significant figures, one in industrial design and one in architecture. Donald Norman is famous for his discussion of how objects signal their affordances to us in his *The Design of Everyday Things*. He first introduced the ideas of affordance as a deliberate design strategy (Norman 1988). He argued that everyday objects with long evolutions tend to do this naturally and that modern design may have forgotten this. Most notably, he pointed out that a flat plate on one side of a door seems to offer the affordance of pushing whereas a long bar-type handle on the other side suggests pulling. Traditional teapots are wonderful examples of such objects with the handle and spout respectively instructing us to pick them up and pour.

This created a whole school of design where new objects suggest through their form how they should be used, thus eliminating the need for labels and instructions. One everyday example that still seems to frustrate us is the way in which a conventional tap suggests turning but we seem unable to come up with a design for a tap that is operated by sensing a hand below the spout. This took Norman into the field of graphical communication on web pages where he developed six principles of design. That is of enormous importance but takes us into a field beyond the scope of this book.

Our architectural example of using the notion of affordance in design is the renowned Dutch architect Herman Hertzberger. His guiding principles include the idea that we should design our environment to be rich in affordances. He wants people actively to see new possibilities in the world around them and to take possession of places by the way they use them (Hertzberger 1991). Hertzberger talks of developing a form of design in which the designer creates 'instruments' rather than 'tools'. In his approach to design, Hertzberger creates both space and form that he thinks of as like musical instruments. The modern flute, for example, is a very complex and sophisticated piece of design created by a man called Theobold Boehm. But it does not restrict a player so much as invite an amazing range of possibilities. This is design in which each user can do things with it that could never have been anticipated by the designer. By contrast, a 'tool' is very specifically designed to carry out a tightly defined action.

There is some argument here about how well certain styles of design perform in terms of offering affordances. Hertzberger, for example, argues that the classical column with its square base offers a choice of sitting in the sun or the shade. By contrast, the minimalist modern column offers no such possibilities. But we are in danger here of getting into a discussion about design styles and that is not the purpose of this book. However, seeing affordances and recognising situations remain vitally important tools in the thought processes of the designer.

Tutors recognising schemata in student schemes

I have often been involved in, or overheard conversations between, studio tutors discussing student progress. It is quite common to hear them using schemata including gambits in such exchanges. In architecture you might hear a tutor say that a particular student has got an axial scheme or is using the idea of a large central volume surrounded by smaller pavilions. Sometimes these conversations might refer to the work of another architect or particular design, and sometimes to a well-known design from the previous year. Some ideas are so well known that they have names and very detailed schemata. One example of this would be the rather well-trodden path of a 'second year hexagon'. For some reason, in the development of students, they seem to discover the geometric properties of hexagons and how they can be nested together. Possibly this might be a response to a tutor urging them to break out of a predetermined rectilinear approach. Most of us, it seems, need to go through at least one of these 'second year hexagon' phases to get the schema, with all its possible gambits, in our heads. Most will usually come to realise the tyranny of such geometry and learn to put it aside save for quite special circumstances. It seems, though, that we must all learn these sorts of lessons for ourselves.

When tutoring and examining at industrial design schools, I have often heard a tutor bemoan the fact that a student has gone into the display screen phase. Of course such devices are now in many objects, not least my car, but during student development they can sometimes be a way of avoiding the creation of form that is ergonomic or invites a particular action. In landscape design a commonly recognisable schema is the idea of geometric human interventions with landscape allowed to grow naturally across it. Gertrude Jekyll used such a device in many gardens, particularly in collaboration with Edwin Lutyens.

And so it goes on. The point here being that experienced tutors often 'see' a student scheme very quickly and can associate that with a wide range of commonly used or perhaps inventive design gambits. I had a wonderful friend and colleague Peter Blundell Jones who died tragically early during the writing of this book. Peter was well known for his ability to 'get to the heart of a scheme' in crits. He could also immediately go to the weakness of a project. This created trepidation in the minds of students (though he was never cruel in his criticism) and won widespread admiration from his colleagues. Peter was not only a creative designer in his own right but a very fine historian and theoretician. Quite simply, he had studied so much design that he had a huge store of precedent. Peter's particular skill was to find generic lessons from individual pieces of design. I have never known someone more able to 'recognise' design situations and then offer a range of alternative 'gambits'. He was a real expert.

So, what have we learned from all this? Well, to begin with, it reinforces my earlier exhortations to get looking and sketching in order to learn precedents. But clearly the additional skill that is really helpful is to analyse and extract generic principles and possibilities, and to see new and perhaps unintended affordances that will aid your creative potential. It really is all about developing schemata and refining and inter-relating them. No wonder then that design expertise takes a long time to develop for most of us. We just need so much study of solutions and ideas. There are few shortcut theories for us. In our next chapter we look at how the experienced designer can generate not just one idea but many.

References

Ahmed, S., K. M. Wallace and L. T. Blessing (2003). "Understanding the differences between how novices and experienced designers approach design tasks". *Research in Engineering Design* 14(1): 1–11.

De Groot, A. D. (1965). *Thought and Choice in Chess*. The Hague, Mouton.

Dreyfus, H. L. and S. Dreyfus (2005). "Expertise in real world contexts". *Organization Studies* 26(5): 779–792.

Gibson, J. J. (1986). *An Ecological Approach to Visual Perception*. Hillsdale, Lawrence Erlbaum.

Hertzberger, H. (1991). *Lessons for Students in Architecture*. Rotterdam, Uitgeverij 010.

Khaidzir, K. A. M. and B. R. Lawson (2013). "The cognitive construct of design conversation". *Research in Engineering Design* 24(4): 331–347.

Lawson, B. R. and C. H. Dorst (2009). *Design Expertise*. Oxford, Elsevier/Architectural Press.

Norman, D. A. (1988). *The Design of Everyday Things*. New York, Doubleday.

Suchet, J. (2016). *Mozart: The Man Revealed*. London, Elliot and Thompson Ltd.

Chapter 17

Having more than one idea

Design rarely proceeds in a predictable and orderly fashion. We seldom have a clear idea about the outcome early on. Richard MacCormac put it very well when he said 'this is not a sensible way of earning a living, it's completely insane'. We agree to design something without any certainty that we can deliver a decent result. One word that you may have noticed has been missing from our discussion so far is 'creativity'. Designers are expected to be creative. This is a word that can carry so many interpretations that I am usually reluctant to use it, but in this chapter we must confront the problem. What is creativity in connection with design? Almost by definition, designers must be creative because their job is to create things. But we can also say that a mathematician is creative. Sometimes we describe someone as creative if they are prolific. At other times we say someone is creative because they do something new or original. The issue has been clouded by the concepts of 'convergent' and 'divergent' thinking. We have even seen people classified as convergers or divergers (Hudson 1968).

Convergent and divergent thinking

Two simple intelligence tests (Figure 17.1). One requires convergent thinking, which tests the ability to arrive at a logically correct answer. The second requires divergent thinking, which tests the ability to generate many different answers.

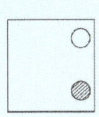 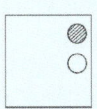 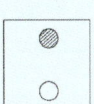

a convergent task:
complete the sequence

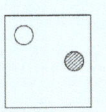

a divergent task:
what might this
represent?

17.1

There is a tendency to associate creativity with divergent thinking. In design this analysis is simply not good enough. It must surely be clear from our understanding of design activities in Chapter 8 that, to get to a good result, designers need both kinds of thinking, an ability to know when to apply which one and the skill to switch quickly. Undoubtedly, one of the skills many design students do not necessarily find easy is the ability to recognise when they are at a dead end with an idea. To put an idea aside, even if only temporarily, and work on another is a vital design skill.

How can you tell when there might be other ideas that you would have preferred? How soon should you focus on one idea? Having interviewed and studied so many expert designers I am sure that this has to be a personal thing.

Generating alternatives

Should you develop more than one idea at a time? Should you develop a design process that is based on deliberately generating alternative solutions? Some highly successful and much admired designers argue quite strongly against this.

An argument against alternatives

There has to be this big thing that you're confident you're going to find, you don't know what it is you're looking for and you hang on.

Richard MacCormac

Unless there is enough energy in this generative concept, you will actually not produce a very good result, because there is this three years or so of hard work to go through and the only sustenance apart from the bonhomie of the people involved is the quality of this idea, that is the food. It's the thing that nourishes, that keeps you, you know every time you get bored or fed up or whatever you can go back and get an injection from it, and the strength of that idea is fundamental, it has to carry an enormous amount of energy.

Ian Ritchie

If you think too much about the scheme you'll probably come up with two or three alternative solutions and with maybe half a dozen other options but if you approach a scheme with a gut feeling there can only be one solution but billions of options.

Ken Yeang
(Lawson 1994)

Richard MacCormac, Ian Ritchie and Ken Yeang all feel quite cautious about deliberately seeking alternatives. In essence their argument is that they feel this might weaken their belief in the one or two big ideas in a scheme. I have heard this idea expressed many times. It is the concern that a scheme may end up lacking what many designers call 'integrity'. This is the coherence that the big idea gives to the scheme. There is a concern that, somehow or other, some features of different alternatives will creep into the design and produce a mish mash. Some designers worry in this regard about showing more than one idea to the client. Ken Yeang makes an interesting distinction between deliberately searching for different overall strategies and the many variants one finds along the way of developing one basic idea.

An argument for alternatives

Michael Wilford uses a design strategy of deliberately mapping out alternatives almost as a way of defining the range of possibilities, 'the full spectrum'. These are all shown to the client. Wilford worries that this is a skill many students do not possess.

> They (students) are locked into a solution without having a full spectrum available to judge whether that is an appropriate solution. Without this the process tends to become ephemeral, whereas I think it needs to be rooted in a very systematic process of investigation of options and selection.
>
> Michael Wilford

John Outram uses a strategy of stopping work in the office and getting everyone to produce a design.

> We have actually won our first competition (using this approach) and we are negotiating another right now. My three associates and I each presented a design to the client . . . I thought this was quite dangerous . . . but in fact it had a very good effect on the client because it winkled out of the client what he was somehow looking for, which meant we could identify much better what the client was thinking about and therefore relate it to what we could offer.
>
> John Outram

> When a project starts we always look at all the options we can think of and see which is the strongest and most appropriate one. I don't think it has ever happened that we would say 'that's it' straight away. There are always alternatives.
>
> Eva Jiricna
> (Lawson 1994)

Ways of generating alternatives

There are many ways that different designers have come up with to force out alternatives. The argument here is that unless there is some formal procedure it is difficult to put one idea aside without losing some enthusiasm. John Outram has the idea of doing this by using all his staff in an internal competition. Michael Wilford and James Stirling seemed to use a particular aspect and often this was overall spatial and circulation organisation. A sort of general disposition of elements.

Stirling and Wilford alternative plans for Temasek Polytechnic, Singapore

A range of major planning alternatives for a large scheme involving many building functions (Figure 17.2). All these and indeed many more were shown to the client and discussed.

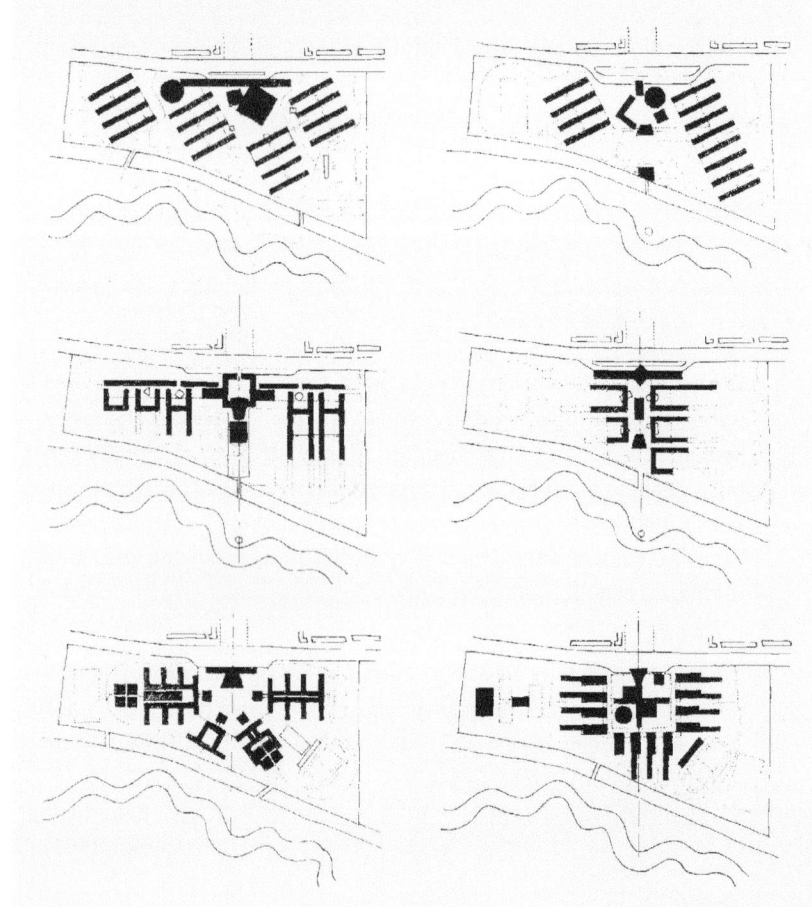

17.2

More alternatives for the same scheme

Even though these are in basic 3D they are still carefully abstract (Figure 17.3).

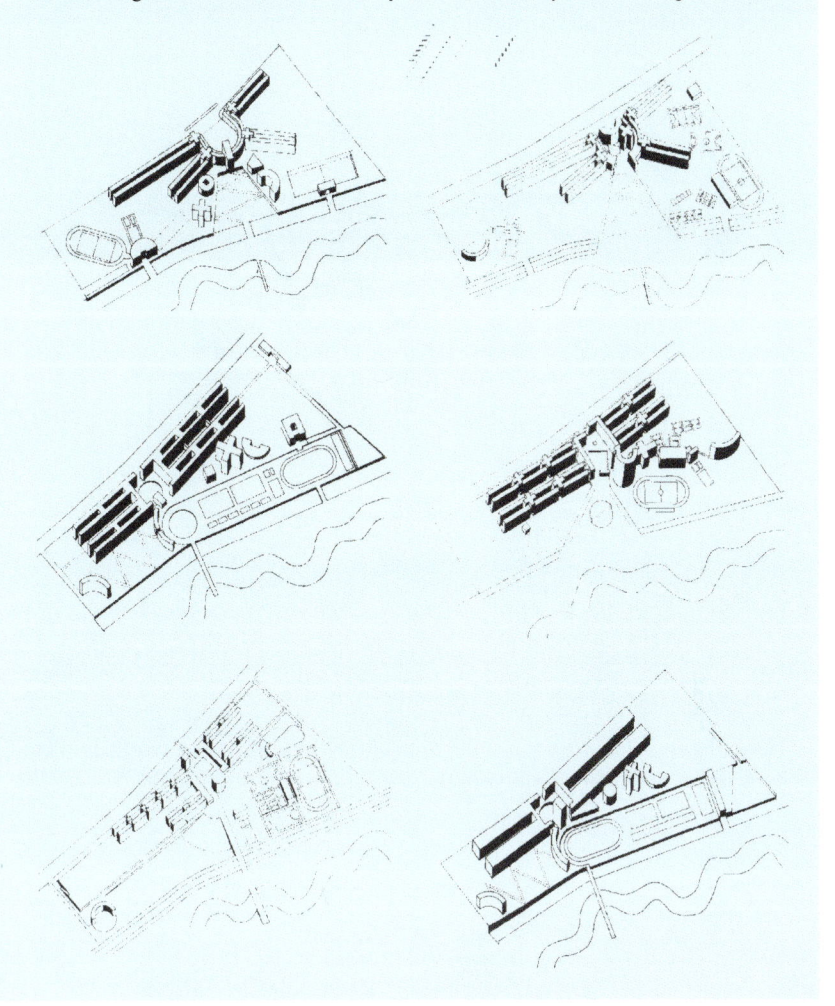

17.3

I asked Wilford specifically about the problem that might arise if the client wanted to pick aspects of different alternatives. He was quite comfortable with that as long as the result could be made to work well. It is interesting to see that the alternatives shown to the client do not give any real impression of how they might look. Wilford explains,

> we make it quite clear that these diagrams are totally abstract . . . actually this is one of the frustrations that some clients have with us . . . we have a long talk at the beginning of this process and say to them 'you're not going to see what this building is going to look like for several months'.
>
> Michael Wilford

Here (Figure 17.4) Stirling and Wilford work up one of their alternatives in more detail but it still remains quite abstract.

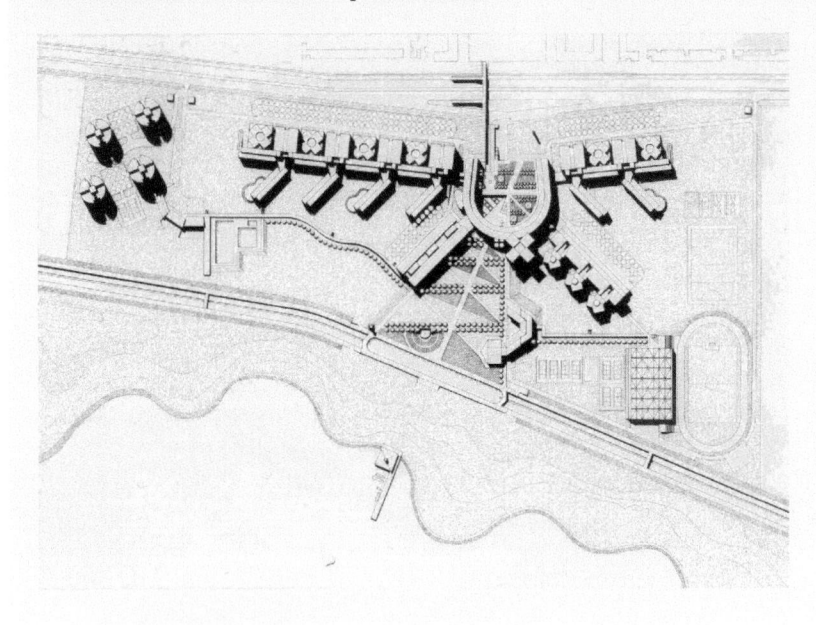

17.4

Here (Figure 17.5) we see a small area of the selected option worked up in sufficient detail to begin the process of deciding how it will look.

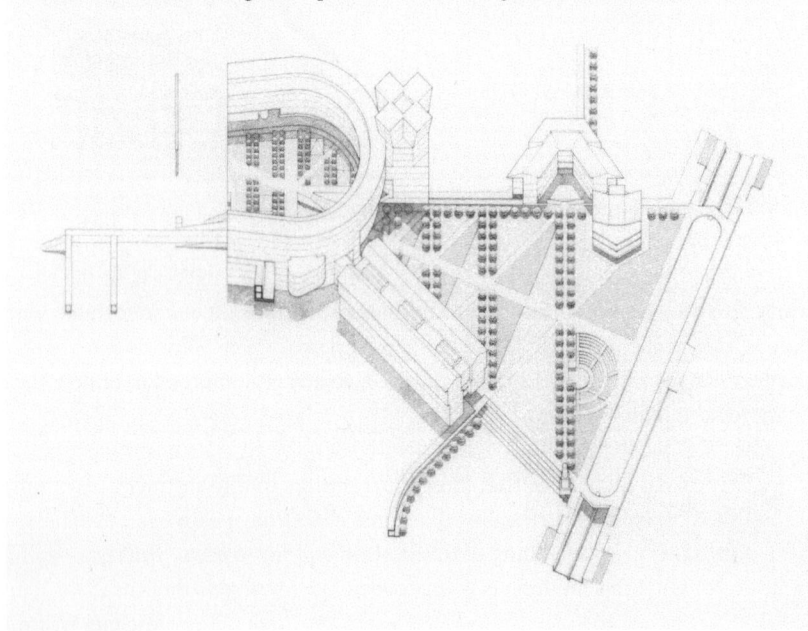

17.5

Temasek Polytechnic as built

Views showing the central area, internal circulation, the faculties and student services (Figures 17.6a, 17.6b, 17.6c and 17.6d).

17.6a, 17.6b,
17.6c and 17.6d
(continued)

(continued)

(continued)

17.6a, 17.6b,
17.6c and 17.6d

Eva Jiricna uses a very different method of generating alternatives. She thinks of different ranges and combinations of materials. She then sees how these would combine by working on the details of their junctions. A good deal of Eva's work is at the intersection between architecture, interior design and product design. She is well known for her avant-garde interiors complete with sculptural staircases often using structural glass.

On the first morning when you start working on the scheme you have got, let's say, ten and they are all equally possible and then you go through a process of analysing it and develop each of them slightly further on, and then you are left with, say, five. That process goes on and eventually you are left with one alternative.

Eva Jiricna

To some extent this idea of starting with materials, looking at intersections and beginning with some detailing might be a product of two circumstances. The first is that Eva Jiricna had, through her own choice, quite a strong engineering background. The second might be the quite small and intimate nature of many of her projects. What is very clear, however, is that it is perfectly possible to start designing from the detailed rather than the general and to do it by creating alternative design languages that gradually get eliminated until the final choice, which then gets worked up in even more detail.

Eva Jiricna on starting from detail

In our office we usually start with full-size details . . . if we have, for example, some ideas of what we are going to create with different junctions, then we can create a layout which would be good because certain materials only join in a certain way comfortably. (Figures 17.7a, 17.7b and 17.7c.)

Eva Jiricna

17.7a, 17.7b and 17.7c *(continued)*

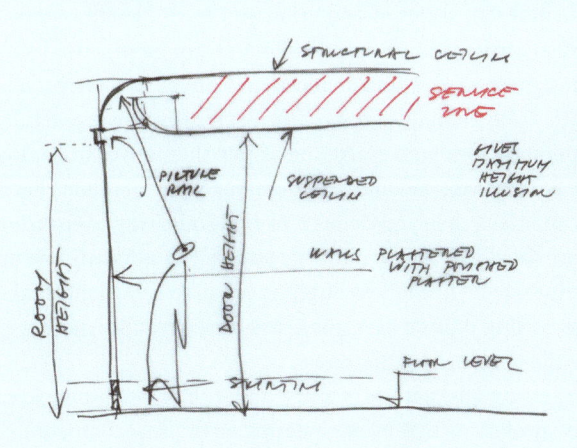

(continued)

(continued)

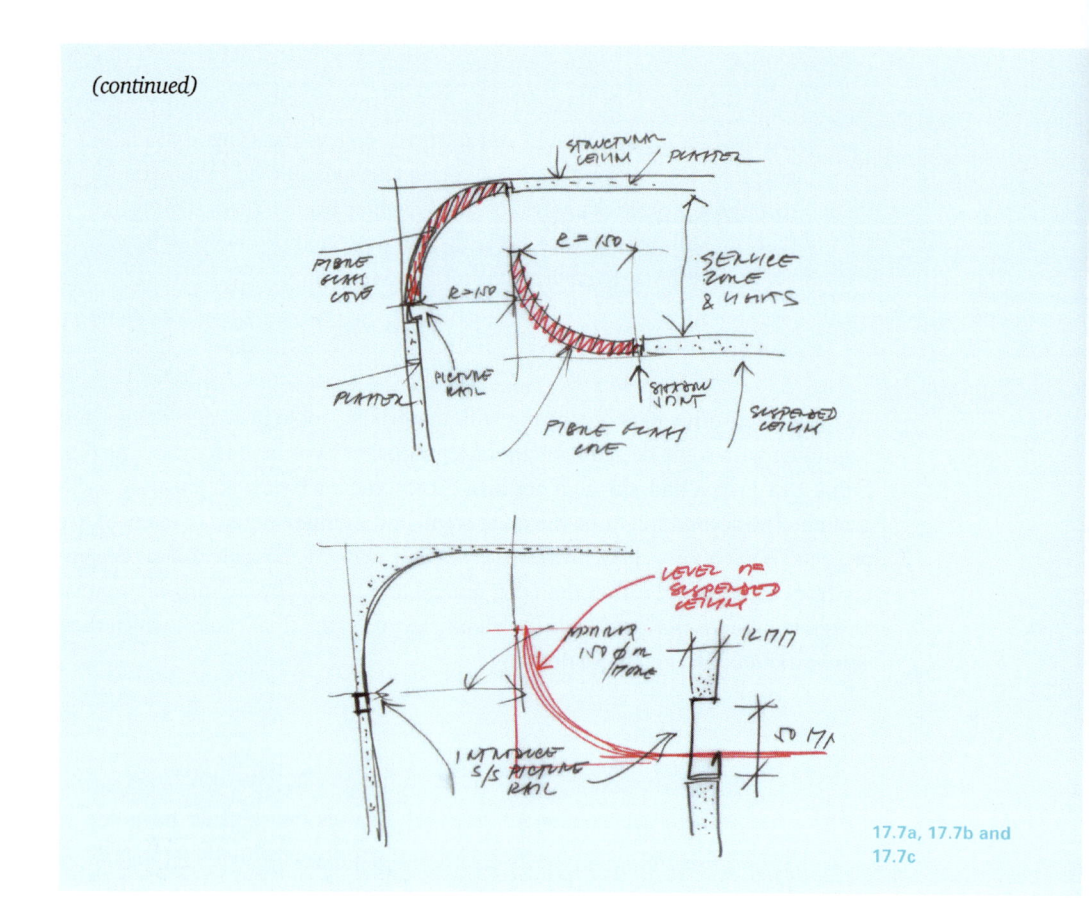

17.7a, 17.7b and
17.7c

So what we see here are two variants of the alternative generation approach but fitting into two quite different scales of operation and sets of guiding principles. Of course many other variants must be possible and can be practised successfully, while other designers remain unconvinced and prefer to work on one idea at a time. What both these great designers show us, however, is a carefully orchestrated way of generating alternatives. Neither allow themselves to get too far ahead with one idea, perhaps worried that this might take over. It seems that if you like the idea of this approach then you do need to find some way of ensuring that many alternatives are organised before allowing yourself to work any one up too far. It also seems likely that you need these alternatives all to be variants of the same set of issues. In the Stirling Wilford case, these are basic layouts, whereas in the Jiricna case they are the languages of materials.

A further way of creating alternatives is to use more than one brain. John Outram has shown us a way of doing that by engineering an internal competition. I have another more anecdotal experience of that system at work; it is quite simply the design school studio project. It is gained from many years of setting students design problems in architecture, urban design, interior and product design as well as landscape design. Typically, a group of students might be between 20 and 60 here, so, by the final crit, we would see effectively 20–60 alternative designs. It was very often the case that, at most, there would be only about half a dozen fundamentally different approaches, with the remainder being effectively variations on one or other of these themes. Of course this really depends on the kind of project, the extent to which the client had briefed and the availability or not of user reaction and so on.

Eva Jiricna and Michael Wilford are not only advocates of alternative generation but have developed skilful ways of doing this. Unless you do this in the parallel way shown here it can be very difficult to put one well-developed idea aside and start enthusiastically on another and so on. The lesson here must surely be that if you want to generate alternatives it is a good idea to have an almost mechanistic way of creating the initial ideas. At the more engineering end of the design spectrum the number of fundamentally different possibilities may actually be finite, and here the problem becomes one of methodically discovering and mapping them out. There are a number of ways of doing this and one of the most interesting is that of morphological charting. This can also have its uses in more open-ended design when working on some of the detail. This technique depends on being able to map out a theoretical range of physical possibilities.

A morphological chart for designing vehicles

This example is not comprehensive but is used to illustrate the morphological approach to design. First you map out all the elements that are required by the object being designed. In this case it needs supporting, propelling, steering and stopping.

support	wheels	rails	air	water	
propulsion	wheel drive	air jet	cable	water jet	screw
steering	wheels turn	rails	air jet	water jet	tiller
stopping	brakes	air jet	ratchet	water jet	

Then against each of these elements you list all the various ways of doing this you can think of. The design process then consists of taking an example in each row, combining them and looking for a way of doing this. If you look carefully you can see such exotic vehicles as funicular railways and such innovative vehicles as hovercraft.

This morphological approach, while suitable for engineering, is highly unlikely to be able to act as a general tool for architecture or industrial design. However, there are times when it might help to generate alternatives for parts or aspects of a design problem.

Alternatives or variants

The difference between alternative solutions and variations on one solution may not seem obvious but the two ideas can lead to quite different design processes. So far we have really discussed alternatives. These may be different from each other in one or more fundamental ways. Variants are changes that are not fundamental or significantly different and usually along one dimension or parameter. In practical terms, large numbers of parametric variants have really only been made possible by the advance of computer generator software. Here the computer, in response to human direction, can generate virtually unlimited sets of variations on a theme. Such software can often produce variations along two or more dimensions, setting up grids of possibilities to choose from. An example of such a parametric study would be to take the mathematical descriptions of a complex curved surface, such as the famous Sydney Opera House shells, and tweak one of the inputs to the mathematical equation defining the surfaces, making minor changes each time. The human designer can then choose between all these variations, finding the one that seems the most pleasing, the best compromise or by looking for some optimal condition.

Alternatively, a whole series of variants may be employed in a single design, allowing for a flexible form of repetition. This is demonstrated in Figure 17.8. Some have gone so far as to claim that such techniques will eventually create a new unified approach to design for the twenty-first century (Schumacher 2012). Whether such claims have any real basis or not remains pure speculation. While such ideas can no doubt enable new forms to be contemplated, there is less certainty that this will automatically create better design or a form of design that is universally accepted and applauded. There also remain real doubts about this enabling a form of design process that will supersede what we have known through the last century (Lawson 2011). What is certain is that such techniques have a particular value in adding a new and powerful way of creating variation in design to the designer's toolkit. There is not room here to discuss such ideas in detail but examples of the results of such a software-based approach can be found in Carlo Aiello's beautiful book (Aiello 2014).

The Singapore Opera House by Michael Wilford

The large enclosures over this complex building are like inverted kitchen sieves (Figure 17.8). Below are the performing, circulation and ancillary spaces. This geometry probably looks simpler than it is. In fact, every cell in a kitchen sieve is unique and slightly different from its neighbours as the square grid of wires is resolved onto a curved form. In the hot tropical climate of Singapore all these cells need shading to avoid the otherwise intolerable solar gain. In this building every cell also has its own unique orientation and so is partially covered by a uniquely designed shade. In addition, each hood shading a cell depends not only on the shape of the cell but also its orientation in relation to the movement of the sun. Such a task would never have been contemplated without computers.

17.8

The time taken to generate such variant alternatives using manual methods would be prohibitive. This is a rather nice example of the computer not just aping what the human can do but really introducing a new capability. One downside of such a technique is that it probably required quite specialised knowledge to generate the solutions. The inputs required for the Singapore Opera House, for example, would involve complex three-dimensional curved surface geometry. The mathematics of Bezier curves of non-uniform rational B-splines are not for the faint-hearted. In this example however, the designers knew that they could generate all these variants at will and the resolution of this could be left to a later stage in the design process. However, such software makes it possible for the designer to consider creating buildings or objects with much more complex geometry and rely less on outright repetition of form.

More about alternatives

Alternative ideas in design can be generated in one other very important way. And the ability to do this certainly seems to be common among highly admired designers. This is such an important idea in design that it deserves a whole chapter so it is the subject of Chapter 18.

References

Aiello, C. (2014). *Digital and Parametric Architecture*. New York, eVolo Press.

Hudson, L. (1968). *Frames of Mind: Ability, Perception and Self-Perception in the Arts and Sciences*. London, Methuen.

Lawson, B. R. (1994). *Design in Mind*. Oxford, Butterworth Architecture.

Lawson, B. R. (2011). "Of sails and sieves and sticky tape". *Distributed Intelligence in Design*. T. Kocaturk and B. Mejdoub. Chichester, Wiley-Blackwell: 3–15.

Schumacher, P. (2012). *The Autopoiesis of Architecture: Vol 2: A New Agenda for Architecture*. London, John Wiley.

Chapter 18

Parallel lines of thought

More than one way

We have explored the deliberate generation of alternatives as a conscious design process. However, there are other ways of looking at more than one design idea at a time. I have observed this in a number of highly successful and well-known designers and I have seen similar observations elsewhere in the literature (Rowe 1987). I have also seen it used by design students, rather less often but particularly under the guidance of their tutors. I have called this technique 'parallel lines of thought' (Lawson 1993).

To understand how this works we need to remind ourselves of some concepts explored earlier in this book. The first of these is the use of a 'primary generator', a way of framing the problem–solution situation in order to narrow it down temporarily and therefore make it more malleable. Often these primary generators grow out of the 'guiding principles' of experienced designers. I have, however, sometimes suggested this approach to students in the studio who report being 'stuck' or 'blocked'. To see how this might work let us return very briefly to an example quoted in Chapter 8.

There we saw a pair of students working on the design of a day nursery for small children. In this protocol, one student said 'the problem is how to make a protected outdoor play space that is safe for the children'. They then started to explore ways of using the building to block off ways into an outdoor play space. These students had framed the problem in a very precise sort of way. As a result they created an L-shaped building up against two site boundaries.

Let us imagine that this line of thought did not lead them anywhere very useful or interesting. As a tutor, you might well suggest they put that aside for a while and frame the problem differently. For example, you might suggest they looked at the aspect of the site and how the sun moved around it so as to create an outdoor play space that was sunny for most of the day. Or you might suggest they did something completely different and looked at how their building might relate to neighbouring buildings. Either of these suggestions could lead to another line of thought. It may eventually be combined with the first line of thought or they might discover some conflicts between the two. Either way, they would be pushing their design along a little bit further.

A first example of parallel lines of thought

So now we can turn our attention to a couple of extraordinary masters of this sort of process. The first of these is Robert Venturi. His guiding principles tend to be about the language of his architecture and especially a rejection of the modern movement tendency to minimalism. Venturi took on a high profile and rather controversial project in the form of a major extension to the National Gallery in London. This was no easy project as his process and end product would be very much in the spotlight. A previous design for this had been completed by another practice we have already studied, that of Ahrends, Koralek and Burton (ABK). The ABK practice had won a competition to design this building but had a difficult time working up their winning entry, partly because the project had two separate clients. There was the 'using' client of the gallery itself and the 'paying' client since this building was to be known as the Sainsbury Wing. During the later stages of this difficult process the Prince of Wales had barged in when giving a speech at Hampton Court Palace. He described the extension as 'a monstrous carbuncle on the face of a much loved and elegant friend'. The ensuing furore eventually led to the dismissal of ABK and the appointment of Venturi. He found similar difficulties and, in this regard, spoke to me about 'the need for a client to let you be on their side', and the problems of designing in the full glare of the press. While Prince Charles claimed the original Wilkins Building as an old friend, it was not without its architectural weaknesses. There are some curious inconsistencies of scale and the entrance is hardly well resolved and this leads to some planning problems internally.

Robert Venturi's first drawing for the National Gallery extension

Robert Venturi was staying at the Savoy Hotel, which is just a couple of hundred metres down the Strand from Trafalgar Square. He had just visited the site for the first time and, over dinner, had begun to sketch on the menu (Figure 18.1). The sketch above the Savoy logo is remarkable in the extent to which it foretells the eventual plan. What it also clearly shows is a line of thought about circulation. On the left of this sketch plan is the proposed extension, while to the right is the existing building with the entrance and major circulation routes roughly indicated. (This image was also shown in Chapter 8 but it is included again here to make this sequence easier to see.)

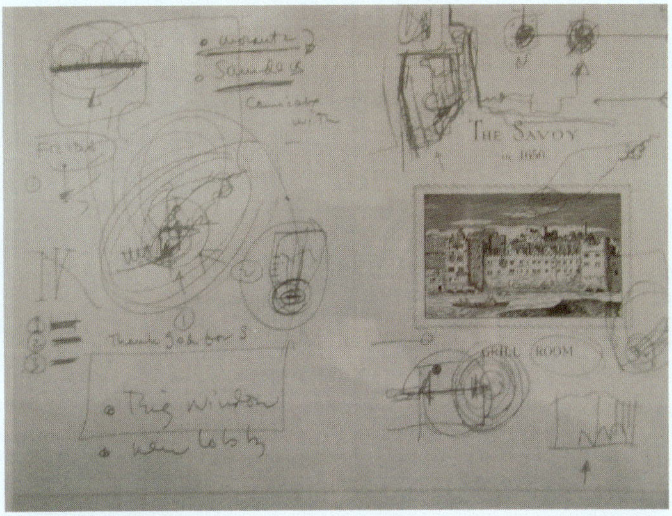

What we can see from Venturi's design sketches, which are shown here in the order they were drawn (Figure 18.2), is a developing line of thought. This is primarily focussed around a specific problem and thus is framed to narrow down the concerns explored in this sequence. This building typology in general poses a particular problem of designing for flows of people in some reasonable order. At the most popular times there can be many visitors here and major flow needs to be strongly suggested while also allowing for specific journeys. In this case there is the added problem of creating a new entrance in the extension and then linking movement into the main building circulation. Venturi already makes the note on this first drawing of the need for a new lobby so that the Sainsbury Wing can offer a specific exhibition.

A sequence of sketches by Robert Venturi of his ideas for the National Gallery extension

Normally we could only guess at what was actually in the designer's mind during the production of these drawings (Figure 18.2). However, what is clear from conversation is that he was exploring the plan and, in particular, the circulation issues. He also branches out briefly to investigate building structure. The rough circles that appear show Venturi having a conversation with these drawings about how to turn a strong axis into a different direction of flow. Even the sketch perspective included in the third plan shows an investigation of a sequence of spaces.

(continued)

(continued)

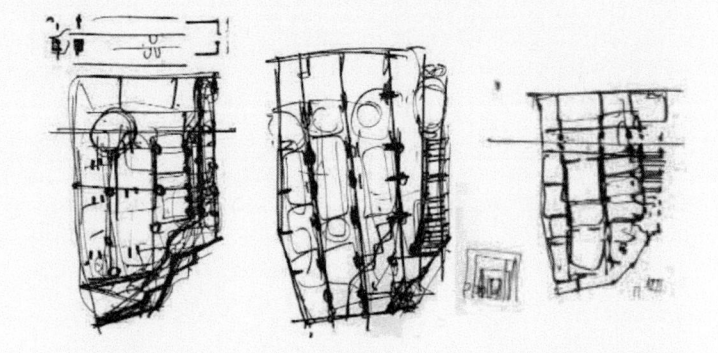

18.2

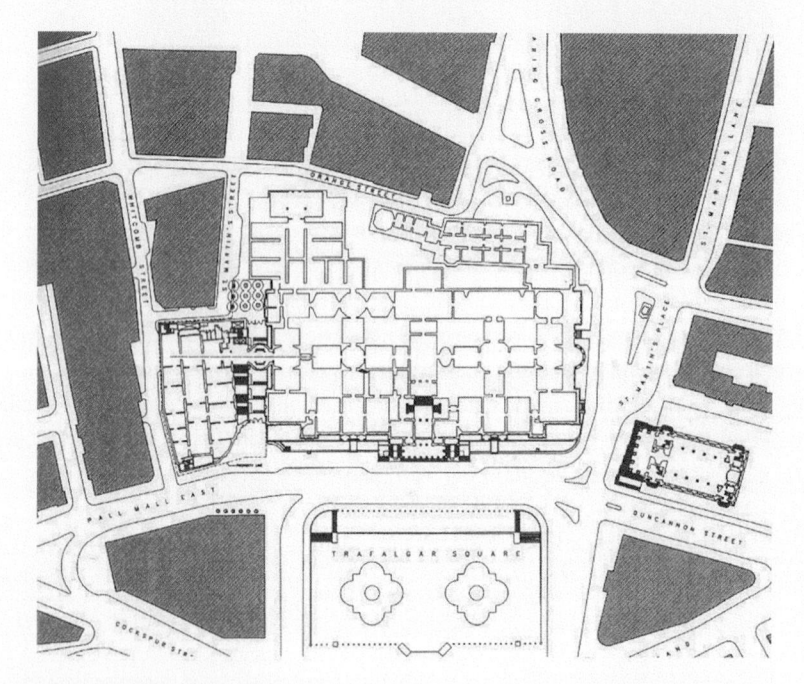

18.3

The final plan of the National Gallery extension

Of course, during his design process, Robert Venturi was to go on to frame the problem in many ways. However, this line of thought about plan and circulation can be seen to have strongly influenced the eventual plan form (Figure 18.3).

What is quite interesting about the final plan for us here is the axial line being drawn from the existing main galleries through a circular form into the new building. Robert Venturi explained that the new building had to respect some street boundaries and orientations. As can be seen, it takes the main facade out and beyond the limits of Traflagar Square and down Pall Mall East. In order to reconcile the new grid with the original strong axis Venturi was looking for some kind of 'hinge'. In the earlier sequence of drawings this round 'thing' appears in several places. In the final design is it expressed as a hinge both internally and externally. This line of thought then started right at the very beginning and persisted for a significant amount of time throughout the process.

The 'hinge' as built

18.4a and 18.4b

(continued)

(continued)

The 'hinge' showing an external walkway passing through below (Figure 18.4a). The second illustration shows the hinge joining the new gallery to the left and the original to the right (Figure 18.4b). The internal circulation joining them goes across through the hinge.

We turn now to another sequence of Robert Venturi's design drawings for this project.

The first drawing of a second sequence

Venturi was travelling back to his home and office in Philadelphia when his mind must have been turning over the Sainsbury Wing project. He sketched

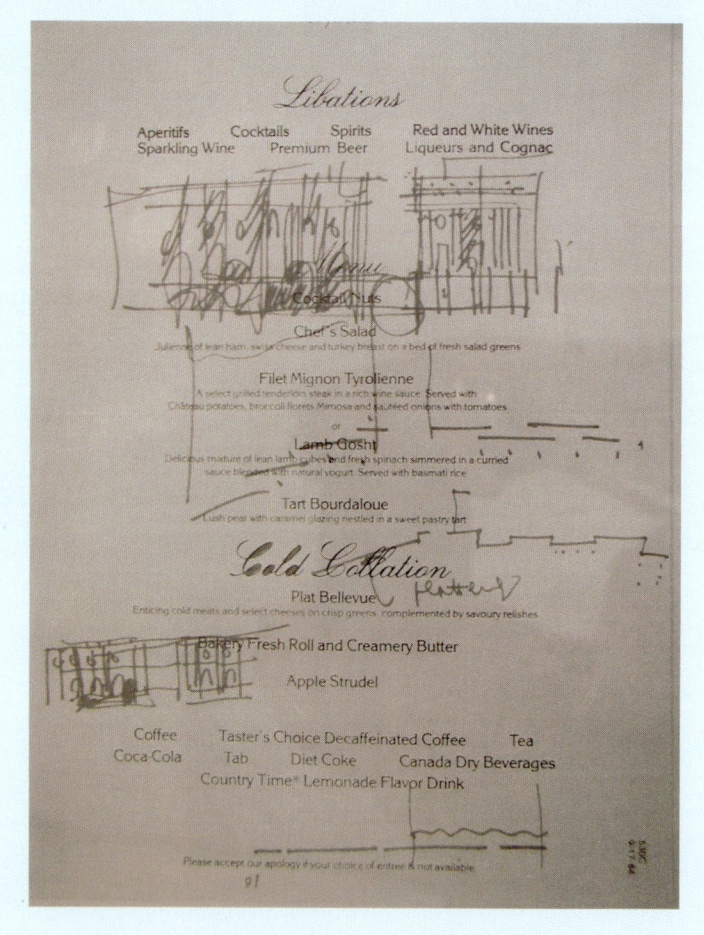

18.5

some thoughts on the menu on his Pan Am flight. There is another special issue here about why Venturi uses menus to draw on. That was discussed in Chapter 8 where this drawing also appears. What you can see here (Figure 18.5) is a very rough sketch by Venturi of the front façade of his building (to the left) and its relationship to the main Wilkins front elevation of the original National Gallery, a few bays of which appear to the right.

This is a line of thought about the façade of the new building and its relationship with the original building, which opened in 1838 and was designed by William Wilkins. Before going on to analyse the sequence of drawings which follow, it is also just worth noting that Venturi drew a circle between the two buildings to remind him of the need for a 'hinge' in a form yet to be determined.

More of Venturi's drawings exploring the second line of thought

These drawings (Figure 18.6) show a consideration of the main façade and its relationship to the original building. We can see elevations with many overdrawn lines suggesting a conversation. Other small drawings seem to explore the mouldings and detail language used by Wilkins.

18.6

Any study of Robert Venturi's work, both drawn and written, would lead you to expect the language of elevation as façade appearing as a primary generator (Venturi 1977). The lower sketch in Figure 18.6 begins to explore the possible way forward in Robert Venturi's mind. The idea here is somehow to transition between the Wilkins' architectural language and one that clearly expresses the time and thinking of the late twentieth century. This can be seen in both sketch and model form in Figure 18.7.

The idea develops

Robert Venturi told me that

> the main idea for the National Gallery façade . . . came on the second day I was thinking about it in London. I was standing there in Trafalgar Square and it came like that, and it has lasted, although it took many months to refine it.
>
> Robert Venturi

These images of sketch models are part of the process (Figure 18.7). Venturi had the original Wilkins façade surveyed and drafted on the computer. The columns with their complete order could then be printed and cut out. This enabled the experimentation shown in these photographs.

18.7

The final scheme

The design as eventually built (Figure 18.8). The line of thought we have been following comes to its conclusion here. The order as used by Wilkins is faithfully copied on the new elevation. However, as we move further away from the original this gradually loses detail until eventually we end up with a piece of almost blank wall.

18.8

What cannot be determined accurately from the two sets of drawings shown here is when these two ideas came together. However, in my discussions with them, both Robert Venturi and Denise Scott Brown made it absolutely clear that both these lines of thought were allowed to exist and were followed in their own right for many weeks if not months. Gradually the fenestration patterns and structural continuity issues interacted with the circulation patterns to produce the design as built. Before analysing this technique of parallel lines of thought in more detail, it seems sensible to show at least one more example. Hopefully, this will illustrate some other features and leave you in no doubt that this technique is not the exclusive preserve of one designer.

A second set of parallel lines of thought

The second example of this design process technique is taken from the great architect/engineer Santiago Calatrava. There surely cannot by now be any doubt that Calatrava will be seen as one of the most significant figures of his time.

He studied architecture in his native country of Spain followed by degrees in civil engineering in Switzerland. With countless honorary degrees from universities around the world, offices in Zurich, New York and Paris and a command of several languages, he is a truly international figure. He has become known for many remarkable high-profile projects in recent years but, for this example, we shall look at one from an earlier phase of his work that is perhaps less well known and never built. This is the proposed completion of the Cathedral of St John the Divine in New York, which was an invited competition. I was fortunate indeed not only to have access to Calatrava's work but also to the man himself for several days. I am also very grateful to Domeng Raffeiner who runs a model-making workshop in Zurich that was very intimately involved in Calatrava's design process.

We are also fortunate that Santiago Calatrava maintains a number of bound sketchbooks. I observed him sitting with several of these open. Most of them are small, perhaps A5 or less. The largest I saw was A3, in which he did freehand watercolours. One of the other sketchbooks had calculations and notes but the others were all kept for drawings, some of which were annotated. For this reason, we know what order the drawings were done in each sketchbook and that the sketchbooks allowed Calatrava to follow more than one line of thought. It is therefore clear that the use of parallel lines of thought is integral to Calatrava's design process.

Early sketches from the first sketchbook of Santiago Calatrava

This set of sketches shows the early ideas about structure (Figure 18.9). You should particularly note the extensive use made of the section drawing in thinking about structure. These sketches deliberately omit any detail of the external skin. Only the barest single line is used to indicate where external walls might be and the roof is not represented at all.

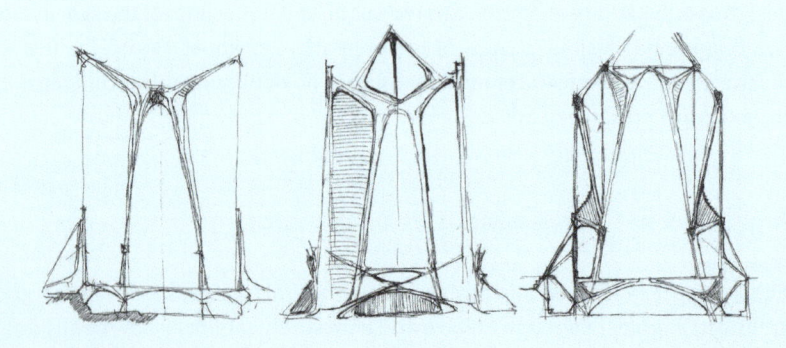

18.9

The first sketchbook of Santiago Calatrava

Since Calatrava is qualified both as an engineer and an architect we might expect his guiding principles to be about structure. This is certainly true but it is a far more sophisticated set of ideas than that. There are many other ideas involved in Calatrava's theories but two in particular will get our attention here. The first is a passion for understanding and using materials. In particular, Calatrava is fascinated by putting two or more materials together and exploring how they might comfortably make a junction. We saw this interest explored at a much smaller scale by Eva Jiricna in Chapter 17. Calatrava also readily acknowledges the influence of Viollet-le-Duc (Harbison 1992). It is not hard to see this when looking at the use of both concrete and steel together in his structures.

The second theme running through Calatrava's work dates back to his time studying engineering at Zurich University where he wrote his doctoral thesis on folding and moving structures. Some early design work included ingenious examples of moving and folding loading-bay doors that opened to then form a canopy to cover part of the vehicle and operators. So began a keen interest in structures that not only move but maintain a balance. Calatrava has since further refined these ideas to include the notion of what he calls 'dynamic equilibrium'.

Calatrava's use of dynamic equilibrium

Santiago Calatrava making reference to the human frame as a source of structural support (Figure 18.10). The development of the structural frame for St John the Divine is clear in these sketches.

18.10

For Calatrava 'dynamic equilibrium' is achieved by structures that can move (dynamic) and yet remain structurally stable (equilibrium). Calatrava is fascinated by the way in which the human body can assume so many postures and also support loads. He demonstrated this to me in discussion by imagining the problem of designing a swimming-pool diving board. He would stand feeling how the human body would stabilise at the moment of diving.

The second sketchbook of Santiago Calatrava

We turn now to a second sketchbook. While working, Calatrava would have several books open before him. He would move from one to another and sometimes change media. This, like the previous one, was in plain pen and ink.

The building envelope

Now we see a line of thought not so much about structure but about the enclosing envelope of the building and how it relates to the ground, nearby trees and the movement of the sun (Figure 18.11).

18.11

The contrast between this and the previous notebook is remarkable. Now for the first time we see the building in context. Its relationship to the ground, the movement of the sun and nearby shading trees are all examined. We also see a very sketchy elevation treatment examining the possible formation of the transepts as they might appear in relation to the nave. Interestingly, this sequence generates a new idea, that of locating an ecological gallery in the roof space. This is explored by returning to the section drawing.

The second line of thought develops a new idea

An 'ecological gallery' in the roof space is envisaged in more detail as the sequence progresses (Figure 18.12).

18.12

In further discussion, Calatrava also revealed an additional feature of his guiding principles, which he said had developed a little later than his structural ideas. Calatrava is an amazing inventor of form and his process has surely generated many ideas that will influence others. But he also reflects in an extraordinarily humble way and admits 'I can no longer design just a pillar or an arch, you need a very precise problem, you need a place'. We can see this attention to context in his second line of thought here.

Other parallel lines

In a valuable and more controlled piece of research Rowe (1987) observed designers and analysed their drawings. What was reported here seems to confirm what we have seen with Venturi and Calatrava. He does not use our nomenclature of 'primary generators' and 'parallel lines of thought' but it is clear that he is describing the same phenomena. So, although our studies are of two of the greatest masters of our era, we can be reasonably sure these are generic design processes.

Rowe's study of designers and their drawings

Rowe reports observing lines of reasoning that are based upon some formative design ideas rather than analysis. He records 'the tenacity with which designers will cling to major design ideas and themes in the face of what, at times, might seem insurmountable odds' (Rowe 1987).

In one case study Rowe reports 'several distinct lines of reasoning can be identified, often involving an a priori use of an organising principle or model to direct the decision making process'.

In one of Rowe's protocols designers were working on a waterfront site in Chicago. Rowe showed that two primary generators remained for most of the design process.

> Perhaps the most distinctive features of the protocol is the attention paid by the designers to the two large themes of creating a focal point, or landmark, and extending the grid pattern of Chicago in a linear fashion out into the lake. Throughout these two themes seem almost to compete with one another. First one dominates; only to recede again as the process unfolds. In the end design effort was focussed on the proposal of a single landmark building, although even then its immediate environs were clearly controlled by the idea of the grid pattern.
>
> (Rowe 1987)

What happens to the parallel ideas?

If there are, shall we say, two parallel lines of thought, then what are the possible outcomes? One possibility must surely be that they both eventually lead to some integrated solution. Rowe's data clearly shows this happening. Another possibility is that the two conflict in some way and one comes to eliminate the other. A further possibility, as seen in the Venturi and Calatrava examples, is that the two lines are about sufficiently different ideas as to be able to co-exist without conflict. They deal with different aspects of the problem and can both be included in the overall solution.

Parallel ideas as a tutorial suggestion

I have over the years on many occasions come to see a student part way through a design project who reports being stuck or blocked in some way. Sometimes it is evident that this has resulted from one primary generator pursued to such an extent that it can be taken no further but that the student remains focussed on it. This is often the time to suggest that the idea be put on one side for a while and a totally separate idea be investigated. In a later chapter I will show some ways of doing this that you could use for yourself rather than being dependent on a tutor.

Timing is everything

In the case of this suggestion to a student, the two lines of thought are really investigated serially rather than strictly in parallel. In the case of both Venturi and Calatrava we have clear evidence that the two ideas really were worked on in parallel. It may be that the ability to do this, to maintain parallel ideas without forcing them together but allowing both to mature, is one of the skills more commonly seen amongst master designers.

Calatrava's lines of thought

It is interesting that Santiago Calatrava does not seem to see his parallel lines of thought as being alternative ideas. The example we have seen genuinely seems to be two parallel investigations of issues, with a third emerging.

> You have to let an idea run and proceed with it to be convinced . . . of course you criticise it and you may leave it and start again with something new but it is not a question of options. It is always a linear process.
>
> Santiago Calatrava

Calatrava's skill here seems to be one of letting ideas develop to some maturity and yet not allowing one idea to dominate at the expense of the others. This is probably one of the most sophisticated and mature design processes I have been privileged to observe at close quarters. It is clearly such a valuable tool that it seems sensible to try to practise this way of thinking.

In the next chapter we shall explore other mental devices that good designers characteristically exhibit.

References

Harbison, R. (1992). *Creatures from the Mind of the Engineer: The Architecture of Santiago Calatrava*. Zurich, Artemis.

Lawson, B. R. (1993). "Parallel lines of thought". *Languages of Design* 1(4): 357–366.

Rowe, P. G. (1987). *Design Thinking*. Cambridge MA, MIT Press.

Venturi, R. (1977). *Complexity and Contradiction in Architecture*. New York, The Museum of Modern Art.

Chapter 19

Some expert tricks of the trade

In this chapter we will look at a few of what you might call 'tricks of the trade'. These are ways of progressing a design that designers say they have found helpful. In reality, there are many of these kinds of tricks to prompt a new view of the design problem/solution situation. Those tricks discussed are reported fairly commonly but the examples used here come from masters of their trade.

Analogy

Using analogy as a way of creatively generating design form has long been a recognised trick. Broadbent, in his early book on design methods, explicitly described an analogical approach as one of what he called four design methods (Broadbent 1973). Natural and organic forms have often been used as inspirations from which design forms develop. But all kinds of analogies can be useful. John Johansen has described using analogies with electronic circuitry, and talks about his buildings as having a 'chassis', 'harness' and 'components'. He explained that he 'wanted to borrow the underlying ordering principles and their systematic logic and use them as a model for architectural methodology' (Suckle 1980). Using an electronic analogy for architecture may sound odd to you. However, the important thing is whether or not it helps that particular designer.

The analogy does not have to be exotic for this to work well. At its most basic some designers have used common everyday objects. In his law court building for Northampton, Kit Allsopp recorded using something as simple as a sandwich. In this case the site was triangular and this may have suggested the form. However, it gave the architects the idea of slices through the site to order the design. Having developed that, Allsopp then 'saw' a route across the site within a slice as being like a 'street'. This in turn gave rise to an internal structure of columns holding up the canopy as being analogous to trees planted along the street through which you might glimpse the sky.

Kit Allsopp's design for a law court complex

This scheme makes use of analogies of everyday objects such as a sandwich and a street lined with trees (Figures 19.1a and 19.1b).

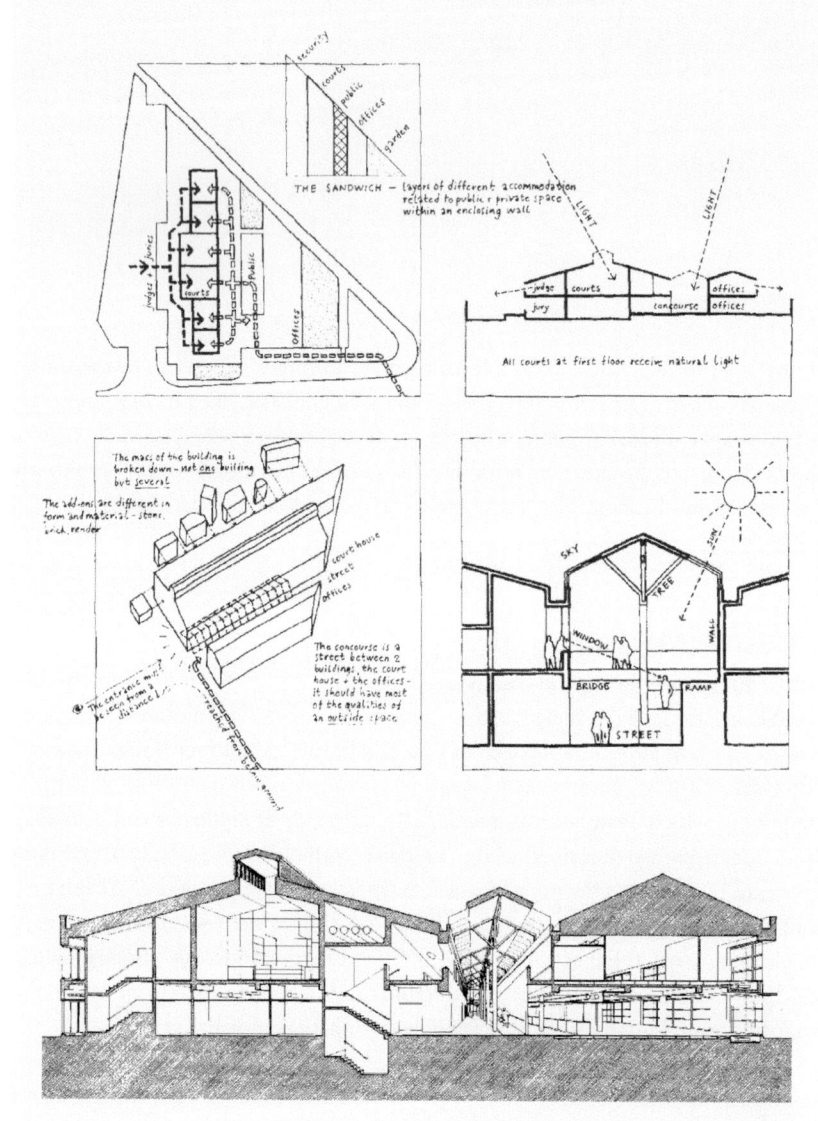

19.1a and 19.1b

What's in a word?

Quite often designers report that some very simple change in terminology can progress a design that has been stuck. This may be only one word that somehow changes their whole perception of the concepts behind the scheme. This seems to work particularly well when a team of designers are working together and trying to explain to each other what their ideas might be. Nigel Cross was studying a video recording of some industrial designers trying to design a device for carrying a hiker's backpack on a mountain bicycle (Cross 2011). For over an hour the team were using the word 'bag' to describe the problem. Then one drew a sketch of an idea and described it as 'like a little vacuum-formed tray'. The word tray carried enough meaning for the team to make progress. Of course we cannot say whether it was the sketch or the word that changed things. However, the word 'bag' was not used again and the word 'tray' was used repeatedly.

The example shown in Figure 19.2 of Richard MacCormac working on his design for a new Headquarters and Training Centre for Cable and Wireless demonstrates very much the same process (Lawson 1994). This shows that it is not necessarily the meaning behind an analogy that matters; it can just be a change of a single word. Perhaps a synonym but it can even be a homonym. Whatever works, works.

A design process relying heavily on analogy

The architect Richard MacCormac described to me in great detail a sequence of events when designing a new Headquarters and Training Building for Cable and Wireless. This image (Figure 19.2) shows an overall sketch from an intermediate stage of the design process. This building had to combine both large-scale spaces for the headquarters and training spaces (seen in the V formation) with single-room residential spaces for students on courses (seen at the top of the sketch). Very early in the process the centre of the scheme became a circular courtyard. MacCormac describes how they then had the idea 'in which the building opens out in a V shape rather like the wings of a bird'.

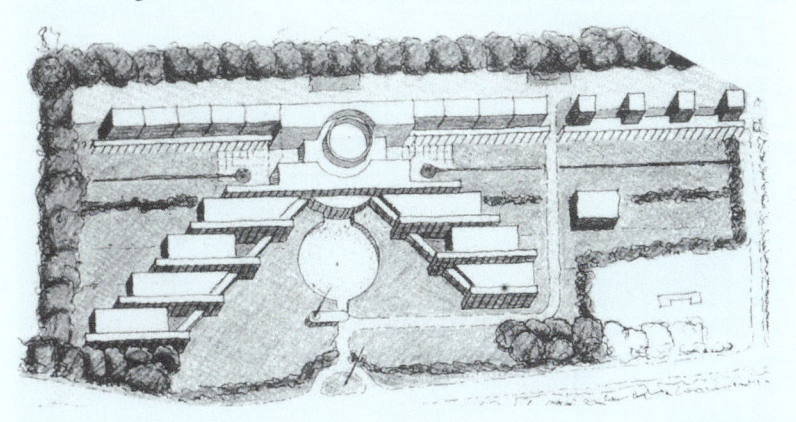

19.2

(continued)

(continued)

The design progresses

MacCormac then began to feel that the circular shape of the courtyard was no longer quite right and that it might be pulled out into 'an oculus, a sort of eye shape', which would reflect the dynamics of the whole scheme (Figure 19.3).

19.3

19.4

Some expert tricks of the trade

A major problem is solved

The team began to feel unhappy with the change of scale between the necessarily rather grand headquarters and the much smaller bedrooms. Then, as MacCormac describes it,

> I can't quite remember what happened but either Dorian [his assistant] or I said "it's a wall it's not just a lot of little houses, it's a great wall 200 metres long and three stories high . . . we'll make a high wall and then we'll punch the residential elements through that wall as a series of glazed bays which come through and stand on legs".
>
> Richard MacCormac (see Figure 19.4)

This can be seen as the idea of 'framing' so famously introduced by Donald Schön and discussed in Chapter 8. It also reminds us of the importance of both words and pictures in design as discussed in Chapter 13.

Narrative

Narrative can be seen as a rather elaborate version of analogy in which a story is told that forms and structures some aspects of a design. The architect John Outram has devised one of the most highly developed versions of this that I have come across. He has created a story that he can adapt and use on many projects. It involves the imagining of a long-ago history of the site. He imagines it going through cataclysmic events, carving out the site as it might be when occupied by his buildings. He effectively builds a sort of mythological story in which the site passes through a number of rituals or rites. This leads to notions of the design emerging through an evolutionary process rather than the normal, more revolutionary, process. Not surprisingly, he acknowledges that the vast majority of users of his buildings will have no real understanding of this and even argues that this is of no consequence. 'I am arguing the reverse, that it is sufficient for most people that they know there is a meaning, this enables them to engage with the architect at what ever level they choose' (Lawson 1994).

John Outram's Seven Rites of Architecture

This is a very elaborate and carefully constructed narrative in which the site undergoes a series of evolutionary changes (Figure 19.5). Actually it

(continued)

adds up to almost a theory of architecture. What matters, however, is not whether it makes any sense to you the reader but whether it acts as a powerful aid to the design process. For Outram it certainly seems to.

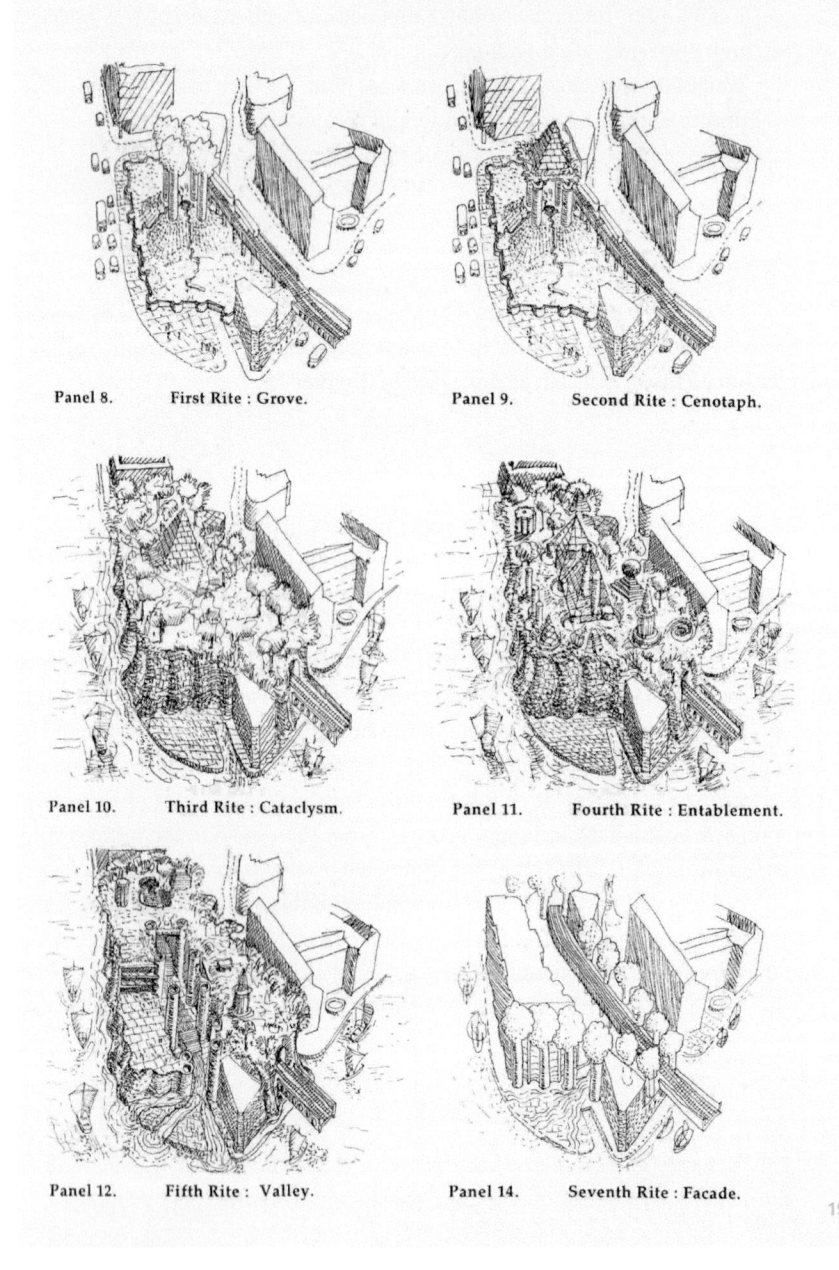

Panel 8.   First Rite : Grove.

Panel 9.   Second Rite : Cenotaph.

Panel 10.   Third Rite : Cataclysm.

Panel 11.   Fourth Rite : Entablement.

Panel 12.   Fifth Rite : Valley.

Panel 14.   Seventh Rite : Facade.

19.5

Sometimes the narrative can emerge during a process rather than being imposed on it as with the Outram method. One rather delightful example is that of the chapel at Fitzwilliam College in Cambridge by Richard MacCormac. MacCormac was fond of using a journey as a metaphor for the design process. His guiding principles include a fascination with geometry (Lawson 2010), which clearly developed during his time at Cambridge where he was influenced by the work of Leslie Martin and Lionel March.

> We look for a clear geometric analogy for the content of the problem. All our schemes have a geometric basis, whether it is the pinwheel arrangement of Westoning, the courtyard system of Coffee Hall flats and Robinson College, the specific tartan grid of the Blackheath houses or the circle-based geometry of Hyde Park Gate.
>
> (Lawson 2010)

Both these geometric guiding principles and the use of narrative can be seen in the process that created Fitzwilliam College chapel.

A geometric analogy

'Very early in this process an idea of playing circles and squares together began to emerge.' The worship space itself was located on the upper floor. 'At some stage the thing became round but I can't quite remember how' (Figure 19.6).

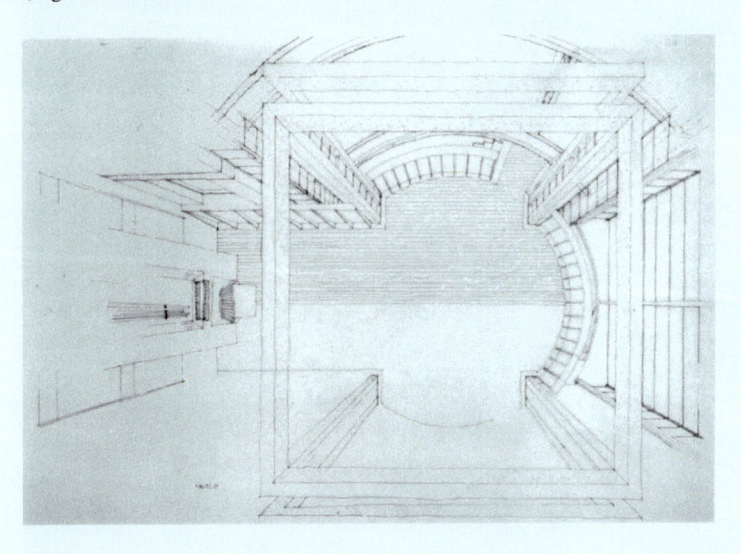

19.6

(continued)

(continued)

A narrative begins

'The congregational space became a sort of ship.' This form began to 'float free' of the structure supporting it (Figure 19.7).

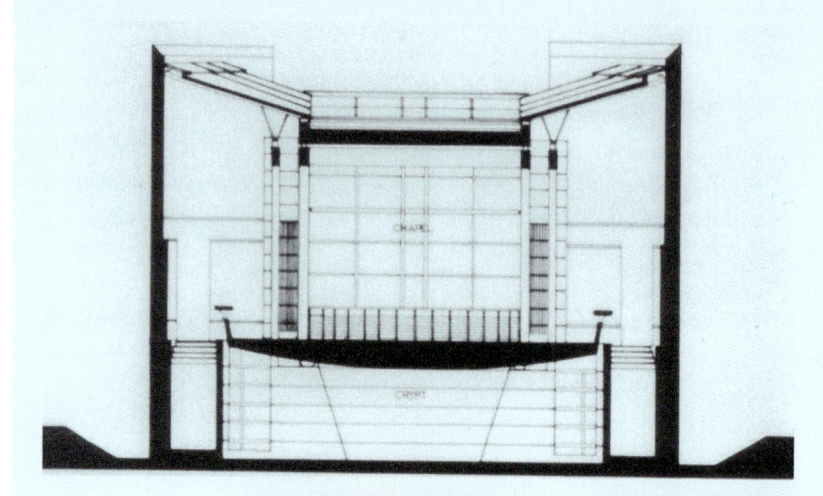

19.7

19.8

Some expert tricks of the trade

The narrative gives rise to form and detail

The design team began to see the upper space as the hull of a ship that was about to dock at the end of a long journey (Figure 19.8).

MacCormac argues persuasively that this narrative can be used by a design team to generate both form and detail. Many people can work on the design and yet it retains an integrity that is given by reference back to the narrative. Like Outram, MacCormac is not concerned that this narrative is appreciated or even understood by visitors to the building. For him it is enough that the result holds together and that it helps to advance the design.

The finished building

Richard MacCormac's delightful chapel for Fitzwilliam College, Cambridge (Figure 19.9).

19.9

Imposing discipline

Sometimes a design may be developing well in terms of satisfying a number of requirements in the brief and thus is showing promise and yet it lacks any distinguishing features or clarity of idea. There are several well-known devices available to designers at this stage. One, most applicable at the architectural scale, may be to impose some sort of geometrical discipline such as a planning grid or modular proportioning system.

Analogy of sails or peeled oranges

Jørn Utzon is said to have seen sailing boats in Sydney Harbour, which gave him an idea about the 'sails' in his famous opera house roofs (Figure 19.10). This rather lovely story has been repeated so often because it feels so natural. In fact, in 1992, *The Sydney Morning Herald* revealed that Utzon had told them in an interview that it was actually a segmented orange that gave him the idea for the roof shapes. 'It is like an orange, you peel an orange and you get these segments, these similar shapes. It was like this in my models' (Ellis 1992). To what extent either of these explanations (and others) depend upon accurate memories seems open to debate. What matters to us here is that Utzon applied discipline to previously irregular forms using such ideas.

19.10

Less rigid and more well known is the way Jørn Utzon resolved the design of his famous entry for the Sydney Opera House. His original competition submission showed entirely irregular form for the famous sails that enclose the opera house and concert hall. At that time we had not yet developed the mathematics and software to model irregular curved surfaces and there was no way of creating the working drawings and instructions to the contractors to build them. After much discussion and debate, which has been described in several slightly conflicting versions, an answer emerged. In the final constructed building all the major surfaces are defined as belonging to the same notional sphere. Not long before he died I had some communication with Utzon about this. By then, irregular curved surface modelling had been created for use in aeronautical body and ship hull design. Also some well-known architects, most notably Frank Gehry, had started to use this software. I asked Jørn Utzon what he would have done if designing the building now, since it would be possible to construct the original irregular forms.

His reply was unequivocal. He would still construct it as built, and said he had all along been looking for some structuring discipline to impose on the form. This discipline is shown in a small model outside the building so most visitors come to understand this, but Utzon felt that everyone would sense the discipline without quite knowing how it was achieved. Of course other designers, in architecture most notably Frank Gehry, apparently feel little need for such discipline. In his communication with me, Utzon was quite explicit in expressing his disapproval of Gehry's forms. There are no right and wrong answers in design. It is all a matter of what you want to achieve.

The imposing of order

The so-called 'sails' of Sydney Opera House started life in the design process as irregular curved surfaces. Later the architect Jørn Utzon, or the engineer Ove Arup, or both, whichever account you believe, imposed a discipline on the design. As built, all the sails belong to the surface of the same notional sphere. This solved a number of technical problems but also gave the design a visual discipline that Utzon believed people perceive even though they might not know why. When seen side on, as in this view (Figure 19.11), it is perhaps easier to 'see' the underlying spherical geometry.

19.11

Pre-conceptual thinking

Another box of tricks that has been used to apparently good effect is what the architect Ian Ritchie describes as 'pre-conceptual thinking'. Effectively this is a combination of several well-known ideas for developing creative thought. What Ritchie seems to believe are two major ideas. The first of these is to delay the point at which thought becomes too concrete. Many writers on creative thinking have advocated this on the grounds that firm ideas about a design solution can become too rigid and dominate thought. Ritchie prefers to think of issues surrounding the design in more abstract terms. As an example of this we can see Ritchie working on the design of smoke vents for a London Underground station. His 'pre-conceptual' thoughts here were thus about air movement rather than the physical design. 'We came down to air and it wasn't the pragmatic and practical issues about how to move air but would air provide us with the central notion of how we could develop a building.' Similarly, when thinking about his glazed pavilions at La Villette outside Paris, the team talked about notions of 'transparency' and 'panorama' before beginning to design.

Pre-conceptual thinking

An example of Ian Ritchie's pre-conceptual thinking as applied to his project for a house at Eagle Rock (Figure 19.12).

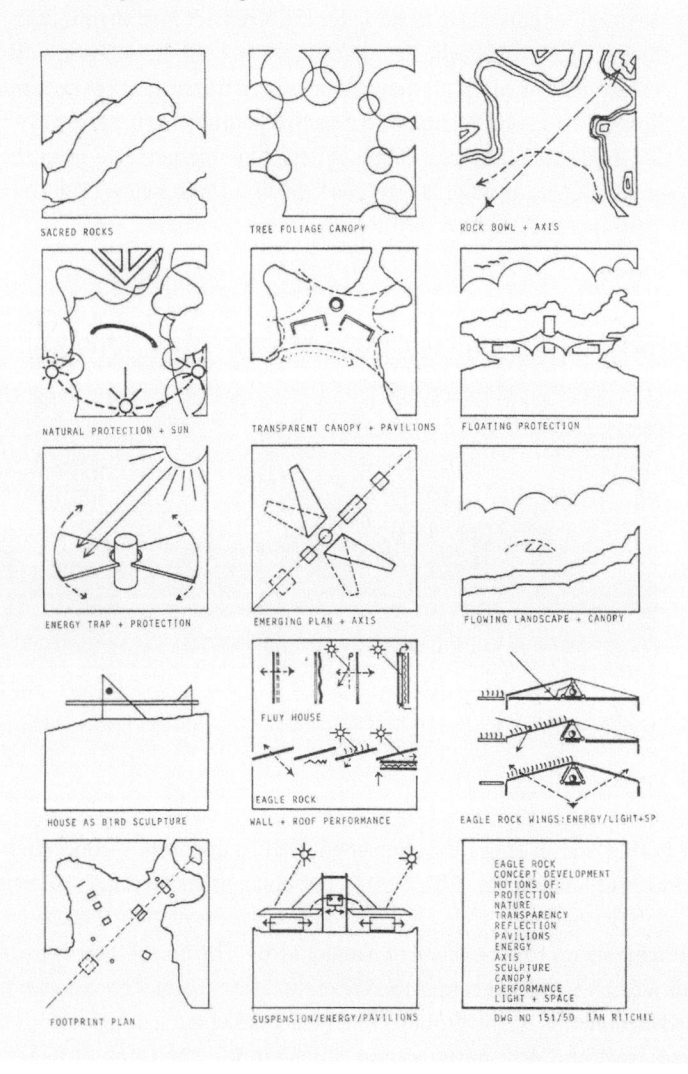

Some expert tricks of the trade

The second important idea behind Richie's method seems to be that of collating all the ideas and issues together in a very succinct format. The example shown here (Figure 19.12) for his house at Eagle Rock is a formal drawing that even has a drawing number for the project so it is clearly intended to have value beyond its creation. The ideas discussed here range from issues about a very special site to some thoughts about geometry and structure. Reducing them all to the same graphical iconic language probably provides an intellectual discipline that helps to clarify vague but important notions and creates an aide-memoire insuring that they all have equal value and none are forgotten.

The result

You can see the impact of some of the pre-conceptual ideas in the final design (Figure 19.13). As with all our examples here, what matters is how the process was pushed along by the ideas rather than by the extent to which the ideas are apparent to the viewer.

19.13

Are these tricks useful?

Whether or not these ideas will work for you depends on many factors. These are not procedures that will automatically generate results. Even if you like these ideas you may need to practise them for a while before they become useful. Design processes are highly personal matters. As we have seen here, some highly successful and experienced designers use tricks like analogy and narrative as normal ways of proceeding. Others may find this unattractive.

The words of caution from Ken Yeang show this. On the other hand, the designers we have studied here are working in what they feel is a natural way. Perhaps this can only come from practice and familiarity. As a student designer, it may be worth trying any of these ideas about process to see if they might fit you.

References

Broadbent, G. (1973). *Design in Architecture*. New York, John Wiley.

Cross, N. (2011). *Design Thinking: Understanding How Designers Think and Work*. Oxford, Berg.

Ellis, E. (1992). "Utzon breaks his silence". *The Sydney Morning Herald*, 31 October. Sydney.

Lawson, B. R. (1994). *Design in Mind*. Oxford, Butterworth Architecture.

Lawson, B. R. (2010). "Geometry, pattern and typology". *Building Ideas*. I. Latham. London, Right Angle: 14–33.

Suckle, A., Ed. (1980). *By Their Own Design*. New York, Whitney.

Chapter 20

More on conversations with media

Seeing design drawings

We saw in Chapter 13 how designers have conversations with the design situation through their drawings as well as in words. In this chapter we are going to look at some more sophisticated practice and alternative ideas about design conversations.

I have interviewed many master designers about their process. Quite early on I began to notice that most would be drawing as they spoke. John Outram once stopped our conversation because he did not have his box of pencils to hand. He went off to find it and returned with a metal case containing various types of drawing media. During the rest of our conversation he sketched incessantly, sometimes showing me the drawing and sometimes not. So some of these drawings were quite simply accompaniments to his speech. It seemed that they facilitated his thoughts. Quite often he would take up a different pencil or pen. It seemed that the degree of precision in his drawing implement was intended to match the kind of thinking he was doing.

Richard MacCormac described this dependence on drawing in order to think quite explicitly, 'I cannot say anything until I've got a pencil in my hand . . . I feel the pencil to be my spokesman as it were'. The architect Ken Yeang also drew extensively, though he hardly ever showed me the drawings. It seems many designers are so used to drawing while talking that it appears to have become an essential accompaniment to their thinking. The much loved English architect Ted Cullinan is in the habit of drawing while lecturing. During one public lecture at my university he drew with a felt-tip pen on an overhead projector. Most of his charming drawings were of motorcars with only a tenuous link to his subject. His audience was obviously as fascinated by the emerging images as they were by his marvellous arguments about design. When I did a lecture tour of design schools in Brazil, I was given a gift at the end of my talk in Belo Horizonte. It was a large drawing done by the legendary architect of Brasilia, Oscar Niemeyer. Like Ted Cullinan, he had drawn throughout his recent talk there. But he had worked on a large flip chart so I was lucky enough to be given a drawing (Figure 20.1). It is a much-treasured object but it could have hardly illuminated his words, and you will be able to make little sense of it.

Oscar Niemeyer drawing while lecturing

This is a large A0 flip chart sheet drawn on by Oscar Niemeyer while lecturing at the school of architecture in Bello Horizonte in Brazil (Figure 20.1). If you are familiar with his government buildings in Brasilia you may be able recognise the shape of some of the major elements in the drawings. Some sketches are quite small and could barely be seen from the back of the lecture theatre. None of the drawings are sufficiently detailed or self-explanatory. They seem just to accompany and prompt Niemeyer's thoughts as he spoke. It is as if his pen was exploring his own designs and reminding him what to say.

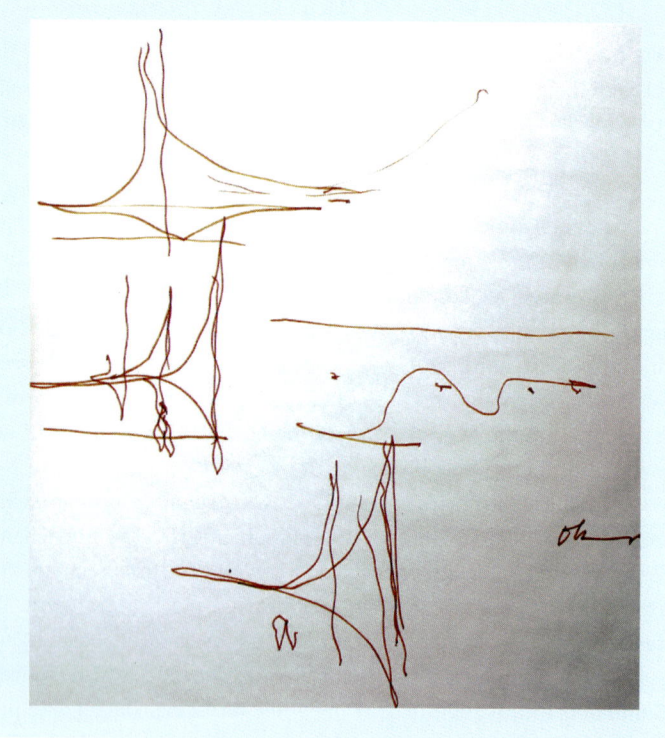

20.1

The audience at a school of architecture in Brazil would almost certainly be very familiar with all Niemeyer's work as he was deservedly a national hero. None of these drawings could possibly have shown members of his audience anything new to them. Each sketch was done at a size to help the lecturer rather than the audience. An interesting question, then, is why Niemeyer was drawing.

Niemeyer looked very carefully at these very basic images as he spoke. It seems likely that he was drawing as a way of reminding himself how the arguments went during the design process. By recreating these images he was forcing out of his memory the most important messages he wanted to communicate.

Size of drawings

Watching designers at work, I gradually became aware of a striking common feature that did not seem to have been discussed in the literature before. This is to do with the size of design drawings. Included here are a series of quotations with major designers that all make explicit reference to this.

Size of drawings (original quotations from *Design in Mind* (Lawson 1994))

'I like to see things encapsulated in one small image. We have a rule never to to draw at a size larger than necessary to convey the level of information intended . . . we always use the smallest possible image' (Michael Wilford).

'I could take a big piece of paper and draw the whole thing but I prefer to concentrate' (Santiago Calatrava).

When in the office Eva Jiricna normally prefers to sit at a table with a small sketchpad rather than at her own drawing board. Most of her drawings were on an A3 pad or smaller.

Richard MacCormac produced endless small drawings, 'I cannot say anything until I've got a pencil in my hand'. He felt both the size and the medium were important to his thinking process. He worried about a recent urban design workshop where large rolls of paper and felt-tip pens were supplied; 'I was drawing whole chunks of Bermondsey without any feeling for it at all. The felt-tip was drawing things that I didn't like at all. It was being a felt-tip pen and not a piece of Bermondsey'.

Ian Ritchie 'retires to his kitchen table in the early hours of the morning' where he does his 'thinking and doodling on an A3 pad'.

At no time in my extensive conversations with Ken Yeang did I see him not drawing. The vast majority of these drawings were smaller than A3.

I was wondering just why so many designers seem to like small sketchbooks and sketch pads. Of course, while out on the road, the small sketchbook that fits easily into a pocket has obvious advantages. But these comments and behaviour related specifically to the design process and were mostly in the drawing office where larger drawing boards were always available. It was another of our quotes from Herman Hertzberger that set a train of thought in motion because he explained and actually said: 'I insist upon having my concentration on quite a small area, like a chess player. I could not imagine playing chess in an open place with big chequers'.

Size of drawings and recognising

The architect Herman Hertzberger explained his use of small drawings to me as follows:

> It's an imperative for me, you know. I insist upon having my concentration on quite a small area, like a chess player. I could not imagine playing chess in an open place with big chequers.
>
> (Lawson 1994)

This outdoor chessboard was just around the corner from his office and surely must have made him think of this explanation (Figure 20.2).

20.2

Just up the street from Hertberger's office in Amsterdam there is such a large-scale chessboard that he must surely have had this in mind. It reminded me of an awful experience playing on a similar 'urban' board in the Canary Islands many years ago. Others gathered around would occasionally murmur to each other as if they could see more or better moves. I eventually lost, having failed to notice a bishop sitting on one edge of the board threatening my king right over the other side. The problem of course was that I could not 'take in' the whole board at one glance. For those further away this was just possible. So now we should return to De Groot's famous book on the psychology of master chess players. In Chapter 16 we saw how he revealed that the masters of chess do not often need to analyse a situation, they simply recognise it at a glance (De Groot 1965). To understand this we need to look briefly at the structure of the eye and its connection with the brain. Only a small area of the centre of the retina known as the fovea can 'see' in detail. By contrast, the outer regions of the retina are more sensitive to movement. Recognising a complex pattern seems to be much easier if the whole of it is projected only onto the fovea, enabling it to be seen as a single entity. Psychologists often refer to this as a Gestalt after a school of research of the same name that showed how we see and recognise single entities from complex stimuli.

It turns out to be the case that normal chessboards are about the maximum size at which this works. It seems likely that designers are reporting the same effect. An A3 pad is right at the limit that allows you both to reach it to draw and yet far enough away to be seen entirely by the fovea.

Starting the conversation

In Chapter 18 on parallel lines of thought we saw two drawings that Robert Venturi sketched on the covers of menus, one in the Savoy Hotel and the other on Pan Am business class. As far as I am aware, Robert Venturi had sufficient resources to buy his own paper and almost certainly in any size and of any type he wanted. So why did he use menus? In fact, you may remember some discussion of this in Chapter 8, but we need to explore these ideas again here.

After a lifetime of attending and chairing university committees I can say that many are long and not often productive. Academics are not known for their brevity. The minutes are invariably printed on paper headed with the university, faculty or departmental crest or logo. I have seen more ways of elaborating these crests than I can remember. The design-related academics were particularly adept at this form of 'art'.

If you doubt this, then listen to some significant artists and one of the UK's most ingenious of inventors, Rowland Emett.

Starting the conversation

Rowland Emett was an artist and cartoonist and creator of wacky and pointless inventions (Figure 20.3). When asked how he came up with his strange designs, Emett replied,

> It is a well-known fact that all inventors get their first ideas on the back of an envelope. I take slight exception to this, I use the front so that I can incorporate the stamp and then the design is already half done.
>
> Rowland Emett (Emett n.d.)

(continued)

(continued)

Rowland Emett's amazing contraptions are apparently useful inventions but in reality they are dynamic sculptures. One can almost see him scribbling to create them, adding a piece here and a piece there to the drawing.

'It's so fine and yet so terrible to stand in front of a blank canvas' (Paul Cezanne).

> But it's like the horror of being in a studio with a blank canvas. I used to always run out of ideas because there are so many possibilities and I would just think, well what am I going to do now?
>
> Damien Hirst (Hirst n.d.)

20.3

Which of us has not been the tongue-tied teenager desperate to start a conversation with someone we most want to impress? But, once the ice is broken, small talk flows much more easily.

Quick, slow, quick

Back in Chapter 9 we saw how design often has to be both rapid and intense. Some designers talked about it as juggling. We also saw that, sometimes, design needs to slow down to give you time to reflect. I was, for a couple of years, part of a design consortium responsible for a major project near the centre of Dublin (Lawson 2014). It was run by the architects Moore, Ruble and Yudell, based in Santa Monica on the western coast of the USA. Other members of the consortium were based in Dublin, London and Berlin. You might think designing under such conditions would be cumbersome and problematic. Not so! The lead architect, James O'Connor, was experienced with such international design teams as he frequently worked on sites around the globe. To begin with, we had to come up with a competition-winning design and then work this up in detail. There were many 'using' clients and stakeholders, including longstanding neighbours of the site. James came up with a remarkably clever set of procedures from which there are some good lessons to be learned. The first was that the whole team would meet in Dublin on a regular basis, perhaps every four or five weeks for about four days. These meetings were held in the offices of the Dublin architects DMOD so we had all the facilities of a design office. During the four days or so we also usually met other stakeholders, often putting proposals to them and getting feedback and developing our understanding of the brief.

Grangegorman: an urban quarter with an open future

The competition-winning masterplan for a major area of central Dublin (Figure 20.4). Something this large has many complexities. There were multiple clients and users, including, of course, the general public. Funding came from a variety of sources. Specialists were needed for the many different building types involved as well as for urban and landscape design and conservation of historic buildings and places. This obviously needs a team, and to win an international competition you will need the best you can get regardless of national boundaries. The design team was spread over several countries and time zones. This required an interesting and carefully planned design process that had many lessons for us about the way designers think.

20.4

You might think that these days would be the periods of intense activity in the design process. Mostly, however, this was not so. There were of course social times over meals and in the evenings and debates about the project amongst us, but in reality little real designing took place. What did happen though was an intense getting together. Most of us were away from home and staying in hotels so we had few if any other distractions. You might call it team building but it was much less contrived than that. We told each other about our work and previous experience. We talked about projects and designers we admired and so on.

Then we all went back to our countries and communicated with each other by email. I have had teams working in a distributed manner many times and often a crisis grows due to misunderstandings about emails. A problem with email is that you do not see the smile or wink on faces and messages can often be interpreted as criticism or apportioning blame when none is intended. That did not happen here as we had got to know each other socially. There was a substantial level of trust.

The large time difference with my colleagues in Santa Monica meant that we only shared a small part of the working day. I would usually wake up to emails from them full of suggestions or responses to my work of the previous day, or questions they thought I could answer and so on. These often prompted a period of extremely intense activity for me, as I worried that I might hold them up unless I got back to them quickly. In fact, they would not be back in their office until near the end of my day. So, although I often worked frantically, I then had most of the day to reflect on my responses. There was simply no point in sending them imme- diately. All this worked extraordinarily well. I would have time to reflect and often change my mind or come up with a new idea long before Santa Monica came on line. Mostly it went well because of the enforced delay. It is not unusual these days for major projects of this kind to be 'handed' around the world, with people work- ing in all the major time zones and passing it west at the end of their day.

Physical models

I saw a similar effect when I was visiting Santiago Calatrava's design office in Zurich. One day, on the way back from lunch, he wanted to take a short detour in our walk through some charming narrow streets to visit the office of his extraordinary model- maker, Domeng Raffeiner. The latest piece of modelling was ready for inspection. This was an extraordinary encounter and one that obviously happened frequently. The model in question was, as usual, in plain white and showed a couple of highly sculpted structural members and their intersection. It was absolutely clear that Domeng Raffeiner was part of the design team in a similar way to my Dublin project team. The two men constantly held and rotated the proposed structures and gestured about how they might be refined. It seemed like an equal partnership with either allowed to criticise or make suggestions. There were no drawings but many words, including references to previous models which were sometimes also picked up and reviewed. I have rarely seen such an intense period of collaborative designing.

However, it also became clear that Calatrava would leave these ideas for Domeng Raffeiner to use to resculpt the models and they would meet again, perhaps the next day. Calatrava made two things very clear. The first was that he saw Domeng Raffeiner not just as a model maker and craftsman but as an integral and important member of the design team. The second was that the two men had developed a way of communicating and collaborating.

> Sometimes you know it is very difficult to explain through the drawing board or by a sketch that maybe something has to turn around perhaps with a double curve on top . . . I would say that the language I have developed with the model maker is very much related to these things and to models, and I can only do this because he is not a simple man, he is someone who is gifted and enthusiastic.
>
> Santiago Calatrava (Lawson 1994)

On the way back to his own office, Calatrava explained that the delay while a piece of model was made and the walk to the model maker's studio was part of his process of reflection. This collaboration and the use of models, changes of scale and refinement, together with a slower and quicker pace of working, reveal one of the most creative design processes I have ever been privileged to observe. There are multiple lessons for the design student everywhere here.

Calatrava's use of models and sculptures

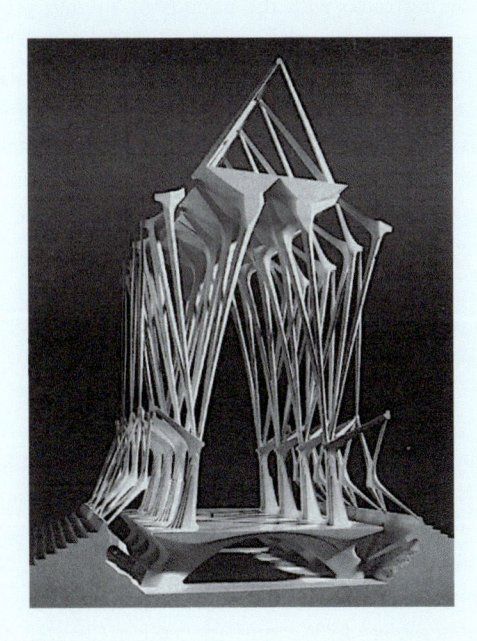

20.5

(continued)

(continued)

This shows a model of the project we have seen earlier (Chapter 18) at an early stage of resolving the structure (Figure 20.5). Calatrava's work is in so many ways as near to industrial design as it is to architecture or civil engineering. So much of his work and thinking can only be understood directly in three dimensions.

> It is very good to do a sculpture because you can have it at home and look at it every night, you can meditate on it and turn it. This is the only quiet moment in the whole process to bring a project to realisation . . . this focus is very important because it gives you a certain authority . . . you can also show it to people and they understand.
>
> (Lawson 1994)

Calatrava also makes creative use of dramatic changes of scale through models and sculptures. 'The change of scale can be a beautiful pattern of creativity.' Sometimes he might make, for example, a table lamp inspired by the forms that hold up a cathedral. 'You see form from a different angle and it changes.'

We see here how various ways of slowing down or delaying design can be extraordinarily helpful when orchestrated with the periods of 'intense juggling'. I cannot explain this more, nor can I tell you how to achieve it for yourself. However, it is vital to appreciate the now widely recognised need for both quick and slow periods. Even when you are in a rush, take time when it feels right. Learn to look out for the times when it is better to just let things go around at the back of your mind rather than pestering away at them. Collaborating with others and having conversations with them can provide this regulator of pace that can be a force enabling creative reflection without feelings of guilt.

Conversations with computers

Since we have mentioned drawings and physical models it seems only right to mention computers. After all, computers can be used to produce three-dimensional models on the screen and even physical models through 3-D printers. As computer technology, particularly artificial intelligence, becomes more powerful, computers are likely to play increasingly important roles in our design processes. One of the problems of conversing with computers about design is that they do not 'know' about solutions in the same way that designers do. We touched on this in Chapter 10 about the way designers know.

When designers are using computer systems in an organised way we have a new research tool, since we can get those computers to record all the events that take place (Cooper et al. 2005). So far, this research has shown that many of the important design moves and decisions are still made outside the computer and are not recorded (Cerulli et al. 2001). Together with my research group, I spent many years trying to discover how we might enable computers to show some understanding of the meaning designers would normally infer from drawings (Lawson 1981). For example, an architect looking at a plan may 'see' a series of components such as walls, windows, doors, and so on. But at another moment the same architect may 'see' spaces and envelopes. Yet again, they may 'see' systems such as circulation, services, cladding and structure (see Figure 10.7). In a normal design conversation over a drawing, experienced designers may flip between all these, and many other ways of seeing, as they discuss the strengths and weaknesses of the design and potential ways to develop it. We had some limited success at developing software that could infer two or three of these meaning systems from a single drawing (Lawson and Roberts 1991).

Perhaps, in the future, AI will give us more power and CAD systems will be able to use such knowledge and we will be able to converse with them more smoothly. To use Adrian Stokes' terms, they may be able to carve as well as model (Stokes 1934). Once that happens, then computer-aided design systems might begin to look very different. They will be able to interact with the designer in similar ways to another designer, but also have the ability to search the internet for relevant information as well as to generate new ideas, so they could become tools to substantially enhance creativity.

The structure of a proposed computer program to converse with designers

My research group has identified five roles necessary for a design agent to be able to converse with us usefully in the design process (Figure 20.6; Lawson and Loke 1997). We have called these 'learner', 'informer', 'critic', 'collaborator' and 'initiator'. To explain these roles we can imagine that the great Le Corbusier might have had access to such a system. He famously said that 'a house is a machine for living in' (Le Corbusier 1923[2007]). The computer would have had to 'learn' this association and possibly request any words it did not understand. As a 'critic' the computer might have reminded him of the differences between a house and a machine, perhaps relying on 'a house has rooms and furniture but a machine does not'. In its 'collaborator' role the computer might have tried to extend or elaborate the metaphor by suggesting that 'a house performs functions' and 'a house uses

(continued)

(continued)

fuel'. As 'initiator' the computer might have given the conversation a new dimension by suggesting that 'a family lives in a house' thus focussing on the occupants rather than the house itself. All these ideas can be used to search across the whole internet for possible creative links, examples and successes and failures.

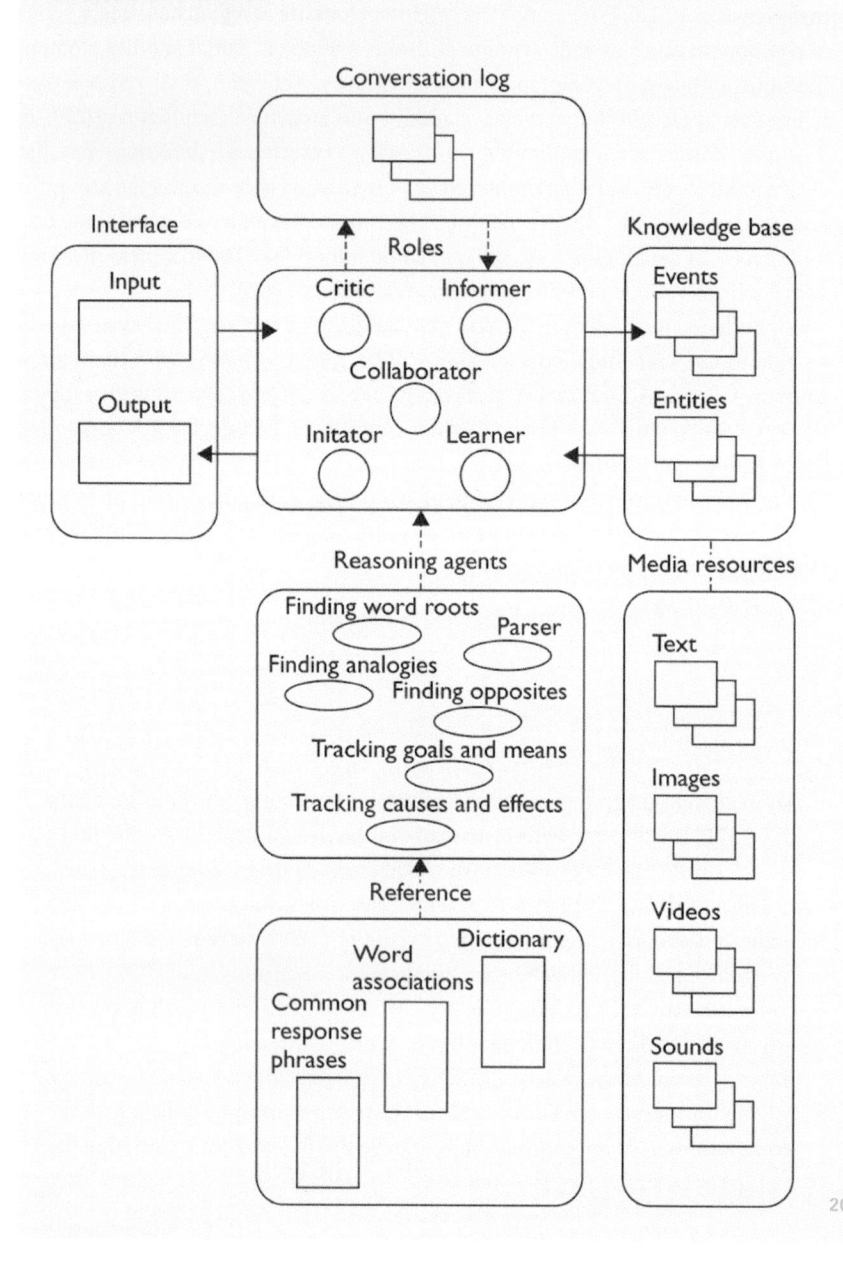

20.6

The computer as agent

We are now used to the computer as a drawing device or as a problem solver and even as a generator of alternative parametric variations (see Chapter 17). But it may just be that, once we can converse with computers through our designs themselves, they may have the greatest potential to impact on our design process. We already see computers as 'agents' in everyday life. When you buy something on Amazon and it tells you what other people have looked at as well you are seeing an agent at work. This is really quite a simple process of storing associated searches. We have seen the development of such systems as Siri on the iPhone that can go off and look for information that might help you. Increasingly such software may be able to be proactive rather than responsive. Perhaps computers will eventually be able to read our drawings and analyse them to find issues that we are working on and search for similar ideas or design precedent on the internet. The Apple Photos application can already recognise faces in your photographs and catalogue your pictures in terms of the people in them. These ideas may seem rather futuristic at the moment but, in due course, computers may be able to act as design agents and recommend examples and ideas to us. Developing such artificial intelligence may take some time but it does not seem beyond us. It really depends on understanding how we converse about design.

Moving on

At the beginning of this chapter we saw some advice about getting started. Although there are occasions when it may not be a good idea to get going quickly, usually the problem is how to get started. That will be the subject of the next chapter.

References

Cerulli, C., C. Peng and B. Lawson (2001). "Capturing histories of design processes for collaborative building design development: field trial of the ADS prototype". *Computer Aided Architectural Design Futures 2001*. B. de Vries, J. van Leeuwen and H. Achten. Dordrecht, Kluwer Academic Publishers: 427–438.

Cooper, G., C. Cerulli, B. R. Lawson, C. Peng and Y. Rezgui (2005). "Tracking decision-making during architectural design". *ITcon* 10: 125–139.

De Groot, A. D. (1965). *Thought and Choice in Chess*. The Hague, Mouton.

Emett, R. (n.d.). Quotation from the website of the Rowland Emett Society. Available at: www.rowlandemett.com (last accessed 18 September 2018).

Hirst, D. (n.d.). Quotation from WikiQuotesX. Available at: www.wikiquotesx.com/quote/damien-hirst-192402 (last accessed 18 September 2018).

Lawson, B. R. (1981). "Gable: an integrated approach to interactive graphical techniques for modelling buildings". *Computer Graphics 81*. London, On-Line Publications.

Lawson, B. R. (1994). *Design in Mind*. Oxford, Butterworth Architecture.

Lawson, B. R. (2014). "The healthcare campus at Grangegorman". *The Grangegorman Master Plan in Dublin – An Urban Quarter with an Open Future*. J. M. O'Connor. Kinsale, Co. Cork, Oysterhaven.

Lawson, B. R. and S. M. Loke (1997). "Computers, words and pictures". *Design Studies* 18(2): 171–184.

Lawson, B. R. and S. Roberts (1991). "Modes and features: the organization of data in CAD supporting the early phases of design". *Design Studies* 12(2): 102–108.

Le Corbusier (1923[2007]). *Vers Une Architecture* [Toward an Architecture], trans. by John Goodman. Los Angeles, Getty Research Institute.

Stokes, A. (1934). *The Stones of Rimini*. London, Faber and Faber.

Chapter 21

Getting into a design project

We have seen that designers tend to be solution focussed and that they often employ what has been called a primary generator. This means that they try out a solution idea and learn about the problem that way. Where do these primary generators come from? This is clearly a matter of skill, judgement and experience and there are no simple or foolproof methods. However, several possibilities and common ways of doing this are worth exploring and might help you.

The designer and guiding principles

For those designers who we might regard as famous, well-recognised or even signature designers, their guiding principles often provide a source of primary generators. Each project is informed by the guiding principles with primary generators growing from this set of values, interests, disciplines and so on. By using these ideas the designers learn more about them and so the project feeds back into a refinement of the guiding principles. This is really a form of action research (Lawson 2002). When I ran a school of architecture we would regularly invite a number of significant architects to be visiting professors for several years. One particular appointment illustrates this research process very well.

Ken Yeang applying some of his guiding principles to a particular project

You can see his early guiding principles set in Chapter 15. Here they are being applied in a live project to build a tower in the outer zone of Kuala Lumpur (Figure 21.1).

(continued)

(continued)

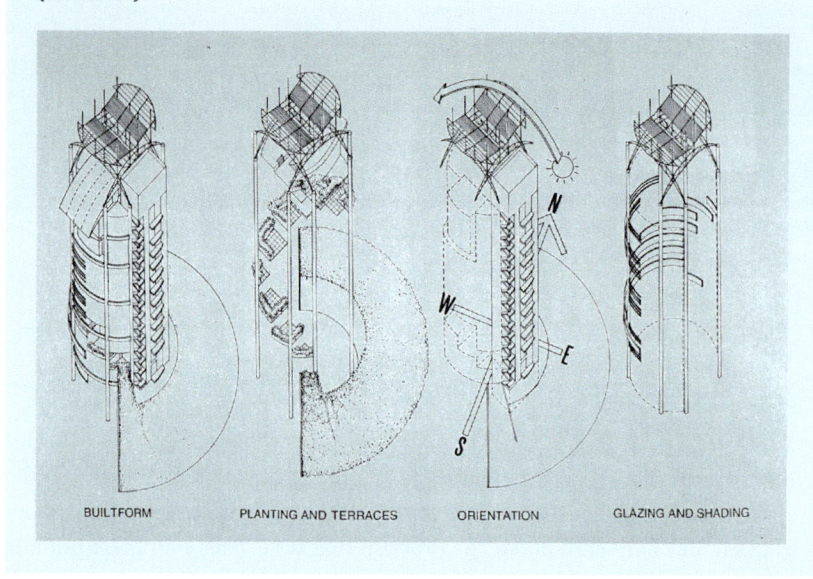

BUILTFORM PLANTING AND TERRACES ORIENTATION GLAZING AND SHADING

21.1

My school had attracted a significant number of students from hot wet tropical countries such as Singapore, Malaysia and Indonesia. Architecture should, to some extent, be a response to both culture and climate. These students had chosen to come to a northern English city to study but I felt they would benefit from some distinguished role models. We invited the well-known Malaysian architect Ken Yeang to be a visiting professor. His guiding principles are concerned with how to make modern buildings in his region but in an environmentally responsive way just as traditional buildings do. In the early years of the development of South-East Asian countries, their economies enabled them to grow major cities like Kuala Lumpur (KL) or Singapore. To begin with, many of the architects helping this process came from northern European or American backgrounds. Their common response was simply to air-condition to counter the hot humid climate. Ken had studied traditional Malay architecture and analysed the principles behind it (Yeang 1978). Like most architects, he did not feel that we could simply imitate the traditional in the context of the twentieth century. As cities like KL grew, land values rose and KL, Singapore, Hong Kong, Bangkok and so on began to spawn high-density needs and high-rise buildings.

The design reaches a more detailed stage

Here we can see a more formal drawing showing the arrangement for solar shading on the main façade and the rooftop structure (Figure 21.2).

Getting into a design project

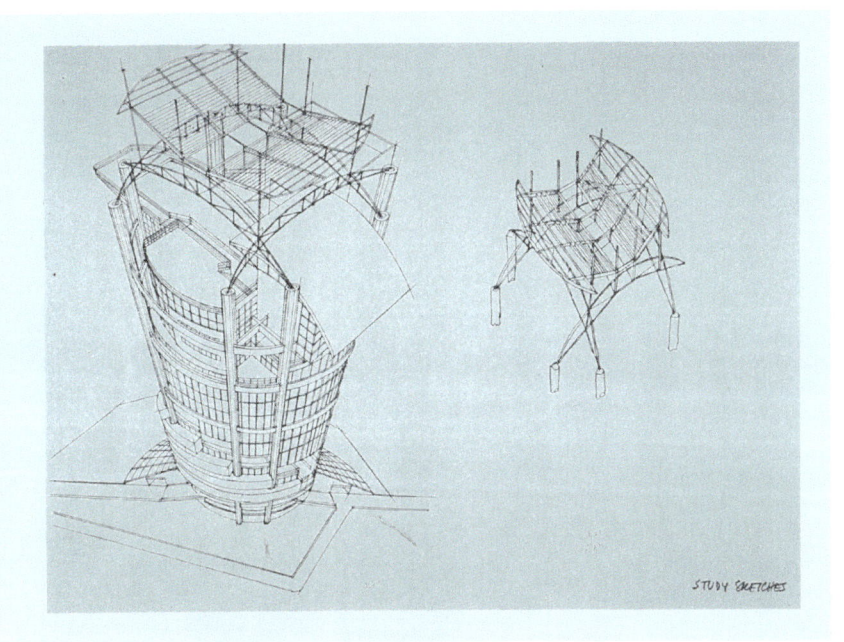

STUDY SKETCHES

21.2

Another advantage of hiring an architect like Ken as visiting professor is that it gave our European students an accelerated form of learning about their own worlds. There is no doubt that architects need to travel and, by seeing how architecture works in foreign cultures and climates, they better understand their own architecture. The need to create cross ventilation, deep overhangs and steeply pitched roofs that throw the torrential rainwater off and into canals, all create features that starkly contrast with traditional north European architecture. These foreign conditions help a young European student to really understand why the buildings around them are the way they are. It stops them taking things for granted and makes them look more carefully.

A reminder of the guiding principles and the final design as built

You can see more of Ken Yeang's guiding principles in Figure 15.2 in Chapter 15. All of these principles were applied to this elegant and revolutionary tower in Kuala Lumpur (Figure 21.3). This began to create a new form of architecture for the region by applying principles mainly learned from academic studies of traditional buildings. This building and many that followed it can be seen as a form of research feeding knowledge back into the practice guiding principles.

(continued)

(continued)

21.3

Each year Ken would show us the latest of his projects and draw lessons from them to explain how his guiding principles were developing. This was obviously research by designing at its best. It took place in a studio rather than a laboratory and was not subject to scientific methods of data gathering and analysis, but this was undoubtedly a productive and effective form of research. Each year Ken would explain how his ideas of natural ventilation, vertical landscaping, solar shading and many more ideas had progressed through his design work. Ken also writes books and explains these ideas in a generic way (Yeang 2006). So, if a client chooses Ken as their architect, they do this in the full knowledge of his guiding principles. They may not understand the technical details but they certainly have a strong feeling about the kind of approach he is likely to take.

Throughout this book I have often referred to well-known designers, sometimes talking about their designs, sometimes about their ideas as expressed in books and articles and sometimes through more detailed studies of observation and interview. There are really two major reasons for this. First, I imagine that you are more interested to find out how the most successful designers work rather than the average designers. Second, our field of design research has been progressed rather too much by studies in universities of students who are captive subjects. This includes some of my own work. If you wanted to know how brain surgeons perform their remarkable and almost miraculous work, you would hardly choose to study students; you would study the best.

However, as a design student, this approach may also be dangerous for you. First, you are not yet a signature designer and have relatively little experience. Even after you qualify you are unlikely to have become well enough known for clients to choose you on the basis of your guiding principles, so it would be inappropriate for you to design as if they did. A further danger here is that you develop some strong guiding principles too early in your development. Perhaps as a young designer you should be trying out more ideas and exploring the range of approaches to your chosen field of design.

What we see here, then, is that the most successful and well-known designers can use their own interests or guiding principles to create primary generators in each design project. You will surely begin to do this yourself as your interests grow and become well enough established but take care that this is not narrowing an early and as yet ill-formed design process. There is, however, nothing wrong in exploring ideas through your design projects as you progress.

Special circumstances (external constraints)

Another fairly common way of finding a primary generator for a project is to focus on the special circumstances or unusual features of the object or place under consideration. This is particularly seen in architecture since buildings are literally grounded in a location.

A unique house

21.4

(continued)

(continued)

This extraordinary house was designed by its original resident to sit on a rocky outcrop overlooking a foaming Atlantic Ocean (Figure 21.4). The island that gives up this site is volcanic and the stone used in construction is lifted from the surroundings.

Many of the most famous buildings of the modern era have been designed on sites that have unique features and these buildings have responded to those special locations to produce memorable stand-out pieces of architecture. We have already discussed Sydney Opera House with its extraordinary site right in the middle of Sydney Harbour. Similarly, Frank Lloyd Wright's masterpiece of Falling Water is a house built over a waterfall. So we could go on. Using these special sites as ways of creating primary generators almost certainly created these highly distinctive buildings.

A special bike for special circumstances

Throughout the process, it was the relationship between front and rear wheel, saddle and handlebars that had to be resolved. But the very special circumstances of high-performance sport and new manufacturing possibilities led Mike Burrows to discard the traditional diamond-shaped tubular frame and adopt a monocoque structure for his LotusSport bicycle (Figure 21.5).

21.5

In industrial design there is less often a grounded location but a project can still have unique or unusual features. Sometimes this may be a circumstance rather than a location. Mike Burrows created a revolutionary design for his LotusSport bicycle ridden to a gold medal by Chris Boardman in the 1992 Olympic Games (Candy and Edmonds 1996).

External constraints generate a new engineering form

The architect's early design sketches for the Cologne Severinsbrucke show a concern about the way a conventional two-tower suspension structure would have seriously obscured the down-river view of the massively impressive cathedral that dominates the skyline (Figure 21.6). As luck would have it, there was conveniently accessible supporting ground in shallow water about a third of the way across the river. The architect's sketch shows his proposal to the engineer so they might be able to design the structure with a single tower at this point. However, not fully appreciating the engineering issues, his sketch shows a catenary structure with its characteristic sagging cables. The engineer replies by changing these to taut cables and an 'A'-shaped tower. Finally, the architect more elegantly resolves the junction between tower and deck.

21.6

Sometimes external constraints virtually determine the whole form of design. What makes one bridge different from another are the site conditions, the span needed and the position and quality of supporting ground. The Severins Bridge across the Rhine in Cologne created a totally new form of structure now commonly employed, but it was originally generated by the particular circumstances found in that stretch of the Rhine.

A special case creates a new pattern

The actual bridge design of the Severinsbrucke (Figure 21.7) was created by special circumstances but this pattern of bridge is now commonplace. So, a particular special circumstance gave rise to what is now a widely used, almost standard, solution.

21.7

External constraints can be just as influential and inspirational at the other end of the design spectrum. In his classic book on graphic design, Paul Rand explains how what he calls 'the given material' forms an important starting point in advertising graphics (Rand 1970). Rand's 'given materials' are in essence the external constraints of graphic design. They might be the product to be promoted, the format and medium of the advertisement and the production process itself. Such factors are not under the designer's control, they already exist and the designer must work with them.

Using what we might call external constraints as a source of primary generators makes a great deal of sense. You cannot move the sun, a nearby road, a view, a river, a cathedral or a particular manufacturing capability. These constraints must be dealt with and therefore starting with them might be useful. It is also highly likely that, through this process, your design will take on some unusual and distinguishing features.

A couple of cautions

We can never divorce a design or the process that created it from the culture, fashion, values and attitudes of the times in which it was created. The modern movement in design tended to play down the role of the specific and special in its search for more general, possibly even universal, solutions. Today we are returning to a period in the history of design characterised by a greater interest in external constraints. In architecture, the great modernist Mies van der Rohe was one of the pioneers of the modern movement international style with his clean minimalist lines. Le Corbusier called for buildings to be like ocean-going liners, keeping a uniform internal environment wherever they were constructed. In fact, there was an alternative tradition of modernism championed by Hans Scharoun, whose famous concert hall in Berlin demonstrated a much more site-specific architecture. Peter Blundell Jones has pointed out that Scharoun's predecessor, Hugo Haring, actually shared an office with Mies and demonstrated how they debated and contested the universal and the specific (Jones 1995). It is interesting to note that the 'universalists' won the debate and it is with the international style that the modern movement is most associated. Perhaps this has more to do with our own laziness in terms of understanding design than with any particular merits of the argument.

Finally, the whole of this chapter should be regarded not as an instruction and certainly not as a way to start a design process that guarantees success. Studying designers shows us how much this process can vary while still producing good results. If you are floundering and no obvious way into the problem strikes you, these ideas have shown that they can be a useful way forward.

Even the best of us can get stuck. For authors it may be the infamous 'writers' block'. In my experience it is quite common for students to begin a design tutorial with the complaint that they are stuck, and it would not be surprising if they are more likely than professionals to encounter this sort of mid-project paralysis. There is no formula or prescription for a successful escape from the block but this chapter and the next two might offer some help. What we will see is a way of breaking down design problems into groups. Moving around, between and within these groups can sometimes help your design process move forward.

References

Candy, L. and E. Edmonds (1996). "Creative design of the Lotus bicycle: implications for knowledge support systems research". *Design Studies* 17(1): 71–89.

Jones, P. B. (1995). *Hans Scharoun*. London, Phaidon.

Lawson, B. R. (2002). "Design as research". *Architectural Research Quarterly* 6(2): 109–114.

Rand, P. (1970). *Thoughts on Design*. London, Studio Vista.

Yeang, K. (1978). *Tropical Urban Regionalism: Building in a South-East Asian City*. Singapore, Mimar.

Yeang, K. (2006). *Ecodesign: A Manual for Ecological Design*. London, John Wiley.

Chapter 22

The structure of design problems (1)

In the previous chapter we looked at two ways of starting to work on a design problem. These are by no means the only ways to do it. It depends on the problem and personal preference. It might seem sensible to start with what Ken Yeang calls the 'key factors for success'. He talks of 'having a gut feeling for which problem to solve first'. All that might seem easy to an experienced and skilled designer but it might feel a bit mysterious to you. If so, this and the next chapter might help.

Analysing design problems

Every design problem is unique. This is one of the features that make designing so addictive. Sometimes it helps to break a big problem down into some constituent parts that might be more manageable. This chapter offers an artificial device that many have found useful during a project. We will build a sort of crude model of design problems that can be used to help manage your design process. It is based on three aspects of problems that we shall call 'generators', 'domains' and 'functions'.

A model of design constraints

I first published this model in 1980. Since then, a few researchers have suggested minor alterations. Some have argued for a slightly different structure (Portillo and Dohr 1994) or have extended and further subdivided some categories (Edmonds and Candy 1996). Other writers have used similar structures or descriptions (Heath 1984). I do not argue that this model is somehow right and others are wrong since there are many ways to deconstruct design problems. Mostly these criticisms are grounded in one or other of the design fields or seem more useful to critics and advanced theoretical researchers. They all have arguments in their favour but this book is not meant as a theoretical investigation but rather as an aid to students. Over the years, many student readers have contacted me to say how helpful they have found this model. So here it is (Figure 22.1).

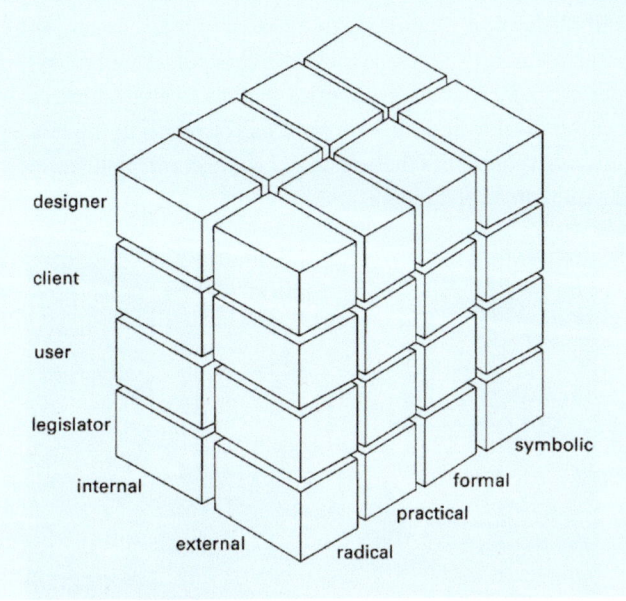

designer

client

user

legislator

internal   external   radical   practical   formal   symbolic

22.1

Generators – the client

The most obvious source of constraints must surely be the client. Normally, but not always, the problem is initiated by a client. Our image of clients can be misleading, especially in studio projects where they often remain imaginary leaving design students to invent their own client. This is unfortunate because discussing the problem with a client can be one of the most useful ways forward at difficult times in a project.

The client as a source of primary generators

The architects Stirling and Wilford have had considerable experience of large institutional clients and have built many civic and educational buildings. Michael Wilford has emphasised the importance of the role of the client in the design process (Lawson 1994). In general, Stirling and Wilford tended to start thinking about the main functions of the building and the context of the site. This illustration of their extension to the Tate Gallery in London shows both these influences very strongly in the final design (Figure 22.2a). The relationship to the adjacent buildings is not only

(continued)

(continued)

obvious on the right-hand side here but also in the semi-circular window above the entrance, which is a direct quotation from the main building as seen in the second illustration (Figure 22.2b). The circulation pattern of this building is a clear generator, even down to the detail of a small relieving area mid-route in the form of the green oriel window to give patrons a refreshing view of the outside and the courtyard half-way round the otherwise entirely internal route. Both these issues of context and circulation featured as dominant themes in discussion with the client.

22.2a and 22.2b

So we can see the client not just as the source of the brief but also as a creative partner in the process. Often clients can be inexperienced in their role. I have worked on many large and complex buildings such as hospitals, where the client had never commissioned an architect before and probably would not do so again. To make matters worse, they were trying to write a brief for one of the most complex buildings that architects design. In reality, such clients are probably learning about the project alongside their designer in a creative way. Some years ago, at my school of architecture, we started a major research project called CUDE. This was about the role of Clients and Users in the Design project in an Educational setting. We found many innovative ways to create a more realistic client role in school design projects. Ideally, someone entirely unconnected with the school but personally interested in the problem can make the best 'client'. If you cannot have a real client, even getting someone to act as one can be helpful.

The client as creative partner

Both Michael Wilford and Eva Jiricna make strong statements about the client as a partner in the design process.

Michael Wilford makes great play of the creative possibilities of working with the client.

> Behind every building of distinction is an equally distinctive client, not necessarily high profile but one who takes the time and trouble to comprehend the ideas of the architect, is supportive and enthusiastic, who is bold, willing to take risks and above all can hold his or her nerve during the inevitable crises.
>
> (Wilford 1991)

The architect Eva Jiricna agrees; 'the worst client is the person who tells you to just get on with it and give me the final product' (Lawson 1994).

Generators – the users

The CUDE project was not just about clients; it was also about users. Sometimes client and user are one and the same as, for example, in the case of a private house. Clients are more often not the end users. Industrial design and graphic design might be commissioned by commercial companies and directed at a mass market. Architects for public architecture such as hospitals, universities, schools or housing often have relatively little contact with the future users of their buildings.

In the public sector, both politicians and administrators may attempt to establish themselves as the communication channel between the designers and the users in order to force through policy or maintain a powerful position in the system.

In his study of 'planning and protest' Page (1972) describes the 'people barriers' erected in many organisations to prevent too much 'disruptive' user feedback reaching designers. On balance, such organisational barriers, whatever advantages they give to the client body in terms of increased control over the designer, serve only to make the designer's task of understanding the problem more difficult.

The 'using client' gap

Even when there are no deliberately constructed barriers between designers and users there are often what Zeisel has called 'gaps' (Zeisel 1984). He referred to 'paying clients' and 'user clients'. He argued that while there might often be good communications between designers and paying clients, both have a gap in their communications with user clients (Figure 22.3).

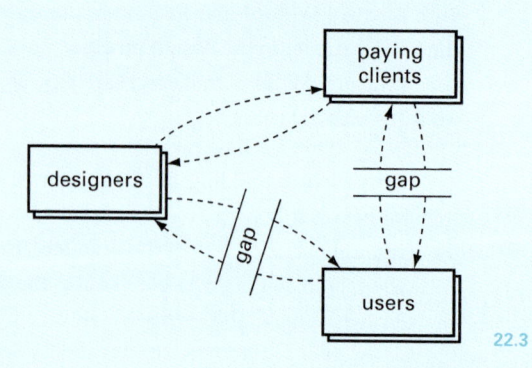

22.3

Cairns not only demonstrated the existence of communication gaps between the users and architects but also showed that architects and their clients were often worryingly unaware of these gaps (Cairns 1996).

Generators – the designer

Occasionally, it might be a designer who sees an opportunity to create something new. The example quoted in Chapter 6 and illustrated in Figure 6.5 of Sir James Dyson and his famous vacuum cleaners is a case in point. In fact, there is a strong history of designers acting as their own clients. This is especially the case in industrial design. Roy studied the design of the innovative bicycle designed by Alex Moulton and Ron Hickman's Workmate® work bench (Roy 1993). In all these cases, the designer started with a personal need or involvement in the application area of the product.

Ron Hickman's Workmate®

Ron Hickman was already a successful designer, having become the design director of Lotus cars. When doing some personal DIY, he was using a chair as a bench to saw some wood. Apparently this unstable situation slipped and he damaged the chair. This inspired him to create the now famous foldable workbench but he could not find a company to make and sell the design. For some years he sold the Workmate® directly until eventually Black and Decker agreed to make and market it (Figure 22.4). There have been several variants and in total in excess of 30 million items have been sold. The designer can make a very successful client.

22.4

Even when designers do not actually initiate the project they can still create their own parts of the overall problem. We have already discussed how 'primary generators' can be created by designers from their own interests or 'guiding principles'. This might have seemed a little perverse. Surely we should begin with the problems in the brief, the problems generated by clients. If you go right back to the first chapter, I showed you my garden 'pondok' and how architecture is greater than mere building mostly because the designer has created additional problems to solve. So, in general, designers are expected to bring their issues and concerns into the design process, and this will undoubtedly be the case in studio projects. In professional life this can also be a source of tension if not made explicit. The extent to which a designer wants to innovate and take risks may not align with a client's position and many of the high-profile fallings out between client and designer are largely due to such a mismatch.

Generators – the legislators

It is probably sensible, then, to think of designers, clients and users as all being stakeholders with interests in the project. These varying interests may sometimes conflict and often drive the dynamics of real-world design. We are not done yet; there is another set of stakeholders to consider. We might rather fancifully refer to them as the 'general public'. Their interests are hardly ever uniform and may be almost impossible to assess by the designer but, in some projects, they are actually very important.

In the case of mass-produced domestic products there is likely to be a whole host of health and safety legislation that will impact on the design process. In some cases, for example the motorcar, this legislation and its accompanying standards represent the interests not just of the potential purchaser but of other road users too. Designing something to be used in many countries often imposes even more complex problems, as several sets of legislative standards must be taken into account.

For architects, an obvious example would be large public buildings. Such edifices have many fundamental impacts on their urban or rural setting. Even the smallest domestic building may have interested neighbours. This is almost impossible to deal with in a design project at university, though there is much research on how we can introduce public participation into design. However, there is a significant element of interest here that is represented through quite formal procedures. We shall call such representatives of the public good 'legislators'. This is a far from perfect title but it will suffice since all the major formal representatives of the public good are empowered and controlled by some form of legislation.

It is all too easy to fall into the habit of seeing legislator-generated constraints as being over-restricting and negative. This is often far from the case and Gordon Murray, the successful designer of the Brabham and McLaren racing cars, is reported to regard the regulations imposed on Formula One cars as fundamental to the necessity to innovate (Cross 2011). In fact, designers like Gordon Murray and Colin Chapman were to develop ideas that created a better understanding of how aerodynamics could be used creatively in vehicle design. It is clear that all this was as a direct result of the ever-changing F1 regulations.

Designing inspired by legislative controls

Every year the Formula One body introduces new sets of regulations governing a wide range of aspects of the design of the cars racing under the formula. Gordon Murray, one of the most successful designers of racing cars, has a history of overcoming the formula restrictions to produce winning cars. Most notably his BR49C Brabham car (Figure 22.5) had dynamic hydropneumatic suspension, which compressed when under speed to allow the car to achieve the ground effect, giving greater grip. The suspension, however, relaxed when stationary, so the car sat the legal height above the road when measured.

22.5

The impact of generators on the process

So our model has four groups of generators of problems: designers, clients, users and legislators. They are put in that order for a reason that is to do with their flexibility. The designer cannot interact creatively with them all on the same level. Designers are entirely at liberty to introduce whatever problems they choose. Equally, they can decide to set their problems aside or to describe them differently at any stage in the design process.

Designers usually have a direct line of communication with their clients but not necessarily with the users, as Zeisel has pointed out (Zeisel 1984). We can discuss problems with our clients, especially when solving them seems to create other problems or when a client has generated problems that are in conflict. Such things often happen in the messy real world.

Legislators are rather more problematic. Those who created the legislation have usually done so generically and are in no way connected with the specific design problem at hand. Those operating the legislation are often powerless to make exceptions or alterations. This is more often an issue than you might imagine. Drafting legislation to govern any future design project is difficult to do without causing new problems. When the British building regulations were first drafted it proved impossible to design some types of building that had already existed. Notoriously this included multi-storey car parks, which some might argue are often a blight on the urban landscape but they seem necessary in the modern world. I have worked on many hospital projects where the fire regulations actually make the building more dangerous. It is easy here to sneer at the unimaginative legislators but it is impossible for them to foresee all the situations that may arise in future designs.

Legislation unintentionally inhibiting design

There is no point in disguising the tension that exists between designers and those who administer the legislation within which society has determined they must work. The designer may, at times, see the legislator as

22.6

mindlessly inflexible, while to the legislator, the designer may appear wilful and irresponsible. This conflict is exemplified in Richard Rogers' account of the problems he encountered with the Parisian Fire Department when designing the Pompidou Centre (Figure 22.6).

> As this was the first public building of grand hauteur, every regulation ever promulgated in the city of Paris since antiquity was applied in the

> most stringent manner conceivable to the tune of 50 million francs, some 10% of the total construction budget.
>
> (Suckle 1980)

> As Rogers puts it, no architect would want deliberately to construct a dangerous building. However, regulations often have to be applied in situations that were not predicted when they were framed; since no designers had previously conceived such extraordinary architecture as that of Piano and Rogers, it seems unreasonable to expect this of the legislators.

This concludes our initial discussion about problem generators and we must now introduce the second dimension of our model of design problem structure.

Domain

This is a very simple dimension, and actually you already know quite a lot about it. In the previous chapter we have already discussed the idea that you might start a design project by looking for the problems that are special or even unique. They might be the site and its surroundings in the case of architecture. Other examples in industrial design, graphic design and urban civil engineering were explored. In our model we shall refer to these as 'external constraints' since they require the designer to relate to something outside the project and beyond his or her control.

The other category, then, in this dimension must obviously be 'internal constraints'. Internal constraints are the more obvious and easily understood in that they traditionally form the basis of the problem as most usually expressed by clients. Thus, for an architect, the internal constraints frequently comprise the majority of the client brief. The number and sizes of spaces of various kinds and qualities form the most obvious client-generated internal constraints. The structure or pattern of the problem for the architect lies in the nature and desired relationships between these spaces. These relationships may be in terms of human circulation and the distribution of services, or in the visual and acoustic connections and barriers necessary to house the various communal and private functions of the building. Architects conventionally begin to grapple with these internal constraints early in the process by drawing bubble diagrams and flow charts that graphically represent the required relationships. The flow of people into and around a building was a central issue of the Beaux Arts architectural design process, and this was carried into the 'functionalism' of the modern movement.

For the product designer, internal constraints might include the problems of fitting an object together. Some relationships may need to be quite close, particularly where mechanics are involved. However, other items that need linking electrically may be rather more loosely connected. Thus, in the design of a power drill, the motor, gearbox and chuck are inevitably very directly connected. The switch is linked to the motor but only electrically and therefore loosely, while any reversing control could be mechanical thus restricting its location rather more.

We can now see that all four of our generators can be responsible for both internal and external constraints. Some generators, especially legislators, may be highly specialised and only generate constraints in one domain. In architecture, town planners are most likely to generate external constraints, as they mostly govern the relationship of a new building to its surroundings. By contrast, building control officers govern such things as construction methods, fire control, heat loss and so on. These are mainly internal constraints.

Domain of constraints

In our model, internal constraints appear before external constraints since the latter are less flexible. To illustrate this at its most basic, we can take the example of a single private house. The client may reasonably say that the kitchen should be near to the dining room. This is an internal constraint and the architect has control over the location of both the kitchen and dining room. The same client might wish for a view across the valley from the living room, or perhaps wish to have the early morning sunshine into the bedroom. These are external constraints and less flexible since neither the view nor the sun come under control of even the best architect.

The structure of design problems

Now we have discussed the first dimension of our model of problem structure that we have called 'generators'. In fact, the second dimension, 'domain', was introduced in the previous chapter. In that discussion we saw that problem constraints could be either 'internal' or 'external' and we called this dimension 'domain'. So far, then, we have two of the three dimensions of our proposed model of the structure of design problems. The third dimension, 'function', must wait until the next chapter, as it is rather more difficult to describe and understand. So our model is only partially complete but still acts as an aide-memoire of what we have discussed.

Generators and domains

What we can see here (Figure 22.7) is that each type of generator can be the source of both types of domain. Overall, because the external domain is one that designers have less control over than the internal domain, our diagram shows a diagonal line across this model indicating the relative flexibility or rigidity of problems.

22.7

References

Cairns, G. M. (1996). "User input to design: confirming the 'User-Needs Gap' model". *Environments by Design* 1(2): 125–140.

Cross, N. (2011). *Design Thinking: Understanding How Designers Think and Work*. Oxford, Berg.

Edmonds, E. A. and L. Candy (1996). "Supporting the creative user: a criteria based approach to interaction design". *Creativity and Cognition*. L. Candy and E. A. Edmonds. Loughborough, LUTCHI: 57–66.

Heath, T. (1984). *Method in Architecture*. Chichester, Wiley.

Lawson, B. R. (1994). *Design in Mind*. Oxford, Butterworth Architecture.

Page, J. K. (1972). "Planning and protest". *Design Participation*. N. Cross. London, Academy Editions.

Portillo, M. and J. H. Dohr (1994). "Bridging process and structure through criteria". *Design Studies* 15(4): 403–416.

Roy, R. (1993). "Case studies of creativity in innovative product development". *Design Studies* 14(4): 423–443.

Suckle, A., Ed. (1980). *By Their Own Design*. New York, Whitney.

Wilford, M. (1991). "Inspired patronage". *RIBA Journal* 98(4): 36–42.

Zeisel, J. (1984). *Inquiry by Design*. Cambridge, Cambridge University Press.

Chapter 23

The structure of design problems (2)

The function of constraints

In the previous chapter we discussed two of the three dimensions of our model of the structure of design problems. We saw that design problems can be generated by several different kinds of players in the process and can be found to be either internal or external to the problem in hand. There is a third and final dimension to the model, which we shall call the 'function' of the constraints. It is the very reason that the constraints are imposed in the first place. It tells us what they do. In fact, this dimension could be categorised in many different ways and there is no one definitively correct structure here.

The general assumption must inevitably be that constraints exist in order to make the final design perform its main purpose at least satisfactorily and hopefully excellently. The question before us here, then, is whether or not we can identify some characteristics of the function of constraints that hold good for design in general rather than for any specific problem or field of design. If we can, then this analysis may be useful during the design process.

Many writers have expressed opinions and discussed ideas that might be useful to us here. Mostly these writers are discussing a particular field of design such as architecture or industrial design, so we need to see if their ideas have more generic value before we can build them into the model.

Hillier and Leaman proposed a model of this kind specifically for architecture, with the primary aim of assisting research in that field (Hillier and Leaman 1972). According to their model, buildings can be seen to perform four main functions. They identified these as to modify climate, behaviour, resources and culture. They went on to say that researchers had been over-investigating the activity in relation to its spatial enclosure (behaviour) rather more than climate modification. Since they wrote, the latter has indeed received more attention.

Tom Markus and his Building Performance Research Unit appraised building performance under four headings. They are the physical components of buildings, the environmental system, the activity/behaviour system and the system of the organisation that the building houses. They argued that the cost or resource factors are not an independent dimension but rather implications of each of the other factors. This seems a valid view but, nevertheless, we can see considerable overlap between the Hillier/Leaman model and the Markus model.

Turning our attention to graphic design, Rand has written about the need for the commercial graphic designer to pay attention to both form and content (Rand 1970). It is clear that often the chief job of graphic design is to convey some meaning or other, which is what Rand means by content. However, it should also have some overall geometric order and pattern that makes it striking, unusual or demanding of attention, which is what Rand means by form.

An early British Airways graphic

The Union flag pattern on a British Airways plane is simultaneously geometric and formal but also symbolic and indicative of its origin (Figure 23.1). Seen from the window of an airport lounge, the traveller is in no doubt as to where the plane has come from. The symbolic value of the Union flag remains strong even when it is only shown in part. It is the strong geometric rules that allow this graphic to be applied to a wide variety of tail shapes and yet still appear as essentially the same image. One further clever property of this design is that the fragment of the Union Jack used looks dart-like and thus suggests movement and even flight.

23.1

A later British Airways graphic

Some years later British Airways changed the design of their plane tails to show graphics relating to all the countries they flew to. A number of these are shown here behind the current style (Figure 23.2). The then prime minister, Margaret Thatcher, was shown a model of this at an exhibition and famously took out a handkerchief to cover it up. Her fury was

(continued)

(continued)

of course generated by the lack of British symbolism rather than by the actual content. This so-called 'ethnic' design style was almost immediately withdrawn as it failed to produce one unifying and recognisable meaning. Since then, the Union flag has returned but in a softer curvy format. This is obviously intended to convey a softer more contemporary feel but perhaps lacks the brilliance of the first pattern seen in Figure 23.1, which works at so many levels.

23.2

These two interesting ideas of form and content, as suggested by Rand for graphic design, can be abstracted so as to apply to design fields in general. Take, for example, the design of a church, which clearly must perform a strong symbolic function expressing devotion to a higher being. Also, a commercial building might need to express the values of the company. In the case of either the church or the commercial building, more abstract or formal patterns are likely to be used to hold the whole design together visually.

Portillo and Dohr investigated the criteria being used by designers working on building interiors and their components (Portillo and Dohr 1994). They suggested that these could be grouped into five categories, which they describe as symbolic, compositional, behavioural, preferential and pragmatic. Edmonds and Candy analysed the problems facing a computer interface designer and, in addition to the categories above, added what they called 'performance' and 'contextual' (Edmonds and Candy 1996). While the second of these actually matches up with the external domain in our model, the 'performance' category is clearly to do with the basic need of the system to deliver performance to match the tasks being performed.

Others have written about architecture as if the buildings themselves could be categorised by the kinds of problems they pose. Famously, Norberg-Schulz described buildings as 'utilitarian' or 'monumental' (Norberg-Schulz 1963). Heath classified architecture into 'commodity buildings', 'systems buildings' and 'symbolic buildings' (Heath 1984). Of course, most buildings combine these functions in some way.

There are many others who have written on this topic, usually in relation to one specific design field. Our purpose here is to produce a set of categories or functions of design constraints that are sufficiently generic to cover the issues in most design fields. In our model we will adopt four functions. These will be called 'radical', 'practical', 'formal' and 'symbolic'. Hopefully you can already see from the discussion above roughly what these mean. However, we need to be very careful to define them as precisely as we can while remaining generic. The rest of this chapter is intended to do just that.

Radical constraints

The radical constraints are those that deal with the primary purpose of the object or system being designed. 'Radical' is used here not in the sense of revolutionary or left wing but in its true meaning of 'at the root of' or fundamental. Thus, in the design of a school, the radical constraints are those to do with the educational system the school is there to implement. Such constraints can range over a tremendously wide set of issues and are generally thought to be very influential right from the beginning of the design process.

Although these constraints are central and critical, little need be said about them here. They are generally so important as to be obvious and reasonably well understood by the client. However, there may well be conflicts between the radical constraints generated by the client and the users, or even between different groups of users. In a hospital, for example, often what is good for the patients may be inconvenient for the medical staff, and vice versa. One example of this has bedevilled many hospitals. Research has shown that patients are likely to feel better and recover more quickly if they have a view of the outside world, especially one that shows nature (Ulrich 1984). However, hospital clients usually want to minimise the walking distances of staff such as doctors and nurses. This latter constraint, often given high priority in the brief, inevitably results in compact and therefore deep-planned buildings. This is in direct conflict with giving patients good views out.

These radical constraints are to do with the whole reason for having the design in the first place. In this sense, they may overlap some of the other constraints in some cases but that will become clearer later. In the library of an architecture school you are quite likely to find a whole host of books dedicated to the major building typologies that have emerged to respect sets of radical constraints. Thus, there will be books on hospitals, auditoria, housing, offices and so on.

Practical constraints

The practical constraints are those aspects of the problem that deal with the reality of producing, making or building the design. We can think of them as the technological problem. For the architect, such problems include the external factors of the load-bearing capacity of the site and the internal factors of the materials used in construction. For the graphic designer they might include the practical problems of printing and reprographic technology and the media of transmission. For the industrial designer they can include the properties of materials used as well as the manufacturing processes.

In addition to the making of the object being designed, practical constraints also embrace the technical performance of the object during its working life. For the architect this means making a building that will continue to stand up and resist the weather and modify the internal climate appropriately. The product designer must worry about the durability of the product in use, which may include such events as the object being dropped, left in direct sunlight or used under water.

Formal constraints

The formal constraints are those to do with the visual organisation of the object. They may include rules about proportion, form, colour and texture. There is little doubt that we respond well to a certain degree of formal organisation. Music that obeys no rules becomes random noise whilst overly structured tunes are banal and have little lasting value. So it is with art and design in visual terms. Objects that present a totally disorganised jumble of forms, colours, textures and materials are not only difficult to understand but hard to use in relation to other objects around them. We have a fundamental need for order and structure, whilst also appreciating variety and surprise. One of the tricks of good design is to get an appropriate amount of order to meet the needs of the context or situation. At its most simple, the formal constraints include those of composition of line, shape and form.

Le Corbusier's 'Modulor'

At their most extreme, formal rules may be based on modular systems or grids (Figure 23.3). The chief components to be found in the classical styles of architecture are generally based on clearly defined sets of geometrical rules. The romantic periods of design show less of a reliance on such organisation, but the modern movement showed a renewed interest in geometric systems. Le Corbusier talked of 'the necessity for order. The regulating line is a guarantee against wilfulness. It brings satisfaction to the understanding' (Le Corbusier 1946).

Formal constraints may become extraordinarily elaborate and result in the kind of visual gymnastics seen in Baroque architecture, but they can also demand extreme simplicity, as exemplified by the famous aphorism of Mies van der Rohe, 'less is more', though this was later spoofed by Robert Venturi who claimed 'less is a bore'.

In the United Kingdom, a whole school of ideas was developed by Sir Leslie Martin who designed with, and researched, geometrical rules for the organisation of space and form. His work carried on in the Martin Centre at Cambridge, which influenced a generation of architects and industrial designers. These studies of formal constraints in design can be seen in theoretical terms in major books such as *The Geometry of Environment* (March and Steadman 1974). Several times in this book we have looked at examples of the architecture of Richard MacCormac. Richard was a student at the Martin Centre and often worked with geometrical principles in his designs.

It is worth noting that the formal qualities of the design shown in Figure 23.1 are so strong that they tend to disguise the different tail designs. The image in this figure also shows that the formality of the design enables it to be perceived even when partially obscured.

Symbolic constraints

The pendulum of design swings back and forth. The modern movement, most particularly in its international style, showed rather less interest in the symbolic properties of design. The alternative traditions of architects such as Antonio Gaudi and Hans Scharoun show a much greater concern with the expressive qualities of design and the use of form and space to achieve specific effects rather than as an abstract assembly. Post-modern design has frequently made use of historical styles in a self-conscious attempt to reconnect contemporary life with the past and to express ideas about the contradictions of a more uncertain age. Wittgenstein said 'where there is nothing to glorify there can be no architecture' (Wittgenstein 1953). Perhaps today we might use the word 'celebrate' rather than the more religious 'glorify'. But, as we saw very early in this book, design is always a form of communication. It is seldom mute. It says something, sometimes about those who buy and use it, sometimes about the designers, often about a time and sometimes about a place. It frequently 'tells' us about its purpose and how to use it. Whether intended or not, design has symbolic qualities. But in recent years symbolism has become more deliberate and sometimes, as Eva Jiricna says, designers and critics can be rather pretentious about the symbolic qualities of design.

Whose meaning is it?

We must be careful about the role of symbolism in the design process as opposed to its role in design criticism. Some designers do certainly use the generation of symbolic meaning as a central part of their process, and we have seen this in Chapter 15 on guiding principles. A good deal of what is written about the symbolic content of design is in the form of critical analysis, as the architect and interior designer Eva Jiricna points out.

> You get an idea but that idea is not really of a very philosophical or conceptual thought. It is really something, which is an expression on the level of your experience, which is initiated by the question. I don't think that great buildings have got great symbolic thinking behind them. I leave it to journalists and architectural critics to find a deep symbolic meaning because I don't think that anybody who looks at buildings can actually read the thinking behind them, and to me it's just totally useless.
>
> (Lawson 1994)

23.4

The building shown here (Figure 23.4) is Oscar Niemeyer's chapel at Pampulha, near Belo Horizonte in Brazil. When completed in 1943, it was hugely controversial. The clerics claimed that the shape of the section was that of half a bell and the bell tower tapered towards the ground. Niemeyer was a lifelong communist and the clerics claimed he was trying to bury Christianity and refused to use the building. The mayor of Belo Horizonte even described it as 'the devil's bomb shelter' and it was not consecrated until 1959. Today the waiting list for weddings in this chapel is measured in years, indicating how the meaning has changed and it has become accepted.

In product design, symbolic values can be right at the centre of the problem. They can provide a way of making the product special and giving it a niche targeting a particular audience.

Personality in design

This Blackhawk Stutz electric guitar was designed by Seymour Powell for a rock performer (Figure 23.5). It takes its freedom from the acoustic envelope as a key idea. Richard Seymour spoke of the 'X-factor' in design.

> The X-factor in a product is its essential personality; its desirability quotient . . . we're constantly searching for that elusive product iconography, the psychological bridge between consumers as they are and consumers as they'd like to be.

> (from a personal conversation)

> *(continued)*

(continued)

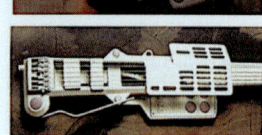
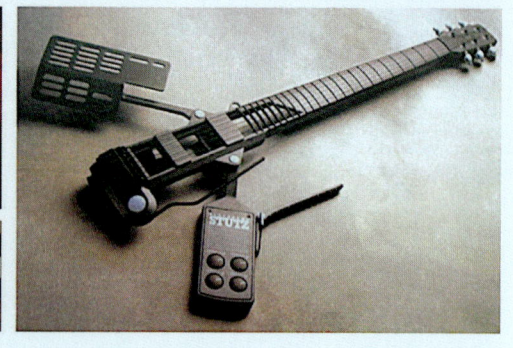

23.5

This design is clearly strongly influenced by external symbolic constraints but it also exploits the removal of the practical constraints generated by the conventional acoustic body and it folds away for more simple transportation.

Our model of design constraints

We have now completed our model of design constraints developed over this and the previous chapter. Hopefully it helps the understanding of design problems in all the major fields of design.

A 3-D model

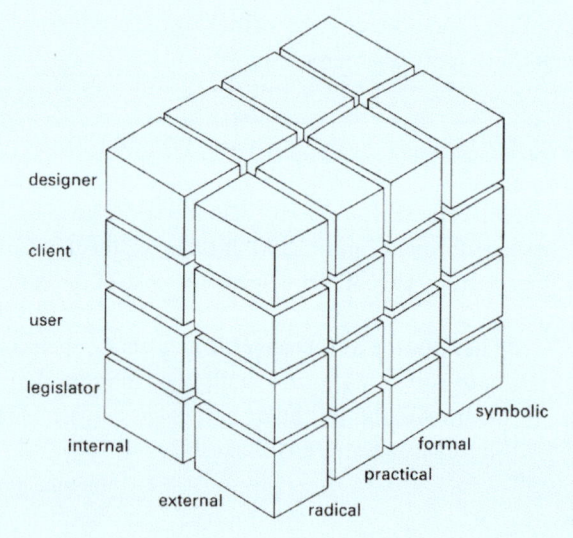

designer
client
user
legislator

internal
external
radical
practical
formal
symbolic

23.6

The overall model of design constraints developed here is shown in three dimensions (Figure 23.6). This is a repeat of the diagram shown at the start of Chapter 22. In theory, all four of the generators can create constraints that could be either internal or external and have any of the four functions. In reality, some of the boxes in this model will be more populated than others. This suggests one of the possible uses of the model.

Each particular design situation may show a different balance of where the larger number or most important constraints are to be found in the model. It is one way of showing differences between design problems and perhaps even design fields. However, there are many other ways the model can be used as a design aid and we shall explore some of them in the next chapter.

References

Edmonds, E. A. and L. Candy (1996). "Supporting the creative user: a criteria based approach to interaction design". *Creativity and Cognition*. L. Candy and E. A. Edmonds. Loughborough, LUTCHI: 57–66.

Heath, T. (1984). *Method in Architecture*. Chichester, Wiley.

Hillier, B. and A. Leaman (1972). "A new approach to architectural research". *RIBA Journal* 79(12).

Lawson, B. R. (1994). *Design in Mind*. Oxford, Butterworth Architecture.

Le Corbusier (1946). *Towards a New Architecture*. London, The Architectural Press.

March, L. and P. Steadman (1974). *The Geometry of Environment*. London, Methuen.

Norberg-Schulz, C. (1963). *Intentions in Architecture*. Cambridge, MA, MIT Press.

Portillo, M. and J. H. Dohr (1994). "Bridging process and structure through criteria". *Design Studies* 15(4): 403–416.

Rand, P. (1970). *Thoughts on Design*. London, Studio Vista.

Ulrich, R. S. (1984). "View through a window may influence recovery from surgery". *Science* 224(4647): 420–421.

Wittgenstein, L. (1953). *Philosophical Investigations*. Oxford, Basil Blackwell.

Chapter 24

Navigating your design problem

Using the model as a design aid

The simple model of design constraints developed in the previous chapters can be an aid in design and many have contacted me over the years to say they have found it useful. There are several ways to incorporate it into your design process if you find it helpful.

It can form a sort of three-dimensional checklist of problems to work on. From time to time you might find it useful to ask where the issues are that you have been concentrating on. Have you become fixated on issues from some part or parts of the model? If so, perhaps it might be worth consciously moving to another part of the model for a while to see what that brings. Are there some areas you still have to work on?

Using the model to get going

Another question that you might use the model to help answer is 'are there some areas of this particular problem that seem critical?' Perhaps you might think of them as what Ken Yeang calls the 'key factors for success'. If so, maybe trying to work on them to begin with might be a useful idea. Perhaps you can create a primary generator by trying to solve these problems. Playing around with this idea might then lead you on to other parts of the problem.

Key factors for success

In using the model it might be useful to think about what Ken Yeang calls 'key factors for success'.

> We look at each project and try to see it from the client's point of view . . . and then we try to have a feel about what is the big idea, what are the key factors for success . . . a useful guideline is to ask early on to what extent the building exists as a symbol, as an enclosure, a marketable product or as an investment.
>
> (Lawson 1994)

There are two little caveats here. First, be prepared to abandon your primary generator later if, when it is tested, it seems to cause more problems than it solves. Even if that happens, it will have still got you going and got you well into the problem at hand.

Second, even though we have used Ken Yeang's idea of key factors for success here, he prefers to work in a more intuitive manner. Of course he is far more experienced than you are likely to be. One of the skills that more expert designers seem to have is to find the core issues in a problem very quickly.

A word of caution from Ken Yeang

We have seen that this model can be used to help think about the process, to check what has and has not been worked on, or what seems critically important. But one of our frequently quoted master designers reminds us that, eventually, this should perhaps all be less self-conscious.

> I trust the gut feeling, the intuitive hand, the intuitive feel about the project . . . you can technically solve accommodation problems, you can solve problems of view and so on but which problem to solve first is a gut feeling . . . you can't explain it but you feel that's right and nine times out of ten you are right.
>
> (Lawson 1994)

Use the model to check your work is comprehensive

It is frighteningly easy to get fixated on an idea that you like for some reason. You can then become blind to the shortcomings of a design that grows out of this proposition. This is another of those common faults that I find when I sit down at a student's drawing board for a design tutorial. Of course you can rely on your tutor or other students to help you see this, but how much better is it to be able to see your own faults? Unless you can criticise not only your own work but also your process you are not going to become an expert designer. Try using the model to find other parts of the problem that you might have given little or no attention to. It might be worth taking a 'timeout' every now and then to look at the model and see if you can find fault with the ideas you are developing.

Use the model when you are stuck

One of the tutors I found most helpful when I was a student had a number of useful prompts that he was fond of, and one in particular is at the root of this idea. He would often listen to me describe where I had got to with my design and why. He would then inevitably ask what I was going to do next. I would usually raise some conflicts that I had been trying to find a way round but just could not resolve. Perhaps my design was not very elegant in some way. I was hoping he would then suggest some clever way forward, but, being a good tutor, he knew it was not his job to create the solution but to help me to do it for myself. His favourite trick was to suggest that I should add in yet another problem. This might sound perverse but it can distract the mind away from its endless cycling around the same issues and thus create new opportunities. So, how do we find a new problem to tackle? You can scan around the model to see if you can find a new problem to work on. See if you can incorporate a solution to it into your existing ideas or maybe find a new set of generative proposals.

This will not always work but when you are stuck you have little to lose. The analogy here is with that simple aphorism promoted in so many books by Edward de Bono. If you are not getting anywhere you can either keep digging the same hole even deeper or you can start to dig a new hole. This is the basis of 'lateral thinking' (de Bono 1967).

Overcoming familiarity

Sometimes you can get so familiar with a design situation that it is difficult to move on from existing ideas. The Dutch industrial designer Theo Groothuizen created a clever triangular design for a telephone booth and became a consultant to PTT, the Dutch telecom company. He admits to having difficulties created by over-familiarity with this area when he designs telephone booths.

Familiarity – Theo Groothuizen

When you have a lot of knowledge in a field, that is comfortable but it is also limiting. I notice when I design telephone booths I know so much about telephone booths that designing one becomes more and more difficult. Because if you did a good job on the last one, then that contains many of the optimal solutions, or the optimal choices that fit me as a designer. (Figure 24.1.)

(Lawson and Dorst 2009)

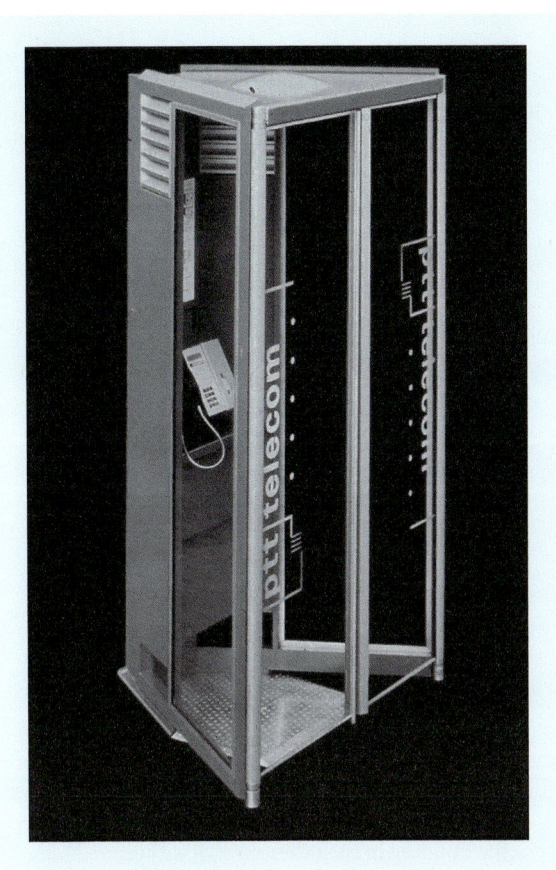

As a student designer, you are not likely to suffer from this problem of having designed for the problem before. You may find, as many students do, that you look at other designs and find them so good that somehow it is difficult to break away from them. When I find this in a student design tutorial I usually suggest looking hard to find a way in which your problem is different to the ones already worked on. Perhaps the model of design problem structure might help you search for this. It is then just possible that you can learn from previous designs and yet find your own way forward.

Integration again

A word of caution here takes us right back to Chapter 5 when we discussed integration. The cartwheel and other examples showed how a single idea in the solution can be used to solve many problems. To achieve this, it is likely that you must first do a lot of work creating ideas from primary generators, possibly using parallel lines of thought, before that single solution idea appears.

A motorway service station

This motorway service station has a cross section that is extruded to form most of the building with only minor variations at the ends (Figure 24.2).

24.2

The interior of the motorway service station

Looking down the inside of the building in the other direction (Figure 24.3). The servery is to the left. The seating areas are to the right. The clever section here solves so many problems.

24.3

The humble motorway services building shown here offers a simple example of the integrative idea. There are just a few key ideas in this design. It is what architects might describe as a 'section building', by which they mean the cross section is the clue to how the building works. This, of course, is a sophisticated schema shared by architects.

In this case you can see that one section runs nearly the whole length of the building with only minor changes at the ends. The major function of this building is indeed a sort of linear activity. People must come in, perhaps queue, and move along a servery collecting food, pay for their food, and find a table at which to sit down and eat their meal. This main activity follows the change in the roof section, creating a strong feeling of circulating along this line. The split roof also separates public space from the 'behind the scenes' kitchen, stores and other working spaces only entered by the staff. The highest part of the ceiling accommodates the most public space, with lower, more intimate, sitting spaces for the area where meals are eaten. The split in the roof that organises the structure also allows for glazing that will flood the lower spaces with natural daylight. Uplighting can be mounted here to create the same feeling at night. In addition, this part of the section allows for air extraction immediately over the servery where the greatest need would be. The whole section creates a 'front of house' to 'back of house' divide, enabling deliveries to be made out of sight and separates deliveries at one end from rubbish collections at the other, as required by legislation. The deep overhanging roof on the public side, together with landscaping, prevents noise from the busy motorway annoying those eating their meals and creates the opportunity to use protected outdoor space. Finally, the boiler room and flue compose well against the section and point to the entrance as the building comes into view from behind the grass banking.

Exterior space

24.4

(continued)

(continued)

The exterior shows how the ground works complete the functionality by combining with the deep overhanging roof to make a quiet sheltered garden free of noise and visual pollution from the adjacent motorway (Figure 24.4).

Whether you like this architecture or not is unimportant but you should be able to see that it is a clever and well-worked-out proposition. Problems of circulation, legislation, structure, ventilation, noise control, lighting, view and scale, and the creation of appropriate public spaces as well as places to sit, are all solved, and mostly this is done through the section. This might look easy to do but probably only came after a lot of hard work. It creates a very useful precedent for future designers.

So now to the word of caution. Simply using the model to solve parts of the problem in each of the boxes will not necessarily lead you to the kind of elegantly integrated solution we see here. Remember that designers tend to work in a solution-focussed manner and the model cannot give us that focus, so it would be unwise to allow its use to dominate your process. It can, however, help when you are stuck, or maybe when you cannot seem to get started, or just to check that you have covered all the important parts of the problem.

References

de Bono, E. (1967). *The Use of Lateral Thinking*. London, Jonathan Cape.

Lawson, B. R. (1994). *Design in Mind*. Oxford, Butterworth Architecture.

Lawson, B. R. and C. H. Dorst (2009). *Design Expertise*. Oxford, Elsevier/Architectural Press.

Chapter 25

How are you getting on?

It is not easy to specify exactly what skills, knowledge and understanding you should have at each level of design-based courses. As we have seen, designing involves a multitude of skills. It is therefore quite reasonable to expect that students studying a design-based course might not all have reached the same level for all the required skills. It is also unlikely that students arrive with the same set of skills. In architecture, for example, there is no equivalent subject that can be studied at school. Some may have studied art and have well-developed graphical skills. Others might have studied maths or physics and be good at the science of buildings and structures. So it is sensible to regard the first year as a sort of foundation; a platform on which all students can build during the rest of the course. In the UK, it has been common practice for the art and design faculties to recognise this and to run a foundation year before students begin the various art and design degrees. Interestingly, this also provides the opportunity for students to change their mind about the specific degree they want to study.

Models of expertise

There are now some fairly well respected models of expertise. In particular, Dreyfus has proposed a generic model with six distinct levels (Dreyfus and Dreyfus 2005). These models are effectively a staircase with distinct steps or stages. Developing skill is not a steady process but often one of fits and starts. It is now generally accepted that people on higher steps of these models do not do the same thing as people on lower steps. Expertise is not just a matter of getting quicker or better at a skill. We saw a very good example of this in Chapter 16 where we used chess playing as a model. The expert chess player does little board analysis but rather recognises a standard pattern or some close variant and immediately knows what standard moves are available, together with all their potential advantages and disadvantages.

However, it is not quite this simple. To see this we return to the earlier example of learning to play the flute (Chapter 8). As with design, there are many skills here. There is the ability to read music, forming the embouchure to make the flute sound, learning the fingering patterns to produce the notes, mastering breathing and breath control to give qualities of sound and so on. Actually, the skills required are a little more complex because the flute does not naturally play in tune across the full range. For our example, we will forget all the sophisticated complexities of making good sounds and reduce the task to one simple objective. How does a flautist learn all the fingering patterns so that all the notes in any scale can be played correctly and in the right order from memory?

The flute fingering chart

This chart (Figure 25.1) shows part of the flute's range and the pattern of keys and fingers that must be used to get the basic notes. In fact, the embouchure (mouth position and shape) and breathing are also needed to get the perfect pitch of many notes and there are many alternative fingerings for tricky situations. However, no one has ever become even a competent flautist without learning at least these basic fingering patterns.

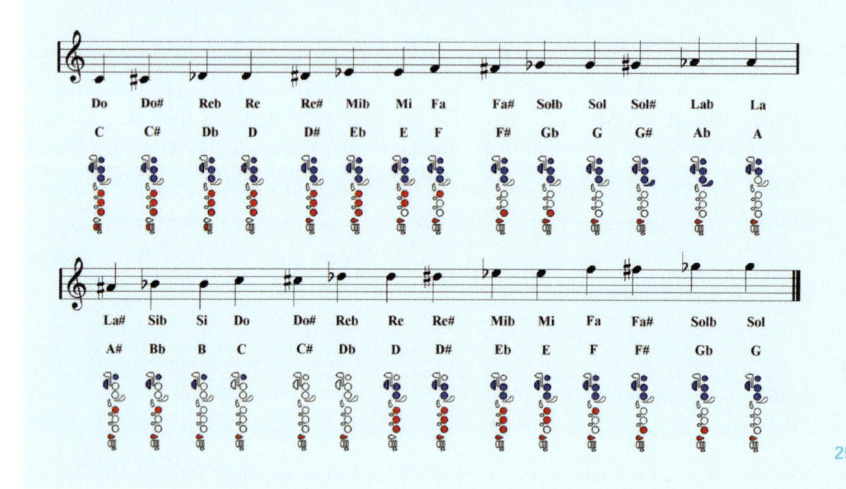

25.1

A beginner on the flute must learn all these fingering patterns and associate them with the notes as written on the music stave. A basic exercise to learn these is to play the various scales in all the common keys, usually starting with C major, which has no sharps or flats (i.e., uses only white keys on the piano). These scales must be so well known that you can play them from memory. The question is, how does a flautist remember all this information?

One way of remembering all this is to imagine the chart you see in Figure 25.1. This chart, however, shows how to play a chromatic scale. That is one with all the flats or sharps included. Another way is to imagine the piano keyboard laid out in front of you as shown in Figure 25.2. The attraction of this is that it represents a left-to-right sequence from low notes to high notes. To play a scale of C major here you just use only the white notes starting on a C, which is the white key immediately to the left of the pair of black keys. A pianist then can just hit all the white keys in the same order they appear on the keyboard and this will result in a scale of C major. Unfortunately for the flautist, the way fingers go up and down does not follow any pattern of rules. You just have to learn them all individually. However, if you link a memory of those fingerings to an image of the keyboard the flautist can also play a correct scale. All this is hard enough to learn, but it remains rather a cumbersome way of storing knowledge. To have to remember all this every time you play a note would be slow and tedious.

The musical scale and the piano keyboard

This piano keyboard is effectively a diagram of the notes available (Figure 25.2). They progress from left to right, going up in pitch as they do so. The familiar pattern of groups of two and three black keys, representing the sharp or flat notes, is also diagrammatic. The flute gives the player no such simple diagram.

25.2

Probably the most reliable and smoothest of all ways of remembering how to play sequences of notes is through body memory. You remember how your body feels for all the positions of all your fingers (and mouth) for each note.

Of course there is no real picture of this, as we cannot represent this kind of memory in an image. However, the picture in Figure 25.3 at least makes the point that the poor flautist cannot actually see their fingers, as both hands are way out to the right-hand side of the head.

Playing the flute from body memory

Flautists may be able to see the music in front of them but they cannot see their fingers on the keys (Figure 25.3). The beginner often stops and moves the flute to see where the fingers are, which is a hopelessly halting way to play. The more expert flautist knows what it feels like to be playing each note.

25.3

This body memory eventually not only includes the notes themselves but what it feels like to move from one note to another. This higher level of expertise only comes after a good deal of practice. However, the earlier memories are not lost. The most skilled of players can think in all of these patterns. In some musical contexts each of these ways of remembering has its benefits and disadvantages. Of course, when playing a real piece of music, so many situations will arise, making it valuable to have many alternative ways of remembering. The important principle here is that experts usually gather more sophisticated ways of doing things but do not substitute these for the simpler methods, rather they add to their toolkit as it were. Designers are no different.

The design expertise staircase

Kees Dorst and I have tried to relate this to designing (Lawson and Dorst 2009) but this model cannot yet be seen to be complete or accurate since so many skills and levels of attainment are possible. It remains to be seen through more research just how well we can map all these onto a single model and whether that would then be sufficiently simple and understandable to be of use when learning to design. For now, it is a useful way to break things down so you can see the sorts of skills and attainment levels you are likely to go through in learning to become a designer.

The design expertise staircase

For several years I have been looking for a way of graphically representing the process of acquiring design expertise. Kees Dorst and I embarked on a project of trying to map this out and our best efforts can be found in the book that has often been referred to here (Lawson and Dorst 2009).

25.4

(continued)

First, we do see this as a set of stages representing the development of different skills. It seems inevitable that the progression must be in a set order. You cannot master the most advanced skills unless you have already mastered the more basic ones. So we portray this not as a continuous ramp but as a staircase. This is in line with general models of skill acquisition. One can even see this pattern in the early years of development of the child. The models of these years do not show a strict timetable but it is a predictable sequence. Each child is likely to work to its own particular timetable but this follows a more or less predictable order.

You arrive at design school already being a designer, an everyday designer. Our discussion of that idea was introduced in Chapter 2. This forms a sort of platform or foundation from which the staircase springs. The first stages of becoming a more advanced beginner may well feel like going around in circles as you try to discover what it is exactly that you are supposed to be learning. There is, after all, a whole new language to acquire that is used by your tutors and professional designers. I remember now with horror the first time I worked in a team of tutors teaching the first year of an architecture course. The course leader told the assembled body of students that they might well be more confused after the first term (it was before British universities adopted the semester system) than they were at the outset. I think this is a fairly commonly felt experience. There is just so much new stuff to take on board and you have so little experience to test it against. However, this course leader went one step further. He said that students must expect that when they went home at the end of this first term they would no longer be able to talk to their parents (who were even then largely footing the bill) about architecture and design. He seemed to think this was a good thing. The rest of his pep talk was to the effect that this was a new world and the students had virtually no useful experience of architecture and design and must now expect to start from scratch learning this from their tutors. Mostly, these days, we think this approach to education is weak. We learn best when we can relate each new idea to ones we already understand. The design schools were, and to some extent still are, populated with academic staff who espouse the notion that their design field is a wonderful separate world and cannot be related to everyday experience. I do not hold that view.

However, there is so much to learn not just about the things you are designing but about the very way you think, that it probably still feels as if you have little useful knowledge to hold on to. Our staircase has no handrail. And the steps are

How are you getting on?

transparent so it feels easy to fall back at any moment. Indeed it is. It is often not a steady progressive climb.

My experience of teaching design across many sectors is that the steps feel closer together to begin with and then gradually they seem to get bigger and it is more difficult to make that upward leap. Remember, too, that we do not all get to the very top. Not all of us will become visionary designers. Some people get to a level they feel comfortable at and fail to develop much for the rest of their careers. Others are permanently dissatisfied and ambitious, revelling in disturbing and challenging new ideas.

At this point it is also necessary to remember that actually you are really climbing many of these staircases simultaneously and you may not necessarily stand on the same step of all of them at any one time. Some students develop more quickly at conceptual idea generation than they do at mastering the technology they must work with, or perhaps their drawing and other representation skills are poor and thus holding them back. There is an almost infinite range of possible combinations of skill levels. So let us summarise, in outline, the various steps involved in this staircase.

Vernacular/everyday designer

What makes all this more difficult in design is the interpretation of the lower expertise levels. You can see that in many tasks, for example playing chess, you normally begin by following rules and using standard patterns. This is probably the equivalent of the everyday designer and, of course, the vernacular/craftsman designer, who featured in Chapter 3. Such design does not really envisage anything new and certainly nothing revolutionary or iconoclastic. It is almost entirely unthinking.

Advanced beginner

In the early years of a design-based degree we would expect students to aspire to become advanced beginners. You are starting to gather precedent and to learn the language of your field of design, and also to understand the current and historical patterns of design more generally. You can appreciate the guiding principles underpinning the work of significant designers and you are beginning to form some ideas about your own principles. You will have a good set of the basic skills such as drawing and other modelling techniques. You are developing an understanding of the technical aspects of your design field.

Competent designer

To become a competent designer you really need to have a good grasp of all the main ideas in your design field, to be able to see the critical factors for success in a design problem and to be able to generate a range of fairly standard responses to achieve workable solutions. You are likely to be able to distinguish between design that is exceptional, good or mundane and to do this without relying on personal preference. You are likely to have started to develop some personal guiding principles and to be able to create original design solutions.

Expert designer

The expert designer can probably recognise design situations and break down problems into constituent parts that can be tackled with parallel lines of thought. If it suited, the style of working of such a designer could generate many alternative approaches and the designer would appreciate their potential and disadvantages. Such a designer could act as a useful tutor and be able to guide students through a design project. Their work is likely to be of interest to other designers.

Master designer

Master designers are likely to be able to see how different approaches can be made by understanding the nature of the problem. They are likely to be capable of producing work that will get published and become seen as standard ideas, forming precedent that other designers might admire and respect sufficiently to study them.

Visionary designer

The visionary designer is capable of extending the field of design they work in to new paradigms, producing designs that change the field in some way. They may well be able to work comfortably in other design fields. Their work is likely to show new possible ways forward, not just in their specific projects but also for the design world as a whole.

Visionary design

Philippe Starck's extraordinary lemon squeezer is surely the work of a visionary designer (Figure 25.5). It has sold an enormous number of products worldwide and yet is probably seldom used. In terms of its radical constraints it is hardly the most effective and practical squeezer but it has become an iconic product. It somehow caught the spirit of its time with playfulness and freedom from earlier minimalist modernism. Starck's vision was of a more adventurous, whimsical and playful form of design and this product expressed that vision perfectly (Lloyd and Snelders 2003).

25.5

So where have you got to?

What this simple attempt to map out the development of design skills shows is that, by the end of your degree, you are climbing the staircase but that there are still at least two or three steps left. Not all of us will manage to reach the highest level but you should be able to see what it takes to get there.

This very rough model should not be taken too literally. Different designers will make different progress and little of it turns out to be steady anyway. So it is really only a rough guide as an indication of where you are going. It also helps to show what we saw at the very start of this book. Becoming an excellent professional designer takes time.

The whole point about creativity in design is to break away from assumed patterns and rules, so it would not be a good idea to begin our educational curricula with instructions to follow rules. However, there is no reason why designers should not study experts and try to see how and why their designs work. What you are not likely to be able to do, though, is to copy their sophisticated design processes. Partly this is because there is much of this still to identify and partly because you will simply not have the experience or knowledge to work that way. It is all a matter of balance. So much of the process of design is hidden in the mind and there is no way you are likely to know how such designers are thinking. The process of climbing this staircase of design expertise will certainly go on well beyond the end of your time in design school. It may well last a lifetime. Good luck with your continuing journey.

As you move towards graduation and professional practice you are likely to find that design becomes much more of a team process. It used to be rare for studio projects to be set for groups rather than individuals, but increasingly this is a more commonly used kind of exercise. Making creative partnerships work is a skill in its own right and we could probably devote a whole book to it. Often, though, it is a matter of luck in finding partners who are sufficiently similar in outlook and yet perhaps bring different skills.

Today, the professional practice of design is often a team activity. Sometimes the teams are multi-disciplinary and there are many potential pitfalls in organising such teams. The next and final chapter in our book recognises that learning to design does not finish with graduation but can continue throughout a career.

References

Dreyfus, H. L. and S. Dreyfus (2005). "Expertise in real world contexts". *Organization Studies* 26(5): 779–792.

Lawson, B. R. and C. H. Dorst (2009). *Design Expertise*. Oxford, Elsevier/Architectural Press.

Lloyd, P. A. and H. M. J. J. Snelders (2003). "What was Philippe Starck thinking of". *Design Studies* 23: 237–253.

Chapter 26

Moving on

Going beyond design school

In this chapter we will catch a glimpse of the life of designers after they leave design school. This can only be a rather brief discussion as it would be far too burdensome to be taking on the problems raised here while still grappling with the fundamental building blocks of a personal design process. It may just be useful and sobering to consider the learning and development that must continue on through the professional life of a designer.

First we need to establish a variety of levels at which this learning and development can take place. Kees Dorst and I proposed that we should think of four levels called project, process, practice and profession (Lawson and Dorst 2009).

The design project

The first of these is the project. This is really the level at which most of our discussion so far has taken place. Learning takes place inside each project and from project to project. This assumption underpins more or less the whole concept of design education in which you learn by undertaking a succession of projects. The project is of course, the very heart of a designer's life. Sometimes this can become dangerously addictive.

As a student on a design-based course, you are likely to find there is almost no time during which you do not have a project of some kind to work on. Of course you enjoy these projects, although often they can also be frustrating. You want to produce the best design work you can. If you do not feel this way about your design work you are not likely to make it as a designer. The best critic of your work must be you. You cannot rely on others being around or being honest. However, here is the paradox. When you look back at the end of an academic year you might realise that how good any one of your designs was is of very little consequence.

Of course, having good work in your portfolio is important for getting work or employment. What really matters educationally is not how well you did on a project but how much you learned. Sometimes having a real disaster in a project can be the most valuable learning experience. Perhaps one of the biggest challenges you face remains that of allocating time to your design projects as opposed to reading and exploring your subject. The design project can easily grow to fill the available time, leaving students not attending lectures or reading books like this one!

I have met and worked with many designers who have taken up academic careers. Usually they enjoy interacting with students and most of us are fascinated by the ideas students can come up with. Seeing a student move forward and begin to develop original, creative and eventually mature work, can be a great joy. And yet, I often find these tutor/designers also feel in a way unfulfilled. They miss the project. There is often a feeling of emptiness in their careers and many try to find ways of continuing their practice. Design schools often employ a large number of part-time studio staff who would not want to become full-time academics mainly for this reason. I have seen many academics who miss their own projects so much that they are tempted to take over their students' projects. I had a colleague who tutored senior students and managed to help them win many competitions and prizes. There was, however, a real question about how much he and his colleagues took over these projects. We academics must encourage and support students, but if we do not allow them to make their own mistakes and to miss opportunities we are doing them a long-term dis-service. This is a thorny area. As a student, you are likely to feel flattered by the tutor who spends so much time with you and helps you to achieve excellent marks and maybe external prizes. In the end, though, you must learn for yourself.

At the professional level I have also seen this obsession with the project damage the long-term prospects of practices. The project may be the only significant income stream in a design practice. Everyone wants to be designing all the time. These two factors combine to form a situation in which the amount of human resource not involved in projects tends to zero. We shall return to this later but it can often become a recipe for disaster.

The design process

We need not say much about this here since this whole book explores the process. Trying out new processes, assessing the success of process ideas and learning new techniques, as well as reading and exploring, are all essential if you want to progress. Just doing another design project, even one where you produce an outstanding piece of design, will not necessarily advance your process. While the project is ephemeral, understanding, controlling and improving your process will last a lifetime.

The design practice

Now we move on to a level that really only begins with professional practice as opposed to student practice. As a student, you begin this process unconsciously. It can be seen to include your style. This word 'style' tends to have a superficial connotation now and your 'design practice' is most certainly not superficial. It is framed by the total accumulation and formulation of ideas, interests, beliefs and attitudes that you have towards your process and the kinds of objects or places that you wish to create. It is, of course, influenced by the kind of experience you have.

Out there in the professional world you may be able to form your own practice or become part of a practice that already exists. In the latter case, you will need to understand the guiding principles that the practice operates. Sometimes these are entirely explicit, often they have to be inferred from what is said and done.

Two ways of collaborating in design

There are at least two quite different ways in which you as a designer might collaborate with others. First, you might work in a team of similar designers. In many professional settings this is almost inevitable. Certainly larger or more complex objects might just need so much work that more than one member of a design practice gets involved. Sometimes design schools will set group projects and here you would apparently be mimicking this way of designing. Actually, working in groups in design school is a really good idea for educational reasons. It means that you often have to understand and explain your own ideas more than you might if left to your own devices. Be careful, though, as this is a very poor way of mimicking professional design practice. I hope by now you can see why.

Throughout this book we have often relied on the thoughts of many professional designers. Almost all of them work in groups habitually. They are part of or, more likely, run a professional practice of similarly qualified designers. Many of the ideas we have seen arising from these designers are ones that work at the practice level. How they work in practice is something we will look at soon. For now, however, let us also identify the other important way of designing with others. This is when you are part of a multi-disciplinary team. Many of us simply cannot work alone because we do not have all the expertise necessary to deliver a design. Unless it is a very small project, an architect is certain to have a structural engineer and probably also a services engineer on the team. There is a host of other specialists who may get involved. In Chapter 20 I mentioned the huge project that I worked on just a few years before writing this book. We were charged with effectively redesigning a substantial part of the Irish capital city of Dublin.

Members of the team included architects, landscape architects, urban designers, town planners, conservationists, services engineers, transport engineers and many others. This results in different benefits and advantages compared with the first way of collaborating with similar designers.

Evaluating design

Throughout this book I have tried to suggest that the design process can be a very personal thing. I have introduced so many ideas about how designers can and do think that it should be easy to see that there can be many different design processes that are both effective and creative. Since we have mostly been concerned here with the development of your design process while studying, we could just leave it at that. The design process is a highly personal thing and we might all do it in our own particular way. Once you leave design school, and hopefully become a successful and creative professional designer, that may no longer be quite good enough.

My research group carried out a substantial study of multi-disciplinary design in practice. We were particularly interested in situations where a constant stream of design projects was carried out by the same organisations. The major question we wanted to answer was to what degree these organisations learned from this experience and improved or adjusted their design processes and passed on knowledge from one project to another. So we began looking at projects after they were completed to see what happened (Lawson et al. 2003).

Product, process, performance

One overall question you ask about a design project in professional practice is how well it went. Our first surprise here was the extent to which the various members of the design team evaluated the success of the project differently. Our second surprise, and rather nasty shock, was the extent to which participants thought mistakes were repeated and opportunities to learn were missed. An analysis of these reports suggested that there are at least three different and important ways in which a design project can be seen to go well or poorly. For simplicity here, we shall call these 'product', 'process' and 'performance'. It should also be said that data was often differentially well gathered in these three categories. Before discussing this we must define these categories.

The product issues are all those to do with the physicality of what has been designed. They include the material components and systems in the designed object. Questions can be asked after the completion of a project about how well all these physical things worked and met the specifications set down for them. We can ask how easy, convenient to use, reliable and cost effective they were.

We might also enquire whether other alternatives were available that might have worked better.

The process issues are all of those this book has focussed on. In the professional world these include not just personal ways of doing things throughout design but also the procuring, manufacturing, construction and commissioning of the design. Other key factors under this heading would include how well the whole process went in terms of meeting deadlines, schedules and budgets. In the professional world large projects are often phased and this brings a new set of questions.

The performance issues are ones we have not even touched on in this book in any serious way. They are about the new design in terms of how it impacted on the performance of the companies, users and clients in their main business. Does a new school, for example, enable teachers to work more productively and students to learn more effectively? To answer many of these questions time may need to elapse to see the effects.

The value of casting post-project evaluation data into these three headings is that they do appear to be rather more independent than you might imagine. For example, a new school might be delivered on time and under budget but its components might prove very expensive to run and maintain and, even worse, its configuration might obstruct teachers in their work, leaving them inconvenienced and frustrated on a daily basis. Sadly there is a history of design awards being made for such buildings.

Different versions of the same design process

It is time to link all this back to the material that has formed the major content of this book. When we evaluated projects we found another problem hitherto unexplored. We saw evidence of at least three commonly mentioned ways of describing design processes. We shall call these 'intentions', 'practices' and 'aspirations'. In simple terms, these views enable us to see a project in terms of what was supposed to happen, what actually happened and what participants would really rather like to happen (Pilling and Lawson 1996).

Intentions

You might like to look at the websites of a range of designers. You may find that the content of these is substantially made up of examples of things they have done. In other words, they really concentrate on 'product' information. However, what most clients tell us is that they are really looking for 'process' information. They really want to know what it will be like to work with these designers, i.e., how they go about their work and involve, or otherwise, their clients.

The client and the designer

I worked with a very interesting client. It was a collection of artists who wanted to build a new set of studios. I was helping them to appoint their architect. First I suggested a range of architectural practices that I knew had successfully completed projects of a similar nature. This is largely 'product'-based information. We narrowed this down to small number who we would approach and ask to appear at a competitive interview. Our artist clients (and users) were, unsurprisingly, anxious to be heavily involved in the process. So we asked the architects to come to an interview and bring the person who would be mostly in charge of the project.

One practice arrived and presented an actual design, of course only in outline form. They obviously thought that doing this un-called-for work for free would impress the client. Quite the reverse was the case. The clients saw this as an attempt to foist an ill-considered design on them, felt they would not be collaborative in their process, and ruled them out.

Another practice failed to bring the actual person who would run the job and they were ruled out as the clients wanted to meet the actual person they would deal with.

26.1

Yet another practice brought the job architect along but the principal answered every question she was asked. The client concluded that he did not trust the job architect to answer the questions and yet would not be heavily involved in the project himself.

All three of these practices were ruled out on issues they had not really thought about themselves. In the case of the second and third, the client thought that their 'intentions' would not be matched by their actual 'practice'.

Persistence Works was eventually designed by Fielden Clegg Bradley Architects and built for Yorkshire Artspace. It has since won a series of awards (Figure 26.1).

Intentions can be expressed at three levels. First, this can be by an individual member of the design team. Second, the design practice might express intended process descriptions, perhaps on their website or in brochures. Third, the profession as a whole can express them. The UK Royal Institute of British Architects lays out a very elaborate set of procedures and phases of work that, it claims, constitute the process of all architects. Intentions, then, are often, though of course not always, generated in a top-down manner.

Practices

This is the most obvious version of the design process. It is what actually happens. The fact that we need to list this separately from 'intentions' suggests that the two may not always be the same and we shall return to this very soon.

Aspirations

These factors are often the property of those 'at the coal face'. These are people involved in projects on a daily basis and who can see ways of doing things which, their experience tells them, might be better, quicker, more reliable, cheaper or more effective than either the usual practice or the expressed intentions. Such users perhaps frame projects differently to those who brief them.

Hearing the aspirations of users

In research on major projects repeatedly completed by large organisations we found the users often lamenting the way design projects were framed in favour of the capital budget. This is a typical comment by end-users of large buildings commissioned by their employers.

(continued)

(continued)

At the end of a project, we normally end up with a product that costs us more to run. Because the people who design and build projects are only interested in the capital figure, to meet their budget requirements is the major factor of success which in order to achieve, they would have made a lot of compromises while the running of the building will be much more over a longer time period.

(Lawson et al. 2003)

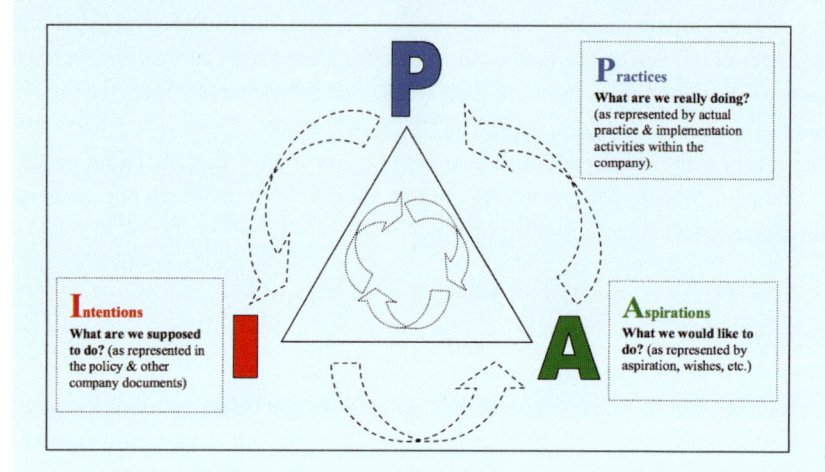

26.2

Intentions, practices and aspirations

Figure 26.2 gives us the three views of the design process, intentions, practice and aspiration. A design practice might find all three at work and might move between them in terms of importance as a project progresses or change them as the practice develops over time.

How these different views of design projects can relate

It became apparent in our research that there are several ways that these different views of a design project can relate to each other. Of course the three pictures, as it were, of intentions, practices and aspirations can be the same. An organisation showing this would express a set of intentions that those on the ground actually realised and about which everyone was happy. You might think such a synchronous organisation would be virtuous but we suspect that it is not necessarily the case. Such an outcome is perhaps a recipe for complacency and may reflect an organisation not open to change and development.

Of course the exact opposite is also possible. This would be a totally asynchronous organisation where the expressed intentions were not realised and, anyway, the people on the ground would prefer to be following yet another view of the process. This seems almost chaotic.

Finally, there are three intermediate states where one of the three views is out of step with the other two that are synchronous.

The varying relationship between intentions, practices and aspirations

In Figure 26.3, it is the middle column of situations is, in our experience, the most commonly found. In each case the letter outside the black line shows one view that is out of synchrony with the other two. All three combinations have their own characteristics.

The top case of asynchronous practices shows an organisation that knows how it would like to work and expresses this clearly but does not actually manage it. This at least offers the possibility of learning and improvement as long as it is recognised. Collaborators may find them difficult to work with.

The middle case of asynchronous aspirations represents an organisation that is actually doing what it claims to do but would rather work

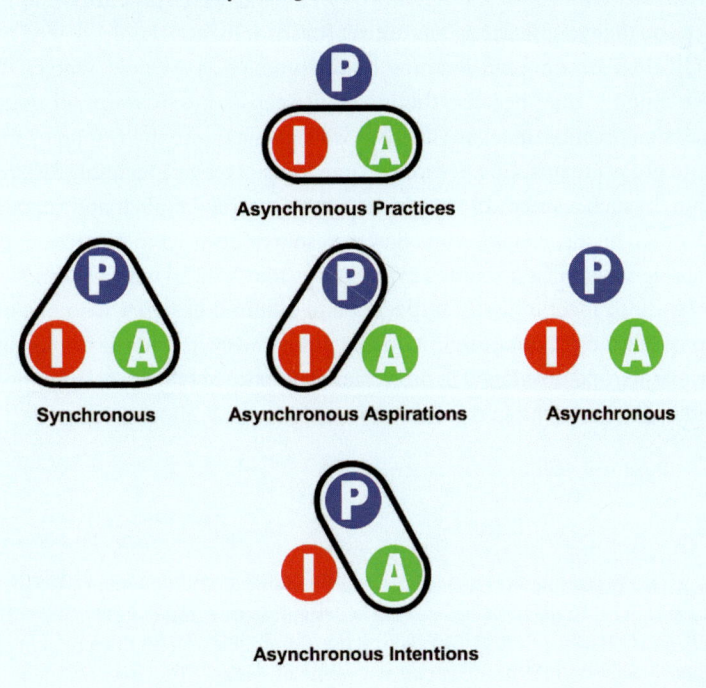

Asynchronous Practices

Synchronous

Asynchronous Aspirations

Asynchronous

Asynchronous Intentions

26.3

(continued)

(continued)

differently. Such an organisation has at least identified a way to improve but has not been able to for practical or contextual reasons.

The bottom case shows designers practicing as they aspire to but describing something different. This is a condition we found clients often expressing about their architects, who they suspected of having a hidden agenda about their own values and priorities.

It may be that a design practice that circles around through the various combinations is learning and thus is a developing organisation. As yet, we simply do not have enough long-term data to arrive at a firm conclusion about this. What is clear, however, is that there is plenty of room for confusion between the various member organisations of a design project, their clients and their users. Working in design professionally is likely to be an interesting ride.

So it isn't finished yet

Hopefully this little glimpse of research into professional design practice is enough to convince you that your learning has not yet finished. In fact, there is a need not just for individual learning but learning by the practice as a whole. One of the dangers we found is that, because the project is seen as the driver of all things good in a design practice, most are likely to want to maximise the resources that they put into project teams. However, over time, project teams inevitably disband and regroup. In such a situation learning is almost entirely implicit and remains inside individual heads. Having some design resource devoted to extracting lessons from projects and disseminating this learning may well be worthwhile.

I have yet to meet a highly respected and admired designer who has not claimed to be learning about design. You may find, however, that the things that need to be learned and developed in professional practice are different from those I have tried to help you with in this book. That, of course, is another story.

References

Lawson, B. R., M. Bassanino, M. Phiri and J. Worthington (2003). "Intentions, practices and aspirations: Understanding learning in design". *Design Studies* 24(4): 327–339.

Lawson, B. R. and C. H. Dorst (2009). *Design Expertise*. Oxford, Elsevier/Architectural Press.

Pilling, S. and B. Lawson (1996). "The cost and value of design". *The Architects' Journal* 203(9–7 March): 46–47.

Index